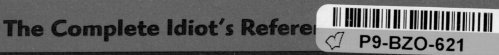

P9-BZO-621

Before You Leave

For a few days or more:

Getting ready to leave on a trip (or just a night out on the town)? Check off these "must-do" items to batten down the hatches at home before you sail away.

- ❏ Let someone you trust in your office or neighborhood know when you're leaving, where you'll be, and when you'll return.
- ❏ Arrange for a trusted neighbor or the police to make periodic checks on your house.
- ❏ Have a neighbor or house-sitter collect your mail, turn lights on and off, park in your drive, open and close blinds/curtains, and so on.
- ❏ If you have no buddy system in place, cancel the mail and newspapers, and set light-timers to various schedules around the house.
- ❏ Arrange for lawn-mowing or snow-plowing while you're gone.
- ❏ Unplug heat-producing appliances (toasters, coffeepots, irons, hair curlers, and so on) before you leave.
- ❏ Leave a list of contact phone numbers and information:
    - Your location and schedule
    - Your phone/cell-phone/beeper number
    - Your home address and phone number
    - The local emergency number (911 or other)
    - The names, ages, and weights of your children
    - The phone number of a poison control center
    - The names and phone numbers of nearby neighbors
- ❏ Post a list of house rules that the baby sitter has read and understands.
- ❏ Make sure that your baby sitter knows where to find a flashlight and what to do if there's a power outage.
- ❏ Tell the baby sitter how to use your security system, and run through the essentials.
- ❏ Lock all doors and windows before leaving, and show the baby sitter how the locks work.
- ❏ Tell the baby sitter specifically whether she is allowed to take the children anywhere outside the home and whether guests are allowed during your absence.
- ❏ Make sure that your baby sitter knows how to get the children out of the house in case of fire.
- ❏ Leave a second vehicle (if you have one available) parked in the drive when you go out for the evening, to give the illusion that adults are at home.
- ❏ Demonstrate the proper door-answering procedure (call someone on the phone before answering the door).

When traveling abroad:

- ❏ Prearrange contact times with someone at home, and plan to register with the consulate as soon as you arrive at your destination.
- ❏ Familiarize yourself with the location you're traveling to before you leave so that you know where you need to go once you arrive.
- ❏ Take notarized photocopies of your passport with you.
- ❏ Pack necessary medication and, if traveling for extended periods, any necessary medical records.

tear here

alpha books

Identity Theft Prevention

Identity theft is on the rise. When someone steals your identity, that person can ruin your credit rating, empty out your bank account, and even get access to your 401(k) or retirement funds. What can you do? Here are some guidelines for protecting your good name:

- ❏ Don't leave or store credit cards in unsecured places, such as your car or your office.
- ❏ Shred all documents that contain personal information before you throw them away.
- ❏ Don't print your Social Security Number or other personal identifiers on your checks. If the bank needs some ID, it will ask you for it.
- ❏ Never give out personal identification to someone who calls you on the telephone. Get the caller's name and a call-back number, and ask for the name of the company he's working for and his reason for requesting the information. Then, say that you will call back.
- ❏ Pay attention to your billing cycles. Thieves have been known to submit a change of address to your creditor to buy more time and to hide their activities.
- ❏ Carefully review your monthly credit card statements. Quickly question any suspicious purchase.
- ❏ Before giving out your credit card number or other personal information on the Internet, find out how secure the transaction is and in what other ways your personal information may be used.
- ❏ Never lend your credit card or driver's license to anyone, no matter how trustworthy you think they are.
- ❏ Get and inspect a copy of your credit report annually.
- ❏ Don't carry unnecessary credit cards, your passport, or your Social Security card.

At the first sign that someone is using your identity, take inventory of all your credit transactions, check the status of your driver's license, report the fraud to the police and to your creditors, and check with your motor vehicle department to see what measures you can take to protect your driving record.

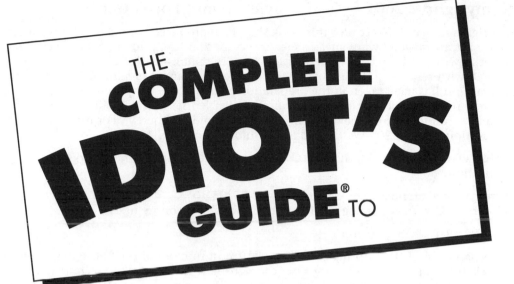

THE COMPLETE IDIOT'S GUIDE® TO

Home Security

by Tom Davidson and Lorna Gentry

alpha books

201 West 103rd Street
Indianapolis, IN 46290

A Pearson Education Company

Publisher
Marie Butler-Knight

Product Manager
Phil Kitchel

Managing Editor
Jennifer Chisholm

Senior Acquisitions Editor
Renee Wilmeth

Development Editor
Joan Paterson

Production Editor
Billy Fields

Copy Editor
Krista Hansing

Illustrator
Jody P. Schaeffer

Cover Designers
Mike Freeland
Kevin Spear

Book Designers
Scott Cook and Amy Adams of DesignLab

Indexer
Tonya Heard

Layout/Proofreading
Darin Crone
John Etchison

Contents at a Glance

Contents

Foreword

Do you worry each morning when you leave home to go to work that while you are away, someone will invade your home? Do you worry when you go to bed that while you are most vulnerable, someone will sneak into your home during the night? Do you hesitate to go on vacation because you fear someone will know you are away and burglarize your house while you are gone?

As a former federal law enforcement officer, I saw firsthand how vulnerable we too often leave our loved ones and our possessions. Sometimes, people naively believe the odds that they would be victimized are so remote they ignore home security.

Others believe that it is too complex and costly to harden home security. The truth is that the burglar looks for the easy target—the one who failed to take security measures.

It is downright unsettling and outright unfair not to have peace of mind while living in your own home. But *must* it remain that way? Are there measures you can take to increase your security and reduce your risk of loss of property or personal injury to you or your family? *The Complete Idiot's Guide to Home Security* provides the answers to each of these questions. And you don't have to be a genuine idiot to read it. You just may be an idiot, though, *not* to read it! Co-author Tom Davidson, a professional law enforcement officer himself, provides you the benefit of the accumulated wisdom of his 20-plus years with the Indiana State Police in securing your home against invasion.

Notwithstanding the obvious physical dangers to your family, there are profound psychological after-effects of a home invasion. People feel very foolish for not having taken reasonable precautions and security measures that could have prevented the crime. But worse, they feel vulnerable for months or even years afterward, fearing that burglars could return—and the next time the family could be at home. If their peace of mind was *disturbed* before the event, it is *devastated* after the event.

Authors Tom Davidson and Lorna Gentry inform the reader that home security does not have to be a complicated or expensive affair. It just takes some sound, guided attention. *The Complete Idiot's Guide to Home Security* is a thorough, logically ordered, and easy-to-read guide on how to provide yourself and your family the safety and serenity of a secure home. Don't leave home without having read this book!

Steve McVey

R. Steve McVey, an associate professor of Organizational Leadership at Purdue University, retired after twenty-six years as a special agent of the Federal Bureau of Investigation. He is the co-author of two books: *Managing Violence in the Workplace* and *Kids Killing Kids: Managing Gang Violence in Schools.*

Introduction

Lately, you've been seeing a lot of those "This home protected by Mad Dog Security Systems" signs popping up in your neighbors' lawns and windows, and you wonder what they know that you don't. The last time you went home to visit your mother, she mentioned that someone had robbed a home at the end of her block, where the Fraziers used to live (she doesn't really know many folks in the neighborhood anymore). Your business travel schedule gets busier all the time, and you hate leaving your home unattended, but how do you know what kind of security system you need?

Home security is all about feeling confident, safe, and in control, so why should the process of choosing and installing a system be so intimidating? Just because you aren't an expert on risk assessment, alarm systems, and criminal surveillance, you don't have to throw yourself on the mercy of companies that earn money by selling *their* security products and services. (Hmmm ... protection for hire—isn't that how Al Capone got his start?)

Fear no more! *The Complete Idiot's Guide to Home Security* takes you safely through the process of planning, choosing, and using a home security system that's right for *your* needs. In short, easy-to-follow chapters, this book tells you how to take some action:

➤ Do your own risk assessment so that you know what kind of risks threaten you, your home, and your community.

➤ Choose the type of security setup you need to combat those risks.

➤ Use the best low-cost (and no-cost) security measures to protect yourself, your home, and your family.

➤ Choose a professional security system and service.

➤ Install your own security and alarm systems, nanny-cams, and motion detectors.

➤ Protect yourself against liability.

In this book, you learn more than just the basic "lock your windows and cancel the newspaper while you're on vacation" security tips. At the same time, you *won't* be encouraged to build a bunker and install an alligator-packed moat around its perimeter. Instead, I show you, step by step, how to decide *when* you need security measures, *what* those measures should be, and *how* to put them in place. I help you understand how to eliminate or reduce risks, and how to live with the risks you can't get rid of. You don't need to be an FBI special agent, an ex-con, or a rocket scientist to protect yourself against crime, accidents, and disasters—and I'll prove it to you.

How to Use This Book

This book is divided into six parts; you can feel free to read them all, or if you deserve credit for time served (that is, you already know some of this stuff or don't have time to read it all), you can move directly to the information that you need most. Here's how this book is organized:

Part 1, "A Closer Look at Home (In)Security," steps you quickly through the ground-zero facts about the things that threaten and defend your home's security. You learn what types of protection you can count on from police, fire, and other public safety groups. You'll also spend a few moments reviewing our "police blotter" to get a clear identification on the crimes and accidents that most commonly occur in the home, how they happen, and how they could have been deterred.

Part 2, "Risky Business," gives you the information you need to do your own professional risk assessment and analyze the results, so you know exactly what security issues you're confronting and how to face them down. Follow the simple instructions in this part of the book to track down the facts and information you need to create a "susceptibility profile" that tells you what risks really threaten you, your home, and your community. Learn how to analyze the information to understand what kinds of loss you might be facing, and how bad those losses might be if an incident occurs. By the end of this part, you'll have a prioritized list of the security issues you have to address.

Part 3, "Home Security Doesn't Have to Break the Bank," takes the high cost out of high security. You'll review security options, learn to weigh their costs and benefits, and uncover the hidden costs (and surprising cost savings) of some systems. And before you spend a dime on crime, we'll make sure that you know all of the easy, cheap, and free techniques for securing your home and car, guarding your possessions, keeping an eye on your community, and more.

Part 4, "Bells and Whistles: Using Alarm Systems," tells you everything you need to know to choose, install, and use home security and fire-detection systems. You'll learn about burglar and intruder alarms, motion detectors, hard-wired and wireless safety alarm systems, calculating your safety perimeters, evaluating security services, and installing your own system—safely *and* legally.

Part 5, "I've Got an Eye on You, Babe! Setting Up Home Surveillance," tells you everything you need to know about setting up and using your own home surveillance system. Whether you want to see who's approaching your front door, or you want to monitor what's going on when you're gone, you'll find the information you need in this part. Find an affordable system, install it, and be your own "big brother" (or sister).

Part 6, "Putting a Lid on Other Issues in Home Security," touches on some far-reaching but very relevant points in home security. Learn about your rights as a homeowner—and the potential liabilities of home security systems. Find out the best ways to secure your "home away from home" (that expensive car you own), what to expect from the new smart technology, and just what centralized home management and protection might mean for you. And, because even the best home security plans aren't 100 percent effective, I'll show you what to do if you're the victim of a crime or a home disaster.

I don't leave you there, either. At the end of this book, you'll find a full glossary of all the high-tech terms and cop-shop talk that dominates the home protection industry, along with a helpful list of print and online sources for home security information, resources, and products.

Partners in Crime (Prevention)

That's not all you get in this book—I'm throwing in some extra crime and accident prevention information, along with some related information that I think you'll find v-e-r-r-r-y interesting. Staked out in various locations throughout this book, you'll find these characters:

Talk the Talk

These sidebars will give you the inside scoop on all the high-tech (and low-tech) talk that's common among law enforcement, insurance, and security industry types.

Crime Clock

From time to time (so to speak) you'll see these little notes that tell you just how often certain types of crimes, fires, and accidents are occurring every minute of the day here in the good old USA.

Not-So-Anonymous Tip

These tips (which come from a reliable source) will give you the jump on security issues and bring you some bright ideas for building the best security plan for your home and castle.

Security Password

Don't forget these pieces of information, either. You may not need them right now, but make a mental note of them—they'll come in handy at some point during your security planning or installation.

Sound the Alarm!

Heads up when you see one of these sidebars! These cautions and warnings carry must-know information that you need to read—and remember.

Trademarks

All terms mentioned in this book that are known to be or are suspected of being trademarks or service marks have been appropriately capitalized. Alpha Books and Pearson Education cannot attest to the accuracy of this information. Use of a term in this book should not be regarded as affecting the validity of any trademark or service mark.

Part 1

A Closer Look at Home (In)Security

Welcome to the world! You've decided that you probably need some sort of home security system, but you're not quite sure what that system should be (or exactly what you're protecting yourself from). To know how to fight, you have to know what you're fighting—and that's just what you learn in this part of the book.

After a not-so-formal introduction to your local law enforcement folks, firefighters, and nuclear holocaust specialists, you step through a quick review of the most common threats to home security, then move on to a departmental briefing on the ways most break-ins, thefts, fires, and other sorry mishaps occur in homes today. So get ready to look danger in the eye, and read on!

Chapter 1

Why You Need a Home Security Plan

In This Chapter

➤ The role of police and public safety agencies

➤ The "It can't happen to me" mind-set

➤ Mending the holes in your insurance security net

➤ Facing one-of-a-kind losses

If your home security system is made up of a telephone and a smoke detector, it's a good thing you're reading this book. Sure, 911 is a great service, and that smoke detector will definitely warn you of fire (if you clean your oven so that you can put the batteries back in the alarm), but they aren't the total security solution.

The reality is that the person most responsible for planning and instituting a home security system is *you*, and in this book I'm going to show you how to create a safe, logical, and affordable system. When I talk about putting a home security system in place, I'm not necessarily talking about hard-wiring alarms or staking uniformed guards at all entrances. When you boil it all down, security systems include anything that you plan to do and actually do before the fact to decrease the opportunity for a crime or accident to occur.

You don't want to overreact, but on the other hand, you'd rather not be a sitting duck, either. Maybe your car was broken into once or you recently heard about a cat-burglar operating in the neighborhood. Or, perhaps one of your parents lives alone in a neighborhood that's not quite as safe and familiar as it used to be. Or, maybe you just want to secure things at home, so you're looking for information about how to ward off crime and accidents. Whatever the reason, if you're *thinking* about the need for home security, you probably need it.

Before you start planning, though, take a minute to consider the factors that will influence the home security plan you'll create.

Somebody Call a Cop!

Whether you live in Manhattan or Miller's Crossing, your area is probably protected by some sort of public safety organization. From local, city, and state police to sheriff's departments, firehouses, and volunteer emergency response units, the United States does a great job of putting systems in place to protect citizens from danger. But believe me, you can't sit back and have another margarita because three guys in police uniforms are cruising your town.

Talk the Talk

Public safety agencies are government departments responsible for the safety and welfare of citizens (like you and me). These agencies include police, fire, and highway patrol departments as well as emergency medical dispatch teams, disaster relief organizations such as the Federal Emergency Management Agency (FEMA) and so on.

Public safety agencies are responsible for a variety of things in the communities they serve, and loss prevention is just one of those responsibilities. In fact, these folks usually don't get involved in crimes or accidents until *after* they've occurred. In almost any emergency situation, we dial 911 to report the loss after the fact. Unfortunately, most of us don't involve public safety agencies in before-the-fact efforts to reduce our risk of loss.

The next time you're joking about donut-eating cops, remember that these people (like those at most public safety agencies) have a lot more than pastry on their plates. They're responsible for investigating crimes, catching crooks, carrying out crash and fire investigations, patrolling the beat, enforcing traffic laws and helping disabled motorists, looking for missing and lost children, answering domestic complaints, writing reports, interacting with other governmental and justice officials, testifying in court, attending public meetings, and—oh, yes—loss prevention.

Yes, nearly all public safety agencies have loss-prevention programs in place, most of which welcome citizen participation (I talk more about these programs later in the book). For the most part, however, public safety agencies rely on criminal paranoia and some sort of rapid-response strategy to deter crime and prevent loss. Contrary to the popular saying that there's never a police officer around when you need one, common wisdom holds that fear of being busted has deterred many a would-be thief from committing a crime.

Budget cuts and personnel issues abound in public service agencies, so equipment and staffing shortages are a fact of life in most areas. And what happens when the police or firefighters arrive? Well, a lot depends upon their response time; again, common wisdom dictates that the sooner they get to the scene, the better the chance they have of reducing the *gravity of harm* of the incident. That makes sense, but no matter how great your local agency may be, it can't control some of the factors that affect its response time, such as …

➤ The time from when the incident occurs to when it's discovered.

➤ The time from the incident's discovery to when it's reported.

➤ How busy the agency is when the crime or incident report comes in.

➤ The distance between the scene of the incident and the people who are responding to it.

So, no matter how good a public safety agency is, its effectiveness is limited (in part) by its response time, and no agency has complete control over that factor.

The long and short of it is that your local cops and firefighters probably are responsible for a lot of people, a lot of territory, and a lot of incidents. Therefore, it's unrealistic to expect these folks to keep a keen, individual watch on your home and thus prevent you and your family from suffering any kind of loss.

It *is* reasonable, however, to think that you can combine forces with public safety agencies to reduce your chance of losses from accidents, fires, and crime. Block programs, Neighborhood Watch groups, kid-safe havens, drug-free zones, and other citizen/public-official partnerships have made a real difference in controlling crime in cities, towns, and rural areas throughout the country.

Talk the Talk

The term **gravity of harm** is cop and insurance agent talk for the amount of damage suffered as a result of a loss due to a crime, accident, or fire. If the crime is mailbox vandalism, your gravity of harm will likely be slim (unless, of course, you live in your mailbox), whereas the potential gravity of harm for a victim of arson will likely be much greater.

Security Password

You may not have heard of the *Omnia Presence Doctrine*, but it's fighting crime in your community. The premise behind this theory is that the reason most people don't break the law is because they believe that the police are everywhere and always ready to strike. If you're having a hard time imagining that anyone believes this, just watch someone break his neck to go feed an expired parking meter.

Security Password

There are approximately 423,000 law enforcement officers taking care of 274 million people in the United States. This works out to about 1 officer for every 648 people, which is about half the attorneys-per-Americans ratio of 1 to 391.

Neighborhood Watch signs have become common in most American towns and cities. Signs alone won't stop crime, though. Have you called the local police department to find out how to participate in your program?

Talk the Talk

Property crime refers to burglary, vandalism, and motor vehicle theft.

In Chapter 6, "Grade Your Public Safety Agencies," you'll learn more about how to check out your local agencies to determine what you can—and can't— count on them to do.

Your home security plan should be based on combined and coordinated efforts among you, others in your neighborhood, and the local public safety agencies. By taking responsibility for your own safety and welfare, you make it easier for your public safety agencies to do their jobs well. And let's face it—you're likely to benefit from the successes of your local police department.

The Neighborhood Watch program is popular *and* successful in areas across the country. To learn more about how you can work with your local police to help set up a program in your area, see Chapter 13, "Stir It Up: Start a Neighborhood Crime Watch."

It Won't Happen to Me!

The police will do their best to recover stolen property and catch the crooks; the firefighters respond quickly and do their best to reduce the loss from fire and treat the injured. But even with the best heroic efforts of our public safety officials, this country suffers a staggering amount of loss to crime and fire every year.

It's estimated that each year, more than 4,000 Americans die and more than 20,000 others suffer serious injuries because of residential fires. Annually, more than 22 percent of American households report being victims of *property crime*. All these losses translate into millions of dollars of damage, lost wages, lost productivity, and human suffering.

Even if you've never been the victim of a crime or a home-based accident, hasn't someone you know been touched by an accident, fire, or crime that occurred in their home? Although most sources report that violent crime is down in cities, other types of crime have seen little decline. And often, crime doesn't go away—it just shifts to new playing fields. Suburban crime is on the rise, and recent criminal justice surveys report that there's some evidence that street gangs and other urban crime networks are setting up franchises or satellite operations in rural areas.

Crime Clock

Somewhere in the United States, a property crime takes place every three seconds.

All things considered, the odds that you'll suffer some type of crime in your home are actually pretty high. The statistics vary, but none of them are very encouraging. Although more than 22 percent of American households report some type of burglary, other statistics indicate that more than 6 million residents are burglarized annually across the United States, and the National Crime Prevention Council estimates that 1 out of 10 homes suffers a burglary in any given year. So, you can play the odds, but statistically, it *can* happen to you.

Isn't That Why I Have Insurance?

Talk about gambling! Insurance is an odd setup, really, in which we make a bet with this big company that something bad is going to happen to us within the year (or six months, or whatever our premium period might be). The insurance is designed to protect us from financial costs that we might suffer if we "win" the bet and suffer some kind of loss.

Not-So-Anonymous Tip

The price you pay for insurance can vary considerably from company to company because insurance companies offer several types of discounts. Shop around, but remember: Price shouldn't be your only consideration. Ask friends, family, and co-workers about their coverage, service, and overall customer satisfaction with their insurance company when you're looking for a new carrier.

However, like any good gambler, the insurance company ups the ante if it senses that you're on a "winning streak" (you've undoubtedly heard of or suffered from the raised insurance rate that follows an automobile accident or other insured loss). Not only that, but your insurance rates probably depend on the loss experience of your insurance company as well as on your own risk potential. So, your loss as well as everyone else's loss will inevitably raise your insurance rates.

Reducing Your Insurance Premium

Happily, the insurance industry has realized that it can reduce costs (and even pass the savings on to its customers) if its customers do some home security planning and prevention. In most cases, you can cut your insurance policy rate by taking a few simple and often inexpensive steps.

Security Password

Increasing your deductible from $250 to $1,000 can save you up to 24 percent of your insurance premium. That doesn't necessarily mean that you should raise your deductible, though. Consider what you can reasonably afford to cover if you have a loss, and be sure to compare that with the actual cash savings (not the percentage) of a raised deductible.

For example, you can save up to 1 to 5 percent by installing deadbolt locks, simple alarms, and smoke detectors. Combining your auto and homeowner insurance policies may save you between 5 and 15 percent. We will discuss these and other steps in detail in Part 4, "Bells and Whistles: Using Alarm Systems."

Of course, the amount of protection that your insurance coverage offers depends upon the extent of that coverage, the cost of the policy itself, and the amount of your deductible. To be an effective part of your home security system, the coverage has to provide real compensation for your losses. The only way you can be sure of that is to check the dollar amount of your coverage and compare that to the value of the stuff you're insuring.

You'll learn more about reducing your insurance rates through home security installations in Chapter 8, "Calculating Your Security Budget."

What Insurance Can Do for You

As I said earlier, being properly covered by insurance is an important part of any home security plan. Generally, most homeowner's insurance policies cover direct losses due to lightning, fire, tornado, wind damage, hail, theft, smoke damage, and vandalism. And the typical homeowner's insurance policy pays for six different types of things:

Sound the Alarm!

Generally, personal property coverage has lots of limitations and exclusions. If you have antiques, expensive jewelry, or Oriental rugs, for example, you probably have to get extra coverage for those items.

➤ Your house. The total amount of coverage should equal what it would cost to replace or rebuild your house, not its current market value.

➤ Any other structures on your property, such as the tool shed, the detached garage, the aboveground pool, and that storm shelter that you keep Grandma in. Typically, other structures are covered for 10 percent of your total home insurance (for example, you get $10,000 of other-structure coverage when your home is covered for $100,000).

➤ Personal property, which includes things such as your television set, furniture, and clothing. Most companies assign a set percentage of your total home insurance to personal property.

➤ Loss of the use of your home. If you have a fire and can't live in your home while it's under repair, your homeowner's insurance should pay your living expenses during that time.

➤ Medical expenses of people who injure themselves on your property.

➤ Finally, it protects you from *personal liability* claims of someone injured while on your property, including some of the costs of your defense if that person sues you.

If you don't own a home, you probably have renter's insurance. Renter's insurance usually protects your personal property and meets your liability needs without insuring the building you live in. Because of this, renter's insurance usually costs less than homeowner's insurance.

In Chapter 12, "Your Name Here _____: Branding Your Stuff," I show you how to inventory and mark your property. That inventory is an important part of your insurance record, as well as a big help for those who are trying to recover your stolen goods.

Needless to say, maintaining adequate insurance coverage is an essential part of any home security plan, but it won't substitute for prevention. While insurance may be able to help you replace most of the stuff that you might lose in a robbery, burglary, or fire, it can't protect your family's safety and sense of well-being.

Talk the Talk

Personal liability means your responsibility for paying any obligations; your assets are fair game until all obligations for which you have personal liability are met.

Security Password

There are two types of coverage methods: *named* and *all-risk*. Named coverage covers only what is detailed in the policy—if it's not mentioned, it's not covered. All-risk coverage covers everything except what's specifically excluded. Make sure you know what type of coverage you have when you're calculating just how much security your insurance coverage supplies.

How Much Is Your Home Security Plan Worth?

I know I've been preaching, and I understand that you already want a security system, or you wouldn't be reading this book. But as you plan your home security, you're actually going to do a *cost-benefit analysis*. I'm going to show you how to calculate your risk of suffering a loss, how to figure up just how much you can lose, and then how to find the most economical security solution to protect you from those risks that you're most likely to face.

All the stuff I've talked about in this chapter should help you think—in broader terms—about each of the factors that you'll have to weigh in your cost-benefit analysis. Now, without preaching, I want to mention some irreplaceable and intangible losses that you can suffer—factors that should carry a lot of weight in your home security plan cost-benefit analysis.

Some things in life simply are irreplaceable—and I'm not just talking about your wedding ring, the only existing photo of your great-great-great-great-grandmother, or your child's bronzed diaper. Although you can lose irreplaceable items to fire and crime, that really isn't the biggest tragedy you could face. We all know that crimes and fires take lives, and no amount of insurance will replace a loved one or make up for a lost limb.

And even when no one gets hurt in a fire or burglary, you still are likely to lose something that you'll never completely recover: your peace of mind. Crime and losses from fire are really demoralizing problems that affect not just the immediate victims, but also their family, friends, neighbors, and co-workers. And sympathy aside, that broader impact can include higher prices, higher taxes, and increased insurance premiums, not to mention the fear of being the next victim.

So, when you add up the benefits of home security planning, don't forget the obvious benefit of the peace of mind that you feel when you know you've done the best you can to protect you, your loved ones, and your home. Nothing beats a good night's sleep—except waking up and discovering that all your things are just where you left them the night before (including, unfortunately, the beer can and stale cheese puffs that you left on the coffee table in front of the TV).

The Least You Need to Know

➤ Despite their best efforts, public safety officials can't be everywhere at once and protect you all of the time.

➤ Crime and losses due to fire are common and can (and do) happen anywhere.

➤ Reduce your insurance rates by taking prevention seriously, either by getting a reduction through personal prevention steps or by reducing the loss experience of your company.

➤ Proper security planning promotes peace of mind, an important benefit of a good home security plan.

-Keep the bad guys out.

-Don't let the house burn down.

Chapter 2

Principles of Protection

In This Chapter

➤ The breakdown on break-ins

➤ Where are the home fires burning?

➤ What else can go wrong?

Before you can plan how to protect your home from danger, you really need to know what kind of danger you're facing. Everyone's worried about crime, particularly home invasions. Every politician uses our fear of being a victim to craft a "tough on crime" policy that's sure to win an election. But watching the nightly news or listening to political debates won't really tell you what the face of crime looks like in this country. And it won't help you understand the nature of other home emergencies, either.

What's the real danger of suffering from a house fire? Is carbon monoxide poisoning something that you really need to worry about? I'm a firm believer in the "Know thy enemy" strategy, so I'm going to walk you quickly through the profiles of some of the top threats to home security today. Above and beyond the vital statistics of what's happening and where, you'll also learn the basic principles of prevention for each of these "enemies" so that you can prepare a home security plan that offers a good defense *and* counterattack against them.

A Quick Sketch of Crime

"Crime is up!" "Crime is down!" Depending upon what newspaper you're reading or politician you're listening to, you'll get very different pictures of just how common home burglaries and break-ins really are in the United States. Even the experts differ in the statistics they release. So, in a nutshell, here's my simplified profile of home-based crime today, based on statistics from the National Crime Prevention Council, the Federal Justice Bureau, and others:

➤ Approximately 6 million U.S. residences are burglarized annually; some estimates states that 1 out of every 10 homes will be burglarized in any given year.

➤ The National Crime Prevention Council estimates that 99 percent of us will have something of value stolen from us at least once in our lifetimes.

Sound the Alarm!

If someone were to break into your home, would you or your kids be willing to run for help, leaving everyone else in the house? Well, you should, and they should. Your chances of helping your family are a lot greater if you escape than if you try to confront intruders yourself. Your kids should know exactly where to go for help if any kind of disaster strikes your household.

➤ Most break-ins occur during the day, when residents are at work or school; nighttime break-ins usually occur in homes that appear to be unoccupied.

➤ Homes located on corner lots are statistically more likely to be broken into than are middle-of-the-block homes.

➤ Statistically, 88 percent of those arrested for burglaries are male, 35 percent are under the age of 18, and 64 percent are under age 25. Most of these young males are looking for cash or small things that they can quickly sell for cash (jewelry, electronics, watches, and so on).

➤ In 30 to 50 percent of home break-ins, the intruders enter through an unlocked door or window.

➤ On average, each residential burglary in the United States results in a loss of $1,300.

Crime Is a Three-Way Street

So that's crime's profile, but if you want to know what makes a crime happen, you have to look at its "heart." I don't want to blind you with science here, but at the heart of every crime is a "crime triangle," made up of three elements:

➤ **Criminal:** That's anyone who has the ability and desire to commit a crime.

➤ **Victim:** A person, home, or object can be the victim of a crime.

➤ **Opportunity:** That's a likelihood that the criminal can commit the crime without being caught.

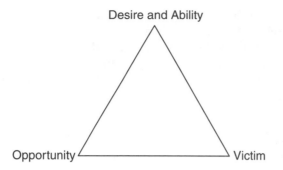

Victim, criminal, and opportunity have to meet in order for any crime to take place. To stop a crime before it happens, you must eliminate one of the three components of the crime triangle. Your best bet for deterrence is to eliminate the opportunity for crime.

In Chapter 1, "Why You Need a Home Security Plan," I told you that you carry the main responsibility for preventing crime in your home—and *preventing* crime should be your main focus. When you're talking about protection, a good crime-prevention plan is *always* a better source of protection than pepper spray, guns, or trained attack-cats. And even the best alarm systems and escape plans will only minimize the damage that occurs when your efforts to deter crime have failed.

Think Like a Crime-Stopper

The best way to break the heart of crime is to eliminate or reduce at least one of the three components of the crime triangle. So, when you're putting together your home security plan, every crime-stopping measure that you use should have at least one of these goals:

➤ Make your home an undesirable target for any would-be criminal.

➤ Make yourself and your possessions harder to get to.

➤ Reduce or eliminate the opportunities for a criminal to invade your home or property.

Unfortunately, you can't really control anyone's desire to commit a crime, and you won't always be able to keep yourself out of harm's way. But your security system will have a huge impact on a wannabe criminal's opportunity to make a crime statistic out of you and your home. By using *target-hardening* techniques that I'll show you later in this book, you'll make it more difficult to commit a crime against you and easier to catch anyone who does.

Talk the Talk

Target hardening means anything you do that makes it more difficult for a criminal to get to you or your valuables (locked doors, fencing, bolted-down equipment, and so on).

If you make it difficult for someone to break into your home, and if you make it clear that anyone trying to do so is likely to be seen or heard, would-be criminals may just move on to greener pastures. On the other hand, if your front door is standing open, the keys are in your car's ignition, and you've hung your mink coat out on the porch for a good airing, you've created the perfect criminal opportunity.

A really good security system forces a would-be criminal to jump several prevention hurdles.

DETERRENCE and DETECTION	DELAY	INVESTIGATION	CONSEQUENCES
Video Cameras	Locks	Police	Arrest
Alarm Systems	Fences	Neighbors	Prosecution
Watch Groups	Safes	Marked Belongings	Fines
Police Presence		Evidence Preservation	Imprisonment
Lighting		Cooperation	
Pets (dog)			
Visible Locks			
Motion Sensors			
Nearby Neighbors			
Light			

In later chapters of this book, I'll tell you everything you need to know to choose and set up a good alarm system, surveillance monitoring, and so on. But as you tackle these or any other specific home security fixes, remember that your first priority in fighting crime is deterrence.

Crime Clock

A theft of some sort occurs in the United States every three seconds. To put that into its proper perspective, that's almost as often as most men change channels with the remote!

Do I Smell Smoke?

House fires are one of the biggest threats to your home security. Thousands of people and millions of dollars in property are lost to house fires every year—in fact, the United States has more house-fire deaths per capita than any other industrialized nation. How is it that we have so many fires and fire fatalities in American homes? If you're curious about where most fires occur and what causes them to break out, take a look at these fast stats:

➤ **What are the numbers?** More than 1.6 million house fires are reported in the United States each year, involving approximately 3,500 fatalities (including 100 firefighters).

➤ **Where do fires start?** Here are the most common places:

Kitchen	29%
Bedroom	13%
Living room/den	8%
Chimney	8%
Laundry area	4%

➤ **How do house fires start?** Smoking is the leading cause of house fires that result in fatalities. Cooking accidents are the leading cause of fires that result in injury.

➤ **Who's most at risk of dying in a house fire?** Senior citizens have more than twice the risk of the gerneral population. Children under five have nearly twice the risk of the general population. Kids 19 and under make up 25 percent of annual fire deaths. Men are twice as likely as women to die or be injured in a fire.

> **Security Password**
>
> Fire kills more Americans than all natural disasters combined, and house fires are the third leading cause of accidental death in the home. In other words, fire is a much bigger threat to your family's health and safety than, say, your teenage son's closet.

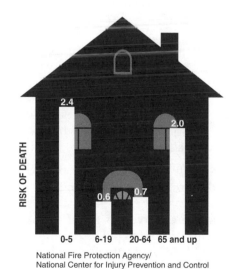

RISK OF DEATH

2.4 — 0-5
2.0 — 65 and up
0.6 — 6-19
0.7 — 20-64

National Fire Protection Agency/
National Center for Injury Prevention and Control

Statistics show that older adults and children under five have the greatest chance of dying in a house fire.

Only You Can Prevent Most House Fires

If you put new batteries in your smoke detectors and keep a few loaded fire extinguishers scattered around your house, good for you. When that fire breaks out, you'll probably know about it (if you're at home), and you may even be able to put it out

Not-So-Anonymous Tip

Every home should have at least one fire extinguisher; if you don't have one in your home, you're almost guaranteeing that you'll lose more in any fire that breaks out. And don't forget to have extinguishers checked by the fire department every year—it's a free service offered in most firehouses.

Security Password

The word *curfew* comes from a fire-prevention law cooked up in the eleventh century by William the Conqueror. To reduce the dangers of unattended cooking fires, William issued an edict that after a certain evening hour, all London residents were to cover the fire. That *couvre feu* order remains with us today as "curfew."

before it causes too much damage. But having a plan to minimize damage isn't really enough. You need to think in terms of fire prevention, and that means taking responsibility for both the condition of your property *and* the personal behavior of you and everyone in your home.

So what are the principles of fire prevention? They're simple:

➤ **Fire-safe home.** Check wiring periodically, keep work areas clean, and use fire-retardant (rather than highly flammable) materials and furnishings wherever possible.

➤ **Fire-safe habits.** Use electrical appliances safely, don't overload circuits, use safe cooking habits, keep matches and lighters away from kids, and pay attention to how you or any member of your family is using fire in your home (this includes fireplaces and stoves as well as cigarettes, candles, incense, and so on).

Think Fire-Free

Putting the principles of fire protection into action really involves a lot of observation (with a little bit of common sense thrown in). If you visually check exposed wiring periodically, make sure that the garage and work areas are relatively clean (with no mile-high piles of gas-soaked rags, for example), you may be getting out ahead of trouble before it starts.

Unfortunately, a lot of us don't think twice about fire prevention, as though we're made of asbestos or something. We'll happily put 100-watt bulbs in our 25-watt nightlight, use converters to get around the need for three-prong grounded plugs (or pull out the third prong), and think nothing of leaving the space heater blasting next to the sawdust pile in the garage while we go inside to nod off in front of a six-hour football game.

Walk around your house once in a while and check to see what's going on behind closed doors. When is your daughter burning those aromatherapy candles, and where is your son plugging in all of those electronic game and music devices that he's using in his room? Does any nightstand in your home have an ashtray on it—and if so, why? No one should ever be smoking in bed. In the end, thinking about your actions and paying attention to what you and your family are doing around the house is the best fire protection you have.

Strong Threads in Your Security Net

When you're preparing your home security plan, you need to think of protecting yourself against more than just break-ins and fires. Your best security plan will include ways to prevent and protect against other types of household dangers and emergencies, too.

Carbon monoxide poisoning isn't a common occurrence in this country, but it's responsible for about 250 deaths a year. Carbon monoxide, or CO, is an invisible, odorless gas that is created when fossil fuels aren't burned completely. In most cases, it's the result of a gas furnace or stove that isn't working right; a car left running in an attached, closed garage; a fireplace that's incorrectly vented; and so on. Lots of people keep carbon monoxide detectors in their homes, and that's a great idea—but it's an even better idea to avoid creating CO in the first place.

Medical emergencies can occur anywhere and at any time, but if you have an elderly parent, a young child, or anyone with any debilitating disabilities in your home, you need to be especially well-prepared. Take time before emergencies strike to know what types of help you're likely to need and how to get it quickly. And, if you live far from help, you'd better be prepared to help until help arrives—that means getting the proper training and having first-aid supplies on hand.

Sound the Alarm!

Your security plan has to take into consideration the special needs of anyone in your home who's very young, very old, or physically disabled in any way. And it's particularly important that you let the 911 dispatcher or other emergency contacts know about those members of your family when you call for help.

Weather and other natural disasters happen in nearly every part of the country, so why do they always seem to take us by surprise? Do you know where to go if your house becomes uninhabitable due to a tornado or flood? Do you know what kind of warning systems are in place in your area?

Your home security plan won't really be complete if you're not prepared to deal with these issues, too.

The Least You Need to Know

➤ Build a good home security plan on a foundation of basic crime, fire, and accident prevention practices in your home.

➤ The best way to prevent crime in your home is to reduce the opportunities for crime around your house and property.

➤ Fire prevention involves both fire-safe surroundings and fire-safe habits.

➤ A good home security plan prepares you to avoid or minimize damage from carbon monoxide poisoning, medical emergencies, and natural disasters.

Chapter 3

Home Security Snafus

In This Chapter

➤ America's most unwanted (but common) crimes

➤ Tales from the firehouse

➤ How car thieves steal your vehicle

➤ Not in my backyard!

Okay, if you read Chapter 2, "Principles of Protection," you have a pretty good idea what kinds of crimes, fires, and other home disasters you need to guard against and prepare for in your home security plan. As I said in that chapter, knowing the shape of crimes and accidents can help you come up with effective ways to prevent them. But even with a good idea of the types of problems that can occur, you might be surprised at the *way* things can happen. It's easy to think that you wouldn't fall prey to some punk thief, or that you'd know better than to let a kitchen fire flare up. But do you really know how most thieves get into a house, or what events lead up to a typical house fire?

In this chapter, I'm going to present brief case studies to demonstrate just what happens in some of the most common cases of crime, house fires, and accidents in the home. These people and their homes were in all those statistics you read about in Chapter 2. I'm hoping that their stories will give you a better idea about just what kinds of problems your home security plan can help you avoid.

Is There a Burglar in the House?

Every crime has its own flavor—the reason the crook does it, the things that make the crime possible, and the individual events that take place during and after the crime. But any police department or insurance agent can probably rattle off the most common types of household crimes and the typical *MO* of the crooks that commit them.

In this section, I'm going to give you a commercial-free look at the unsolved mysteries that became an issue for cops and resulted in some of America's most (un)wanted crimes (okay, I promise I won't do that again).

Talk the Talk

If you've watched any gritty (or supply your own adjective here) crime drama, you probably know that **MO** stands for **modus operandi,** a term common among all police, lawyers, and ancient Romans. It means "method of operation," and it's used as shorthand for "how dem guys diddit."

Case Study #1: A Get-Away for Victim and Crook

Jim and Eileen Goner try to be the type of neighbors they like to have. The Goners keep to themselves; they don't ask anything of their neighbors, and they try to be as quiet and unobtrusive as possible. You'd hardly know they were there!

And for the past two weeks they haven't been there. The Goners have been on a much-needed vacation. Before they left, they made sure to take all the right precautions. They cancelled their mail and newspaper delivery, closed all their curtains and window blinds, and set light-timers to turn their lights on every night at 6:00. Then they locked their doors and drove off.

But their return wasn't very happy. Things looked fine from the front of the house, but when they drove up to the back door, they saw it hanging open, with a huge hole where the doorknob used to be. Inside, the place was a wreck. Someone had gone through every drawer and closet, ripped open mattresses and furniture cushions, torn pictures from the wall, and stolen jewelry, silver, cash, the computer, the television, the stereo, and who knows what else.

When the police came to investigate, they took pictures, interviewed the neighbors, and quizzed the Goners about their activities and associates, but they came up with no significant leads. Other than the two-week span between when the Goners left and returned, the police couldn't even narrow down the exact date the crime had taken place.

Not-So-Anonymous Tip

If you start getting a lot of hang-up calls at different times of the day, you should be suspicious. Try using the *69 callback feature, if you want to reassure yourself that it's just some pesky aluminum siding salesman. Some criminals will call target residences at different times during the day to determine when the houses are empty or occupied. This is yet another reason why using an answering machine to screen your calls isn't always a bad idea. If you rarely answer the phone until you know who's calling, no one can track your absence or presence without speaking up.

Kick-ins are a common way for burglars to get around door locks.

What happened: Breaking and entering, property damage, theft

How it happened: The Goners advertised their absence by leaving their home abandoned and unwatched, and its appearance unchanged for a period of two weeks. The neighbors weren't keeping an eye on things, and neither were the police. The criminals hit pay dirt when they staked out the neighborhood; they could see the house being ignored by the mail carrier and newspaper deliverer. The curtains and blinds weren't being opened at all, and the lights came on at precisely the same time every night. After determining that no neighbors were watching or were nearby, the criminals kicked in the back door and then cleaned out the house of any portable valuables they could find.

Sound the Alarm!

The minute you realize that your house or apartment has been burglarized, leave it and go elsewhere to call for police help. You don't want to disturb the evidence, and you *certainly* don't want to interrupt a burglary in progress!

If only …

➤ The Goners could have made nice with their neighbors, at least enough to ask one of them to collect the mail and newspaper and to keep an eye on the house while the Goners were on vacation.

➤ The Goners could have arranged with a neighbor or a house-sitting service to come in periodically, open and close curtains, check that everything's locked and sound, and generally make the place look more "active."

➤ The Goners also could have notified the local police that the house would be unoccupied during that period so that they could do periodic "vacation checks" while the Goners were away.

➤ The Goners could have forwarded calls to a pre-arranged number so that callers wouldn't get the idea that no one was in the property.

Case Study #2: We Have New Stuff!

Tom and Mary just bought an expensive new state-of-the-art home entertainment center and were ready to sell off their old television, CD player, radio, and sound system. They moved their sale stuff to the garage, priced everything, and then took out an ad in the paper:

> Large garage sale: We have recently replaced many items, and we have a large selection of electronic equipment, used CDs, tools, and children's clothes. You don't want to miss this one.

Tom cleaned up the garage, filling the packing crates from his new entertainment center with junk he needed to get rid of to make room for the sale. The night before trash pickup, he hauled the crates out to the curb.

The garage sale was a huge success. One young guy even brought back a friend, and together they purchased several CDs. When one of them asked if he could get a drink of water, Tom took the young man inside and got him a drink. The guy thanked him, and then he and his friend left.

About two weeks later, when Tom returned home from work he was horrified to see that his house had been burglarized and that all his new stuff was gone!

What happened: Breaking and entering, theft

How it happened: Tom and Mary literally advertised that they had valuable new stuff to steal (remember the newspaper ad?). And the newspaper ad wasn't the only way they advertised their new stuff. Anyone passing by their home on trash night would be instantly clued in that Tom and Mary had just purchased some valuable electronic equipment.

This "burglar bait" is sure to draw a crowd! If you're not interested in attracting thieves to your new purchases, break down packing crates before you take them to the curb.

Finally, Tom took a potential thief right into his home for a quick look around. Any time you allow a stranger in your home, you're giving that person an opportunity to determine the best way of breaking into it.

If only …

➤ Tom and Mary had chosen their words more carefully. Never put in a newspaper ad that you have replaced anything of value; it's enough to say that you have some nice things for sale. Suggesting that you're having a moving sale or a cleanout sale is a better idea.

Sound the Alarm!

Unlike lightning, burglars often strike the same place twice. Victims of burglaries should be extra cautious in securing their home. Thieves often wait until the insurance company has paid off and you've replaced all the stuff that they stole in the first break-in. Then they strike again!

➤ Tom and Mary had flattened or cut up those equipment boxes before placing them on the curb for the trash truck. Flattened boxes don't advertise your new, valuable possessions to anyone. Tom could have set a trash can on top of the flattened boxes, or (even better) cut them up and placed them in the trash can.

➤ Tom hadn't let the young man into his house for a drink. Tom made it easy for a would-be thief to "case the joint." Tom could have asked the young man to wait in the garage or outside while he got the guy a drink.

Case Study #3: The Check Was in the Mail

Ms. Brooster lived alone and was supported by her teacher's pensions and funds from an annuity savings account. Every month, like clockwork, the checks arrived through the mail slot in her door. And that's what happened on this particular day; just as Ms. Brooster picked up her mail and was about to go through it, someone knocked at her door. She laid down the mail on a hallway table and went to answer.

Ms. Brooster saw a clean, well-dressed young couple on her porch; the young lady exclaimed, "I need to use your phone—my car has broken down, and I need to call for a tow truck. Please, I was on my way to a doctor's appointment." Ever helpful, Ms. Brooster directed the young lady to the telephone in the hallway. The young man began to engage Ms. Brooster in conversation and complimented her on the flowers surrounding her front porch and sidewalk.

After a few moments, the young woman stepped back onto the porch and said, "Thanks, we're all set now." The couple left and ran down the street. Later Ms. Brooster sorted through her mail. She was surprised to see that her retirement check hadn't come on time. "Oh well," she thought, "maybe it will come in tomorrow's mail."

A retiree's mail can be a gold mine right after the first of each month. It doesn't take a criminal mastermind to find ways to steal monthly pension or annuity checks, but these thefts can be prevented easily, too.

What happened: Theft, forgery

How it happened: The thieves took advantage of three things. First, by watching the neighborhood, the thieves determined that Ms. Brooster was elderly and at home during the day. That meant she was likely to be receiving a monthly retirement or Social Security check.

Second, like many people, Ms. Brooster was both trusting and helpful. The thieves used this to their advantage by asking Ms. Brooster to help them in a most compassionate and simple way, by letting them use her telephone.

Finally, people are creatures of habit. Generally, after receiving their mail, people quickly sort through it and then lay it down someplace—frequently that place is near a telephone (on a kitchen table or counter, a hallway table, or a desktop). By staging the minor emergency shortly after the mail was delivered, the thieves could be pretty certain that they'd be able to find what they were looking for.

Of course, keeping Ms. Brooster distracted was all part of the scheme. The longer the young man could keep their victim engaged in conversation, the more time his accomplice had to find the check or other easily nabbed items, such as jewelry or cash.

If only …

➤ Ms. Brooster hadn't let the young couple into her house. She could have spoken to the young couple through a locked storm door and told them she'd be happy to call a tow truck or the local police to come help them. That way, she could have helped without increasing her risk of being a victim.

➤ Ms. Brooster had set up direct deposit for her retirement check. Direct deposit is a safe, convenient, and common-sense way to protect the money you earn from mailbox thieves.

Security Password

Thieves often target retired people because they know that most retirement checks arrive in the mail around the first or the middle of the month. Many retirees are quiet, independent people who take pride in their ability to take care of themselves. These fine qualities also make retirees attractive prey for thieves.

Sound the Alarm!

It's common for robbers to try to enter a home under some pretext, even if they're only looking around so they can come back later. The fewer strangers you allow in your home, the less chance you have of falling prey to these characters.

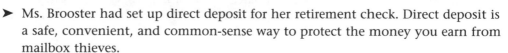

Not-So-Anonymous Tip

Has someone been in your house lately? I mean a stranger, a repairman, a salesman, a neighborhood kid, or even a distant family member or acquaintance? Did you at any time leave that person unattended? If so, take the time to check for missing belongings, particularly your box of checks. Thieves often will tear out a few checks from the back of boxed checkbooks. Victims don't even miss the checks until they're returned with other cleared checks in a bank statement. And if your credit card receipts or other identifying information were left lying around for others to view, you could be in double trouble. Don't leave anyone who isn't 100 percent trustworthy unattended in your home; if you do, be prepared to clean up a potentially ugly financial mess.

Case Study #4: That Darn Cat!

George and Inez Reglar live in a two-story home in an upscale neighborhood. They like living here because it's so relaxing—no loud parties, no junkyard dogs barking all night, nothing to worry about at all. The Reglars lock their doors at night, of course; they even put deadbolt locks on the front and back doors. But at night, they leave the garage door open about a foot so that their cat can get in and out. They don't need to worry about break-ins because they just don't happen on this street.

Like most people, the Reglars' days and nights tend to follow a regular pattern. They both work during the day, come home, throw down their briefcases, purses, billfolds, and so on, and then climb the stairs to change out of their work clothes. After dinner and a little TV, they put the cat out and then go back upstairs to read in bed until they fall asleep. The Reglars had followed this very routine one night when they were awakened by a noise.

They listened, didn't hear anything else, decided that it was the cat, and went back to sleep. The next morning, as George was getting ready to leave for work, he couldn't find his watch. After looking around for it a while, he gave up, grabbed his keys and billfold, and left for work. Inez was late, too (after helping George hunt for his watch), so she snatched her purse and briefcase from the hallway chair and dashed off to her own job.

At lunch, George discovered that he had no money or credit cards to pay the bill. He wondered if Inez had taken them without letting him know, but at about the same time, Inez was at a deli checkout stand across town discovering that she didn't have any cash or credit cards either.

What happened: Breaking and entering, theft

How it happened: The Reglars invited this burglar into their home by leaving the garage door open. Once he was in, they made his job easier by leaving all of their cash and credit cards where they could easily be found and taken, without disturbing the people sleeping upstairs.

Cat burglars know that many people have the habit of leaving their billfolds, car keys, purses, laptop computers, and so on downstairs at night—usually near the door. Cat burglars target two-story houses because they know that the bedrooms are probably upstairs, so they probably can get cash, credit cards, watches, and other valuables of opportunity without having to confront the home-owner.

Talk the Talk

A **cat burglar** isn't someone who steals cats. This unique burglar slips into houses after dark when he (or she—remember the cat burglar in Alfred Hitchcock's *Charade?*) thinks everyone's asleep. This burglar's purpose is to steal valuables such as credit cards, money, and jewelry that people often throw on tables and dressers before they retire for the night.

This opening at the bottom of the garage door yells "come on in" to any would-be house-breaker. In nearly a third of all break-ins, the thieves walk in through the garage. A small pet door would be just as easy for the cat to enter, and a lot harder for a burglar to squeeze through.

By leaving the purse and billfold behind, this cat burglar prevented the Reglars from immediately realizing that they had been robbed. This delay allowed the burglar full advantage of the use of the credit cards.

Not-So-Anonymous Tip

Some cat burglars are very skilled at picking locks, even deadbolts. Often, investigators can tell you if your lock has been picked because the keyhole is left facing one side rather than straight up and down (the normal direction when a key has been used in the lock).

Most locks require that you turn the key back to the up-and-down position to remove it after locking or unlocking; if the lock has been picked, the keyhole will remain turned to one side.

If only ...

➤ The Reglars had installed a cat door instead of leaving that garage door open. A foot-high gap is ample space for a wiry burglar to squeeze into your garage. And the simple button lock on the door that connects the garage to the house offered little resistance to the burglar.

➤ They had taken their valuables upstairs and put them out of sight. Most cat burglars won't stick around to thoroughly search a home, even one whose residents are asleep upstairs.

➤ They had made some effort to scare away any intruder when they heard him during the night. You may not want to call the police every time you hear bumps in the night, but you can do other things, like saying in a loud voice, "Honey, call 911—I think there's a burglar in the house!" Remember, most cat burglars don't want a confrontation with the homeowner, and they may leave when they think you've heard them.

Playing with Fire

If you've ever seen a house fire in action, you know just how quick—and deadly—they can be. But few of us realize how easily we could be the victims of a house fire. Although some fires are caused by faulty wiring or other nearly undetectable sources, most result from simple carelessness. We smoke in bed, leave something burning on the stove, or leave a pack of matches lying around where the kids can get hold of them. If you think you're fireproof, read these case studies of some other homeowners who never thought it could happen to them.

Case Study #5: I Think I'll Smoke for a While

The party was a lot of fun, and by the time Jim and his wife got home, they were both tired and ready to hit the hay. As they'd left, Jim's host had tucked one of his best Cuban cigars in Jim's shirt pocket, for him to enjoy later. Now, Nancy had gone on to bed, and Jim was getting ready to join her. Then he remembered the cigar and decided that he'd watch a little TV and smoke that havana before going up to bed. Three hours later, Nancy was jolted awake by the sound of the smoke alarm in the upstairs hallway.

What happened: Jim fell asleep. His cigar dropped out of his hand and onto the carpet.

How it happened: The carpet didn't burst into flames, but the smoldering fibers ignited a newspaper, which then ignited the upholstery of Jim's chair, the drapes, and so on.

If only …

➤ Jim made it a point to never smoke late at night while everyone else was in bed (and particularly not after drinking); careless smoking is the leading cause of house-fire fatalities in the United States. No smoker ever thinks that he or she would fall asleep while holding a lighted cigarette or cigar, but thousands of them do, every year.

Security Password

An ember can smolder for hours before breaking into flames, but once a fire does flame up, it spreads quickly. A fire can double in volume about every 30 seconds, and it can consume an average-sized room and its contents within three minutes.

➤ Jim and Nancy had installed a smoke detector near the TV room, as well as in the kitchen and upstairs. Because they rarely smoked, they hadn't thought it necessary to have a detector in the family room downstairs.

Case Study #6: I Like My Kitchen Well-Done, Thanks

Everything was nearly ready for dinner. Janet turned down the flame under the frying pan and left the chicken to finish cooking on the gas stove while she walked out to the garden to get some tomatoes for her salad. On the way, she noticed that some animal had been digging in her flowerbeds and had uprooted some of her favorite plants. She got the shovel from the tool shed and began replanting the flowers.

An hour later, Janet was completely engrossed in her gardening and was just finishing pulling some weeds that had been growing near the flowerbed, when she smelled smoke. Looking at the house, she was reminded of the cooking chicken by the flames shooting from the kitchen window.

What happened: The chicken in the unattended cooking pan caught fire, which then spread throughout the kitchen.

How it happened: Janet forgot all about the chicken she had left cooking on the stovetop, and it eventually burst into flames. The fire ignited the curtains at a window near the stove. Because Janet was far enough away that she didn't immediately smell or see the fire, it went undetected until it had spread through the kitchen.

If only …

➤ Janet had turned off the burner while she went outside.

➤ Janet had used blinds rather than flammable curtains on the window near the stove.

➤ Janet had installed a loud smoke detector in the kitchen so that it could have sounded (and she could have heard it) when the chicken first began to burn.

Crime Clock

Every day, 10 people die in house fires across the United States.

A lot of house fires start when people leave the stove or oven going while they're out of the house. Often, they simply forget that they've left anything cooking; other times, a "quick run to the store" ends up in a long and unexpected delay. If no one will be around to watch the stove, you should turn off all burners before leaving the house for any reason. And never keep towels, curtains, or other flammable things near the stove. If a cooking fire does break out, those things will help it spread.

Case Study #7: Kids Love Fire

The Wilsons worked hard to raise their daughter responsibly, and their good training and her natural intelligence had paid off. As a bright, obedient, and happy 12-year-old, Andrea was gaining more independence as her parents' trust in her grew.

The Wilsons had always been careful to keep matches and lighters stored out of reach when Andrea was younger. But lately they had grown confident that she understood the dangers of fire, and now they didn't worry about having a box of long matches located on top of the fireplace mantle. Andrea wouldn't play with them because she knew better.

But one Sunday morning just before Christmas, Andrea woke up early and went downstairs before anyone else was up. She decided that it would be nice to show her parents how industrious she could be by starting a nice fire in the fireplace. This wasn't playing with matches, she reasoned—it was simply doing a family "service." Anyway, Andrea had seen her mom and dad do it plenty of times; she crumpled some newspaper on the grate, laid the kindling on top, and then carefully lit the first long match and touched it to the pile.

The newspaper started burning right away, so she stood up to put the matches back on the mantel, where she knew they belonged. The hem of her long flannel nightgown got too close to the flame, though, and ignited immediately. (Luckily, Andrea's mother was just on her way downstairs, and her quick action saved Andrea's life.)

What happened: A child playing with matches set her clothing on fire.

How it happened: Everyone, young and old, is drawn to the warmth and changing colors of fire, but kids seem to be particularly fascinated with the flame. This little girl knew where the matches were, had seen her parents use them often, and was confident that she knew how to use them safely.

If only …

> ➤ The Wilsons had put the matches away each time they used them to light the fireplace.

> ➤ They had emphasized to their daughter that lighting the fireplace was something that only the adults were allowed to do.

No matter how responsible and trustworthy you think your kids are, don't ever assume that they won't play with matches or lighters, given the opportunity. Where fire is considered, children are particularly vulnerable. Keep matches and lighters out of site and out of reach, and make sure your children know that they aren't to use them until you tell them it's okay.

Security Password

Long, loose clothing often plays a role in starting house fires. People get up early in the morning and stand too close to the space heater or fireplace wearing a long nightgown. People wear loose, baggy shirts while cooking and it gets too close to a lit burner. You really need to think carefully about keeping your clothing back away from any source of flame. And any time you're working around fire, don't wear flowing sleeves, baggy shirts, and long scarves. (The latter aren't advisable when riding in an open convertible, either—right, Isadora?)

Case Study #8: Look up in the Sky! It's Handyman!

Bill considered himself a handyman, and he liked to work around the house and the yard. Bill had long wanted a gas-fueled fireplace, so he decided to buy a gas log insert and install it in his home's traditional fireplace. One cool Saturday, he ran to the home improvement store, got the insert of his dreams, and dashed back home to get it installed. With any luck, he'd be toasting his toes in front of this baby by noon!

After quickly skimming through the installation instructions ("1. Got it. 2. Got it. 3. Already knew that. 4. Yadda, yadda, yadda."), Bill shut off the gas to the house and began to install his new gas log. Bill tapped into the gas line in the basement and ran a line up to the new fireplace log.

When everything was connected, Bill turned on the gas and stood near the meter for a minute or two, sniffing for wayward fumes. He didn't smell anything, so, satisfied that the job was complete, he went upstairs and lit his new log. It worked like a charm, and Bill settled down to enjoy his new gas fireplace. A few hours later, Bill was snapped out of his catnap by a large explosion in the basement, followed by the unmistakable smell of smoke.

What happened: Bill's plumbing left a little to be desired, and the connection that he had tapped into the main gas line leaked. The leaking gas eventually made its way to the pilot light of the gas hot water heater; the gas exploded and then set fire to the house.

How it happened: Natural gas is heavier than air, so the leaking gas sank to the basement floor, where it accumulated until it reached the height of the pilot light of the water heater. The explosion ignited every flammable object within 10 feet of the water heater, including the floor joists above it.

If only ...

➤ Bill had checked thoroughly for leaks in the basement. Although the gas company puts an additive in natural gas to make it smell strong enough for anyone to detect, some people don't smell it as readily as others. But you can find even the smallest gas leak by mixing a few drops of liquid dish soap and water and then dropping a small amount of this "bubble" solution on the joints and connections. If the joint bubbles up, you have a leak.

➤ Bill had a professional install something as potentially dangerous as a gas-fueled heating device. People think that this is like hooking up a new water line, but it's much more difficult—and risky.

➤ Bill had arranged for the gas company to come and check his installation before he turned the gas back on. Although this type of check does require some pre-arrangement (you can't leave the gas off for weeks while the gas company works its way out to you), the inconvenience is well worth the benefit of having a professional eye approve gas connections.

Security Password

If you call the gas company and say that you smell gas, someone will get to your home pretty quickly to check it out. Lots of people are reluctant to contact the gas company if they think they smell gas—they're afraid that it's all in their imagination. Well, this isn't scientific reportage, but a gas company inspector once told me that if a woman smells gas, 9 times out of 10, there *is* a leak. He claimed that everyone in his company agreed that women seemed to be better able to smell gas than men. How's that for one of life's cruel ironies?

Say Goodbye to Your Car

Ooooh, we do love our cars—especially when they have those soft leather seats, great stereo equipment, and a hands-free phone, right? We park them in our assigned space at work, toss our Ray-Bans down on the passenger seat, slam the door shut, click the autolock button, and then, with one fond backward look, head on in to our meeting. And when we return—oops! Someone else loved that car, too!

Forget everything you know about car theft. This major industry is changing faster than all of the security measures we have for preventing it. But the information that you get in these car-theft case studies may give you a fighting chance in keeping your car off the MIA (Missing in Autoland) list.

Remember when a steering-wheel locking device was considered the cutting edge in theft deterrents? Now, these will slow crooks down, at best. Most thieves can break into and steal any car within a matter of a few seconds.

Case Study #9: I Was Just Warmin' It Up for You!

Great morning, yeah. It was freezing cold outside, Tim didn't have a garage, and he was running late for work. He scraped a view hole in the ice-covered windshield and started off on the long drive to work. As was his custom, he stopped at the local convenience store to grab a mug of coffee for the road.

The heater in Tim's car was just beginning to clear off the windshield and warm up the car; he couldn't bear the thought of turning off the car and letting it get cold again. "I'll just be a minute," he thought, and left the engine running while he dashed in for the coffee.

But guess what? There was a man in front of Tim buying lottery tickets—not the computer quick-pick kind, but a long series of tickets with carefully selected numbers that he read slowly from a list. The store windows were steamed up, so Tim couldn't see his car, but he kept thinking, "This'll be it; now I'll get out of here," and the man would begin reading another set of numbers. By the time Tim paid for his coffee and ran back to his car, it was gone. At least someone got lucky!

What happened: A thief saw the car's exhaust, knew that the owner was inside the convenience store, and took his chances on a quick getaway.

How it happened: This was purely a crime of opportunity. No one wants to be out walking the streets when it's freezing cold; a nice warm car was just too attractive for this foot-bound criminal to resist. The

Sound the Alarm!

Some communities have laws prohibiting leaving an unattended vehicle with its engine running. Not only is an idling, empty vehicle an invitation to crime, but it's bad for the environment, too. So, the best answer is to shut off your car when you park it.

guy simply walked up to the car, got in, and drove slowly away. Because he didn't act suspicious or in a hurry, no one paid any attention to him as he stole Tim's car.

If only ...

➤ Tim had "bit the bullet" and turned the car off and locked it up before he went inside.

➤ Tim had kept a spare key in his billfold, so he could have left the car running but locked. Although it doesn't take long for a crook to jimmy a car door, it's not something everyone would do in a busy parking lot in broad daylight.

Case Study #10: Can I Take You for a Ride?

Bobby's wife hated his new motorcycle, and she finally convinced him to sell it. He advertised it for sale in the paper and got several calls. A couple of people came out to look it over, but they didn't want to pay the rather steep price that Bobby was asking for the bike. Eventually, Bobby received a very promising call. The caller seemed excited that Bobby had just what he wanted, and he didn't think the asking price seemed out of line, either. Bobby eagerly set up an appointment with the potential buyer.

The buyer arrived at Bobby's house right on time; he was carrying his helmet with him and said he had a good feeling about this deal and wanted to be ready to ride the bike home. After looking the bike over, the buyer began negotiating the price; he drew a large wad of cash from his pocket, counted through it, and then agreed to Bobby's last offer—provided that the motorcycle was in good running condition. Bobby said go ahead and take her for a spin. The buyer put on his helmet and told Bobby he'd be right back. That was the last time Bobby ever saw the buyer or the motorcycle.

What happened: Vehicle theft

How it happened: The thief raised Bobby's expectations by acting excited and happy with the price of the motorcycle. He also reinforced Bobby's expectations by showing him that he had cash (no worries about a check clearing or the buyer trying to get a loan). Once the thief had Bobby convinced that the deal was about closed, it was easy for him to ask for a test ride.

If only ...

➤ Bobby had asked for a callback number from everyone who wanted to come out and look at the bike. When you advertise something for sale in the newspaper, criminals are going to read the ad as well as would-be buyers. Be cautious if the potential buyer is unwilling to provide you with a callback number; that indicates that the person may not want to be tracked down.

➤ Bobby had asked for identification from the buyer before he allowed the guy to take the bike on the road. When meeting with a potential buyer, introduce yourself and ask for a name. And don't let anyone take your vehicle for a test drive without first examining their driver's license. You can explain, "My insurance company told me that I was responsible for any accidents involving an unlicensed driver on this bike; I can't let you drive it unless I see your license." Be very suspicious if the person refuses to show you a license.

Sound the Alarm!

Unscrupulous auto repairmen and mechanics have been known to copy your keys (house keys, too, if you're foolish enough to leave them on your key ring) when you leave your car to be repaired. A week or so later, these crooks come and visit you—either to steal your car, burglarize your home, or both. How will they find you? Your address is on your check, and don't forget the information on your license plate registration certificate and car insurance card (you probably keep them in the glove compartment or on the visor).

Not in Your Backyard, Eh?

I've shown you just a few ways that really bad things can happen to good people. Can you honestly say that you didn't recognize yourself in *any* of these stories? If so, my hat's off to you. I can tell you that one of the previously mentioned victims was a state police detective and another worked for the Department of Defense as, you guessed it, a rocket scientist.

In any event, this wasn't an exercise in making you feel like an idiot (really!). But I'm hoping that now that you've seen how easily accidents and crimes can unfold, you'll be better able to assess just what risks *you* face for becoming part of a case study someday. By knowing your risks, you're better able to avoid them. And knowing your risks is just what the next part of this book is all about.

The Least You Need to Know

➤ If you're going to be away from home for a few days, ask a neighbor or a professional house-sitter to collect your mail and check on your house every day.

➤ Don't write garage-sale ads that will encourage thieves to see your home as a treasure trove.

➤ Don't advertise your new possessions by placing the packing crates at the curb for trash pickup.

➤ Avoid letting strangers into your home—and if you do, never leave them unattended.

➤ Children playing with matches, food left cooking (and unattended) on the stove, and faulty heating or wiring are common causes of house fires in the United States.

➤ Keep your car locked, and watch your keys at all times.

➤ Don't assume that burglary, house fire, car theft, and other such incidents won't happen to you.

Part 2

Risky Business

Home security plans aren't a one-size-fits-all solution. A risk assessment helps you tailor your home security plan to suit the peculiarities (okay, some call them unique characteristics) of you, your home itself, and the community or area you live in. But you don't have to pay a security consultant (or deal with an insurance company) to get a professional risk assessment of your home, because in this part of the book, I'm going to walk you through the ultimate do-it-yourself risk assessment. By the time you finish these chapters, you'll know exactly what risks your home security system must be built to address.

Chapter 4

Calculating Your Risks

In This Chapter

➤ What a risk assessment's gonna do for you

➤ How to do it yourself

➤ Possible risks + potential loss = ?

➤ Losing some risks and choosing others

If the word *assessment* carries a nasty association in your mind, believe me, I understand. It usually describes an activity that you'd love to avoid but have to endure "for your own good." Well, if the whole idea of a risk assessment conjures up visions of a gray-suited insurance salesmen blathering on about deadbolt locks, rest assured—I'll prove to you in this chapter that it can be a bit more exciting and a lot more useful than that.

Your goal is to put together a good home security plan, and your risk assessment is step 1 toward that goal. By the time you finish this chapter, you're going to know exactly how to do your own relatively painless and infinitely useful risk assessment, and how each step of the process adds another brick to your home security wall.

Is This *Really* Necessary?

Home security systems aren't a one-size-fits-all solution. That's why almost every security firm does a *risk assessment* of a client's home and property before installing any

Talk the Talk

A **risk assessment** is an analysis of the threats or dangers that are inherent for any person or piece of property, based on the physical nature of that person or property, the location in which the person or property exists, the social and environmental forces that surround the person or property, and so on.

system. Insurance companies do risk assessments, too, because they want to know exactly what they're getting into if they insure you (insurance companies take only very, very calculated risks, as you know). For these businesses, doing a risk assessment is just smart money.

But doing a risk assessment saves you time and money, too. You'd never pack for a trip without having some idea what type of climate and weather you could expect at your destination, right? Well, the same goes for planning a good home security system. Before you can determine what type of protection you want to incorporate in your security system, you really need to know what specific security risks you're likely to encounter. Your assessment lets you tailor your security system to fit your needs; you get a safer, more effective system, and you lessen the chance of wasting time and money on stuff that doesn't work or that isn't necessary.

Not-So-Anonymous Tip

As part of a total security plan, your risk assessment may help you reduce your insurance rates. Showing that you've done a careful assessment of the security risks around your home can go a long way toward convincing the insurance company that you're giving serious thought to protecting the assets that *it's* protecting. With your risk assessment and security plan in hand, meet with your agent to explore a potential rate reduction. Let your insurance company know that if it can't reduce your rate, you'll take time to look for an insurer that can.

Your risk assessment will tell you some important information:

➤ What security risks you're facing, and the specific nature of those risks

➤ The magnitude of each risk (how likely it is that an incident will occur, and how much damage it could cause)

The concrete result of your risk assessment will be a prioritized list of the security issues that your home security system must address. Not only will you know which risks your security plan must eliminate, but your assessment also will help you determine which risks your plan can minimize and which it can overlook.

Do-It-Yourself Assessment

Okay, so you're along for the risk assessment ride; where are we going, you ask? We won't even leave the neighborhood. A good risk assessment involves taking an honest, systematic look at you, your habits, your home, your community, and your local hazard-fighting systems (that would be your police and fire departments, emergency medical systems, hospitals, and so on).

The facts that you gather in your investigation tell you what it is about you, your home, and your neighborhood that are likely to open the door to crimes or accidents, what types of crimes or accidents you're most likely to face, and how they're most likely to occur.

Stage 1: Fact-Finding, Sleuthing, and "Neighboring"

The first stage of your risk assessment involves a lot of general information-gathering—and a bit of good old nosing around. In this stage of the assessment, you're going to gather information about

Security Password

Statistically, you're most likely to be the victim of a nonviolent crime if you're between the ages of 15 and 34. Experts think that as we become older and wiser, we get smarter about avoiding risks. But the irony of this statistic is that it seems to show that the more we worry about being a victim, the less likely we are to have reason to worry!

Security Password

You may already be carrying out a daily risk assessment. Newspaper polls show that the "Police Blotter" section of most daily newspapers (the record of police runs, arrests, and so on) is the most popular section of the paper. When you read up on crime in your area, you're doing a risk assessment of sorts (and finding out which of your neighbors was busted for growing pot in the basement).

your habits, the history of your home and neighborhood, and the nature of incidents of crimes, fires, and other accidents that have taken place in your area.

Gathering this information isn't hard; it really just involves three things:

1. **Personal observation.** Write down the things you know or note about the general condition, location, and setting of your home. Include your personal habits and daily routines, the general nature of the area you live in; its history of crimes, fires, and other accidents; and its proximity to the police, firefighters, and medical facilities.

2. **Talk with the pros.** The public safety agencies and insurers in your area can give you both general information *and* statistics on area crimes, fires, accidents, the nature and causes of those incidents, typical response times, and any emerging trends.

3. **Talk with your neighbors.** Your nosy neighbors finally have a purpose when they spill the beans to you about crimes or vandalism that they're aware of in the area (including unreported crimes), neighborhood problems that happened before you came on the scene, response times from local agencies, broken fire hydrants, and so on.

Get over feeling like a neighborhood busybody, and find out what's going on around you. Although you don't want to rush to your neighbor's home to ask why the police car was parked there yesterday, you could check with the local police department to see if any criminal activity was recently reported in your neighborhood.

In Chapter 5, "Pulling Together the Facts," I give you a series of questionnaires and checklists that make the fact-gathering part of risk assessment pretty much foolproof.

Risk assessment means more than just finding out that a lot of folks in your neighborhood have been the victims of *B&E* over the last few months. During what times do most of the break-ins occur? Have the police made any arrests? What kinds of things were stolen? How did the crooks get in? By getting information like this about any type of criminal activity in your area, you can uncover patterns that make the crime predictable—and therefore easier to guard against.

The same can be said for assessing your personal habits or the type of home you live in and its location and landscaping. What kinds of accidents have you had around the house? Do you have an angry—and potentially dangerous—ex-spouse? Do you do most of your banking at ATMs? Does your home-based business require that you keep a lot of expensive equipment on the premises? When the guy at the end of your street had a small house fire last year, how long did it take the fire trucks to get there? Were there any problems with access to the street or the hydrant?

Stage 2: Analyzing the Facts

The checklists and charts that I give you in Chapter 5 will lay the framework for listing the factoids that you uncovered in Stage 1 of the risk assessment. Then I'll show you how to rank each of the incidents, according to the likelihood of their occurrence and the likelihood that you would fall victim to them. I show you how to use a simple three-part ranking system that makes this organization fast and easy.

Stage 3: A Good, Hard Look at Your Weaknesses

When you've finished analyzing your information, you'll find yourself staring straight at your *susceptibility profile*—a clear picture of the security problems that you're most likely to deal with. Based on what you know about the way you live, your history of security problems, the general security conditions of your home's construction and location, and the history and nature of security problems in your area, you know three things:

1. What security problems (including crimes, fires, and other accidents) are you most likely to encounter?

Talk the Talk

B&E is cop lingo for breaking and entering, also known as burglary. When someone enters a residence or business illegally with the idea of committing a theft or felony assault, they're breaking and entering—even if they didn't have to break anything to get in!

HE DID IT!

Not-So-Anonymous Tip

Talking with your neighbors is a good first step in weaving them into your security plan. If your neighbors know who you are and that you're interested in the neighborhood's safety, they're more likely to let you know if they see anything suspicious going on around your property and to call for help if they sense that you need it.

Sound the Alarm!

When you change your personal routines, address, or standard of living, you need to redo your risk assessment. A security plan that's built on your individual circumstances doesn't fit when you've changed (you know, sort of like those jeans you wore in high school).

Crime Clock

According to the crime clock, a car is stolen somewhere in the United States every 23 seconds.

2. How are those problems likely to happen?

3. How bad are they likely to be—that is, how much local control is available to stop or minimize the problems?

So now you know what risks you're facing; next, you need to figure out which of them are bad risks and which of them are bad-to-the-bone risks. Remember, your ultimate goal for this part of the book is to create a prioritized list of security issues that your security plan must address. While likelihood is a big part of an incident's prioritization, cost is another.

What Do You Stand to Lose?

If you ask most insurance agents how much your worldly possessions are worth, they'll say, "About 10 percent of the total value of your home." But if someone asked you, "How much money would you be out if everything in your house was stolen in an armed robbery?" could you really answer? How long would it take you to track down all that new stuff? Could you find a replacement for everything you own? And what would it cost you? And would you ever be able to sleep in that house again?

The answers to these questions would tell you the *gravity of harm,* the big-picture price tag for the financial, physical, and emotional loss that you'd experience if your home was emptied out. Just as no two crimes, fires, or their victims are alike, no two losses from those incidents are alike, either. And when you're trying to figure out which of your security issues is the most serious (and therefore worth the most effort and cost), you can't do it without at least an *estimate* of how much you'd suffer from them.

Now, I can't give you a chart, graph, or formula to calculate each incident's gravity of harm. Everyone's different in circumstances, values, and responses to life's little surprises. But you can figure it out for yourself by considering a few very basic questions about just what you might be at risk of losing.

You need to include the financial, personal, and psychological costs when calculating your losses to any crime or accident.

People vs. Things

I'm really hoping it goes without saying that any loss that could involve people or the use of their fingers and toes would move to the top of the "must fix" list of issues for your security plan. So, based on your understanding of the types and nature of crimes or accidents on your list, which of them could result in the loss of someone's life or good health? The higher the possibility of such a loss, the higher the incident's security priority must be.

Is It Replaceable?

You know that if your car is stolen, you'll have to replace the car, your snow scraper, and all of those empty fast-food wrappers, napkins, and ketchup packets that you keep scattered about under the seat. But what if the loss isn't quite that *contained*? What if you lose your heirlooms, family photographs, and legal documents to a fire? If a thief gets your wedding ring, could you replace that? What about the popsicle-stick lamp that your grandfather made for you during his first year of retirement (remember, we're talking about replacement costs here, not destruction-for-hire).

Not-So-Anonymous Tip

When you think about your potential losses in any security incident, you have to decide which, if any, of those losses would be irreplaceable. If you have a high level of potential for irreplaceable loss from any incident, it should definitely move up on your "to be addressed" priority list of security concerns.

The High Price of Worry

When you're calculating the real cost of any crime or accident, don't forget to take into account the anxiety toll that you'll pay in the wake of some incidents. Peace of mind is a pretty valuable commodity, so you need to think about how much of it you'd lose if your home was broken into, if you had a fire, or even if you found evidence that someone had been

Security Password

Statistics show that, even while the rates of most major crimes (murder, assault, robbery) are falling in many parts of the country, the number of people who worry about being a victim of one of these crimes is actually on the rise. Your security plan needs to bolster both your real safety and your perception of just how safe you and your family are in your home.

standing behind your foundation shrubs and looking in your kitchen window. Even if you never experience certain incidents, will you worry about them if you're not adequately protected?

And remember, when you're calculating how many nights of sleep you might lose over an incident, you have to multiply that figure by others in your house as well. Your spouse, kids, or elderly parents have to get some rest, too, you know. Of course, in most cases, your own anxieties will grow in direct proportion to the vulnerability of the people you live with. For example, because the very young and very old are more at risk of injury in a house fire, you'll naturally worry more about fires if you have kids or if your elderly parent lives with you.

In short, don't forget to add the price of worry or deduct the value of peace of mind when you're calculating the real costs of a particular crime, accident, or other security issue.

Is That a Risk You Have to Take?

At the risk of sounding flippant, you won't necessarily clear your security slate of all the risks that you identify in your analysis. The security plan that you build in Part 3, "Home Security Doesn't Have to Break the Bank," will actually deal with risks in a number of ways. And that's because different risks require a different level of response (you don't need a Howitzer to knock off an ant, after all).

As you read through the following categories of risk management, you'll see that the likelihood and gravity of harm ratings that you assigned will help you determine which risk-management category each incident occupies. And, as you move through the steps for developing your home security plan, you'll probably find that you're including elements of all three forms of risk management in your plan.

Say Bye-Bye to That Risk

Some risks just can't be reasoned with, so you have to show them the door. If a risk has a medium- or high-level chance of causing injury or death, for example, you just have to do whatever is necessary (and within your power) to dramatically reduce the risk or eliminate it completely. You'll eliminate risks if they have these characteristics:

➤ Too costly to allow

➤ Easier to eliminate than to live with or prevent

➤ Less costly to eliminate than to live with or prevent

Not-So-Anonymous Tip

Your security plan will eliminate risks in many ways, including target hardening—you know, making it more difficult for the risk to become a reality. Target hardening at your home might include buying furniture that uses fire-resistant materials, installing deadbolt locks, or installing smoke detectors and alarm systems. Maybe you cut risks down to size by changing your behavior—say, by always wearing seatbelts, not carrying large sums of cash, using the buddy system when shopping, and so on.

To look at a specific example of targeted risk reduction, let's say that your neighborhood has experienced a lot of break-ins lately, and the culprits have been entering through basement windows. Your older son sleeps in a basement bedroom, so a break-in like this at your home could have really disastrous results. To reduce or even eliminate this risk, you might decide to install motion-detecting lights around the outside of your home, individual alarms on all basement windows, or even a full-house alarm system.

In Chapter 8, "Calculating Your Security Budget," I walk you through the process of reviewing security options, estimating their cost, and weighing that cost against their potential benefits.

Encouraging Risk Sprawl by Spreading Risk Around

So maybe you don't have to completely eliminate some risks—maybe you can just spread them around a bit to make them more manageable. (This approach is similar to getting all of your co-workers to join you in complaining about your new director of operations, Attila.)

Spreading the risks cuts down on the losses you suffer if something bad happens. For example, say that you have a large collection of valuable antiques in your home, but

Security Password

A good way to spread out risks is to separate the elements that contribute to the risks. For example, if you keep guns in your house, you may (and should) store the guns and ammunition in separate, locked locations. Create a fake "stash" of a few pieces of your jewelry in a dresser drawer, but keep the bulk of your jewelry stored in separate hidden locations throughout your home.

you use or display only some of them. The others are just stored somewhere in the house. If you have a house fire or burglary, you could very well lose all of this valuable collection. On the other hand, you could stash some of your antiques with a reputable storage company so that no one incident (either at your home or the storage location) would wipe out the entire collection. You've cut this risk in half by spreading it over two locations.

From Me to You: Transferring Risks

Maybe you just want to let someone else carry some of your risks for you. In fact, chances are good that you've already transferred some of your larger and less controllable risks, with health, life, home, and auto insurance. Transferring risks through insurance doesn't really eliminate the possibility that you'll suffer an accident or injury; it just reduces the financial wallop that you'd take if such an incident occurred. And, of course, you could also transfer some risks by hiring someone to take the risks for you—for example, a bodyguard, a tree-trimmer, an electrician, or a roofer.

Accepting the Risks That You Can't (or Choose Not to) Lose

As much as we all may dream of a perfect, risk-free existence, it never happens. When you've finished your list of security issues, it most likely will include some risks that you will continue to live with. Maybe you just aren't willing to take the steps necessary to eliminate or even reduce the risk. For example, you aren't willing to leave your secluded mountain home, even though you know that it raises your risk of losing everything in a fire before the fire trucks could reach you, and it extends the amount of time that you'll have to wait for emergency medical assistance to arrive.

Other risks simply won't seem worth messing with. If you're suffering from mailbox vandalism, you may be willing to replace your mailbox occasionally rather than trying to institute some type of surveillance system to help catch the vandals, or building some bombproof mailbox shelter to thwart their efforts.

Everyone has to make their own decisions about which risks they can and can't accept. But if you choose to accept a risk, it should meet at least one of these conditions:

➤ It has a low level of likelihood.

➤ Its gravity of harm is low.

➤ Its elimination cost is high.

Okay, you're ready to take a cold, hard look at yourself, your home, and the area you live in. Your risk assessment checklists and sample questions await you in the next chapter. With the information that you gain from them, you can create a prioritized list of security problems that your system must protect you against. So what are you waiting for? Put on your rumpled raincoat, grab your investigative journal, and let's get started.

The Least You Need to Know

➤ A risk assessment lists things about you, your home, and your location that make you susceptible to crimes, fires, and other accidents.

➤ Your risk assessment reveals what security risks you face, what kinds of problems threaten you, how incidents are likely to happen, and how much you're at risk of losing from them.

➤ Conducting a risk assessment involves noting your own observations; gathering information from public agencies, neighbors, and insurers; putting the information in a useful order; and then interpreting it.

Pulling Together the Facts

Are you ready to put yourself (and your home and neighborhood) to the test? In this chapter, I'm going to give you a number of risk assessment checklists along with some key bits of information about how to fill them out. If you've read Chapter 4, "Calculating Your Risks," you already know the basics of risk assessment and how this process works. If you haven't read Chapter 4, I recommend that you go back and read it before filling out any of the risk assessment information here. (I'm not being stuffy—you really do need to know what this process is all about!)

How to Fill Out the Checklists

In each of the sections that follow, you'll find a series of questions; answer the questions with a Yes, No, or Not Applicable. Any question that requires you to fill in a number, description, or other information will be marked as such and will include room for you to write the details.

We aren't embarking on a scientific analysis here. I'm showing you what questions you need to answer about your security situation. In Chapter 7, "What Your Assessment Reveals," I'll explain how to rank your answers in terms of the risk they expose. The good news is that on this test, you get to discuss some of the answers with your neighbor. Have fun!

How Safe Is Your Neighborhood?

The questions in this section help assess the safety of your neighborhood. You should be able to answer the majority of these questions based on your own observation and understanding of your corner of paradise. In the next section, you'll probably need to contact local public safety agencies and (believe it or not) talk with your neighbors.

In Chapter 6, "Grade Your Public Safety Agencies," I'm going to give you a series of questions that you should ask about your local police, fire, rescue, and other public agencies. Determining what those agencies can—and will—do for you in an emergency is an important part of your risk assessment process.

Look Around Your Neighborhood

Many of the questions in this assessment aren't applicable for those of you who live in really isolated or rural areas, but even you country folks will benefit from working through this short list.

Answer each question with Yes (Y), No (N), or Not Applicable (N/A):

_____ Are the majority of people in your *neighborhood* homeowners or long-term renters, instead of transient renters?

_____ Does your neighborhood contain local businesses?

_____ Is your neighborhood walkable? In other words, are there sidewalks and crossings?

_____ Do people bicycle in your neighborhood?

_____ Is your neighborhood active during the day? (That is, are there people from the neighborhood at home or outside, gardening, walking, or sitting on porches?)

_____ Is your neighborhood active during the evening hours? (That is, are people working in their yards, sitting outside, or walking?)

_____ Is your neighborhood free from loiterers?

_____ Do you know at least one of your neighbors by name?

_____ Is your neighborhood somewhat self-contained instead of a "cut-through," through which people travel back and forth to get to other neighborhoods or businesses?

_____ Does your neighborhood have an active neighborhood organization, apartment watch, or Crime Watch group?

_____ Is there a police station within five miles of your home?

_____ Is there a fire station within two miles of your home?

_____ Are your streets well-lit at night?

Total number of No responses _____

Talk the Talk

When you say **neighborhood,** what do you mean? In some cities, a neighborhood can be defined as a few square blocks. Some small towns may be just one neighborhood, with everyone in the town sharing proximity to everyone else. And if you live in the middle of the Great Plains, your property and that of your two nearest neighbors could make up tens of thousands of acres. You should give your own definition of neighborhood some thought as you fill in this part of the risk assessment.

Check the Police Blotter, and Chat Over the Fence

In some of the following questions, you need to assign High, Medium, or Low risk rankings based on your own interpretation of the perceptions of others in your neighborhood combined with actual recorded crimes and accidents reported to your local police and insurance agencies. This isn't an exact science, but these questions should lead you to an informed judgment, which is a pretty good indicator.

Your Neighbors' Perception/Experience

Check Yes or No:

Have any of your neighbors been burglarized in the last six months?	Yes ___ No ___
Do your neighbors remember any break-ins, burglaries, fires, or other hazardous happenings taking place in your home before you moved in?	Yes ___ No ___

Break-ins	Yes ___	No ___
Burglaries	Yes ___	No ___
Fires	Yes ___	No ___
Other _____	Yes ___	No ___

Do your neighbors think your neighborhood has a history of:

Frequency/Severity (assign High, Medium, or Low rank*)

Vandalism	Yes ___	No ___	___
Robbery	Yes ___	No ___	___
Break-ins	Yes ___	No ___	___
Assault	Yes ___	No ___	___
Theft	Yes ___	No ___	___
Murder	Yes ___	No ___	___
Rape	Yes ___	No ___	___
Other _____	Yes ___	No ___	___

*For categories other than murder and rape, assign a Low rank if neighbors report that they remember an incident occurring, a Medium rank if they report it happening only a few times, and a High rank if they report it as an ongoing problem. More than a single occurrence of murder or rape warrants a High ranking.

Police/Law Enforcement Record

Does your local police authority have a record of recently (past one year) reported crimes in your neighborhood/area?   Yes ___   No ___

Check Yes or No and note the number of occurrences, if applicable:

Vandalism	Yes ___	No ___	# ___
Robbery	Yes ___	No ___	# ___
B&E	Yes ___	No ___	# ___
Assault	Yes ___	No ___	# ___
Theft	Yes ___	No ___	# ___
Murder	Yes ___	No ___	# ___
Rape	Yes ___	No ___	# ___
Other _____	Yes ___	No ___	# ___

Not-So-Anonymous Tip

Nearly every police department or sheriff's office—even a small one—has a public relations assistant whose job it is to give information to the public. Start with those folks when you're tracking down crime and accident statistics for your neighborhood. They'll be able to tell you what kinds of crimes occur in your neighborhood and how often they happen. They won't give you names of victims, but they'll tell you how the crooks did the crime, what they like to steal, seasonal trends, and so on. The same is true of the fire department; you can find out what types of fires occur near you, what the average response time is in your area, special concerns with water pressure, locally available hydrants, and so on.

Patterns

In regard to crimes in your neighborhood, do the police or your
neighbors see patterns?   Yes ___   No ___

In the following list of typical pattern elements, list any that your interviewees report (use the "Other" space to list other types of patterns reported to you).

Day of the week/time of occurrence

_____

How crimes are carried out

_____

Victims

_____

Objects stolen/damaged

_____

Other

_____

Does your insurance agency have any history of problems with your home or neighborhood? (Vandalism is typically destruction for the fun of it rather than crime that has some end, whether it's gaining property, doing away with someone, or whatever.)

Crimes   Yes ___   No ___

Type(s) of problems_____

_____

Fires   Yes ___   No ___

Type(s) of problems_____

_____

Vandalism   Yes ___   No ___

Type(s) of problems_____

_____

How Safe Is Your Home or Apartment?

The following lists give you a chance to judge the risks that threaten your home, apartment, or farm. As you move through these assessments, keep in mind that few homes are completely safe-guarded against crime, fire, and accidents. But these lists will help you determine how many holes remain in your home-sweet-home's security net.

The Great Outdoors

Whether you live in a home, condo, or apartment building, these questions will help assess the safety of your exterior construction and landscaping.

Answer Yes (Y), No (N), or Not Applicable (NA):

General Placement

_____   Is your home accessible from main supply roads?

_____   Are phone lines buried?

Total number of No responses _____

Landscaping and Lighting

Does your landscaping allow doors and windows to be clearly visible from the street?

_____

Does your landscaping prevent someone from hiding near your doors or walkways?

_____

_____   Are outdoor parking areas well-lighted?

_____   Is the exterior of your house or apartment building well-lighted at night?

_____   Is each outside doorway well-lighted?

_____   Do you have motion-sensor outdoor lighting?

Total number of No responses _____

Construction

_____ Are your doors made of solid hardwood or reinforced with metal?

_____ Do you have metal reinforcement strikeplates surrounding the locks on all doors?

_____ Do your doors open inward and have hinges on the inside rather than on the outside of the house?

_____ Do you have wide-angle peepholes in all outside doors?

_____ Do you have an intercom near outside doors?

_____ Are portable air conditioners built into window frames or otherwise locked in place?

Total number of No responses _____

Locks and Guarded Entrances

_____ Does your garage door have a secure lock?

_____ Does your apartment building have a doorperson or a security system for all building entrances?

_____ For apartment dwellers, does your laundry room have a secure lock that only residents have keys for?

_____ Does the door that connects your home and garage have a secure lock?

_____ Do all sliding glass doors have secure locks and physical stop rods?

_____ Do your windows have secure locks or pins?

_____ Do all basement windows have strong locks and grilles?

_____ Do all outdoor buildings have strong locks?

_____ Did you change the locks when you moved into your home?

Total number of No responses _____

Don't assume that you're safer when you live in a rural area; crimes strike in the 'burbs and beyond. But you also shouldn't assume that you'll have a harder time getting help in emergencies. Many rural areas have developed effective fire, medical,

Not-So-Anonymous Tip

Trashy streets, yards, and houses attract crime. Keep crime down in your area by cleaning up around your home and in your neighborhood. Do what you can to organize a neighborhood cleanup and report broken windows and abandoned cars. You can't escape neighborhood problems by staying inside and putting bars on your windows. The answer to controlling crime often means being more active *outside* your home.

and police services that can be dispatched to remote locations quickly. The only way to know how long it will take emergency workers to get to your door is to ask.

Down on the Farm

If you live on a farm or in an isolated rural setting, you have some special safety concerns. Thieves can steal crops, expensive machinery, and livestock, and vandals can destroy thousands of dollars of equipment, crops, and property in very little time. To assess your special risks, fill out this list.

Answer Yes (Y), No (N), or Not Applicable (NA):

_____ Are all outside buildings and the farmyard areas well-lighted all night?

_____ Do all outbuildings, storage sheds, and grain bins have secure locks?

_____ Are all fences in good repair?

_____ Are access roads gated?

_____ Are all tools and equipment marked with identification numbers?

_____ Is livestock tattooed?

_____ Do you regularly count livestock?

_____ Is all equipment (large and small) kept locked up at night?

_____ Do you have fewer than five people working for you throughout the year?

_____ Do you check the references of any employees working on your property?

Total number of No responses _____

Sound the Alarm!

If you move to a rural area, immediately call your local police sheriff or fire department to find out what emergency rescue services are available (if they can't tell you, they'll give you the number of the nearest 911 operation center). Please, *don't dial 911 to ask these types of questions!* Like any emergency service, these folks won't appreciate nonemergency calls coming in through emergency contact lines.

Inside Your Castle

How safe is the old homestead once you're inside? This list will help you find out.

Answer Yes (Y), No (N), or Not Applicable (NA):

Fire-Safe House

_____ Do you have working smoke detectors throughout your home?

_____ Do you have fire extinguishers at critical spots throughout your home?

_____ Do you clean fireplace chimneys once a year?

Total number of No responses _____

Crime-Safe House

_____ Does every bedroom door have a secure lock?

_____ Do you have a dog?

_____ Do you have an alarm system, automatic phone dialer, or neighbor-signaling device?

Total number of No responses _____

_____ Are your possessions marked with an identifying number?

_____ Do you have a list of all valuable property (and, where appropriate, serial numbers) in your home?

_____ Do you have a safe?

_____ Do you store all large amounts of money and valuable collections in a secure place *other than* your home?

Total number of No responses _____

> **Crime Clock**
>
> Someone is robbed every 30 seconds in the United States. (You'd think all the good stuff would have already been stolen.)

Accident/Incident-Safe House

_____ Does every bedroom have a phone and every nightstand a working flashlight?

_____ Do you have emergency numbers posted near your phone?

_____ Have you installed ground-fault circuit interrupters on bathroom electrical outlets?

_____ Are all medicines stored in a locked medicine cabinet out of the reach of children?

_____ Do you have your furnace/air conditioner serviced annually?

_____ Do you have any portable heaters inspected periodically?

_____ Do you monitor your children's access to all sources of fire and heat in your house?

_____ Do you know where all the cut-off valves and switches are for the utilities that enter your home?

_____ Are any guns in your home kept unloaded and locked away?

Total number of No responses _____

Security Password

Your area may or may not have an active Tot Finders or Pet Finders program with the local fire department. These programs, which use window stickers or decals to list how many children or pets are in the home, have been cancelled in many communities because when new residents move into homes, they tend to leave up the stickers posted by previous residents. If the programs are active in your area, you may need to exchange special information with the department to become a member. Call your fire department or local law enforcement office (police/sheriff) to find out.

How Safe Is Your Lifestyle?

Okay, I'm assuming that if you're a stuntperson, a member of a bomb squad, an alligator wrestler, or a department store Santa Claus, you know the professional risks that you face. But the following checklist will help you gauge just how well you've eliminated risk from your ho-hum daily existence at work *and* at play.

Not-So-Anonymous Tip

Jogging is great for your health, but jogging the same route at the same time every day gives any would-be assailant or home invader an opportunity to pay you a call. Anyone who is checking out a neighborhood for easy-to-hit targets will know that you are out of your house during a specific time every day and that you are alone and (most likely) preoccupied during that same time. Those are two pieces of information that you really don't want some people to have. Varying your routines—even the healthy ones—reduces your opportunity to become a victim.

Answer Yes (Y), No (N), or Not Applicable (NA):

Around the House

_____ Do you have a list of emergency contact numbers posted near your telephone?

_____ Do you keep all outside doors, including your garage door, closed and locked at all times (even when you're in your home)?

_____ Do you inform police when you will be gone from your home for an extended time?

_____ Does everyone in your home ask for identification before opening the door?

_____ Are you present whenever workers or repair people are in your home?

_____ Do you check the references of people who work in or around your home?

_____ Do you know the locations of police stations and sheriff's offices in your area?

_____ Total number of No responses ___

With Your Neighbors

_____ Do your children know how (and when) to call 911 and get help from neighbors?

_____ Do you keep a key with a trusted neighbor rather than stashed around the outside of your home?

_____ Do you speak with one of your neighbors at least twice a month?

_____ Do you participate in a Neighborhood Watch program?

_____ Do you have a buddy system set up with one of your neighbors for keeping an eye on your property, collecting mail and papers during absences, and so on?

_____ Total number of No responses _____

Daily Personal Habits

_____ Do you rarely carry more than $200 in cash?

_____ Do you vary your daily activities (including your route to work) a bit every day?

_____ Do you practice martial arts?

_____ Do you carry a cell phone?

_____ Do you think about your safety regularly?

_____ Do you use ATMs only during the daytime or in well-secured public places?

Security Password

Almost 80 percent of all fire fatalities occur in single-family homes and duplexes—apartment living doesn't up your risk of dying in a fire. But do you know where the fire extinguishers are located in your building? How about the fire exits? Just because the landlord is responsible for smoke detectors and marked emergency exits, you're not off the hook for maintaining your own fire-safe plans and practices.

Sound the Alarm!

You're probably a lot less skillful at breaking into your home than the average burglar. So, if you can get into your home when it's locked, any self-respecting (or otherwise) criminal can, too. Leave a key with a neighbor or trusted friend rather than hiding one under a flowerpot, over the door frame, or in a fake rock near the driveway.

_____ Do you travel with others or regularly check in with someone at home or the office when you travel?

_____ Do you make a point of following safe practices when using power tools and equipment?

_____ Is your personal history free of any major accidents or injuries?

Total number of No responses _____

Fire Safety Habits

_____ Do you have a fire (or other emergency) escape plan?

_____ Do you keep all lighters and matches where children can't reach them?

_____ Do you keep a fire extinguisher next to the stove?

_____ Do you check the batteries in your smoke alarms monthly?

Total number of No responses _____

Your Car

_____ Do you lock up your car and close all its windows whenever it's parked (even in your garage)?

_____ Do you keep doors locked while driving?

_____ Do you look in the back seat before entering your car?

_____ Do you keep your home and car keys on separate key chains?

_____ When shopping, do you make an effort to park in well-lighted lots and try to avoid shopping alone at night?

Total number of No responses _____

Sometimes our normal, everyday behavior makes us a prime candidate for crime. Investing in expensive alarm systems won't give you nearly as much protection against crime as you can get simply by following basic rules of safe behavior.

And Now What ...?

You've put together a pretty clear profile of your home and neighborhood risks. You know what types of problems have occurred in the past and what patterns neighbors and law enforcement officials have noticed in the occurrences of those problems. But what happens *after* the crime, fire, or other incident? Before you know the true risks you face, you need to know what kind of help you can expect in dealing with those risks. That's just what the next stage of your risk assessment reveals.

The Least You Need to Know

➤ You can put together a clear picture of your community (or neck of the woods) by looking around, talking with your neighbors, and asking a few questions of your local public service agencies.

➤ Nearly every police office, sheriff's department, or state police agency has a public relations assistant to answer your questions about staffing and response times.

➤ Your neighbors and local law enforcement, fire protection, and emergency medical services groups are all going to be part of your security plan.

➤ Your personal habits and behaviors play a big role in the overall security of you, your family, and your home.

➤ An honest risk assessment will include a clear profile of just how much your behavior contributes to your personal security risks.

Grade Your Public Safety Agencies

Your local public safety folks are going to play a big role in your risk management plans and procedures. And while no one likes to be judged, you can't really assess your risks or construct a plan to manage them if you don't have a pretty clear notion of just how much you can count on your local cop shop, fire department, and so on.

In this chapter, I'll quickly walk you through the "must-know" information you should gather on these agencies so that you can fit them nicely into your home security plan.

Tracking Down Your Local Agencies

Everyone belongs to someone, whether we know it or not. And in that vein, your home lies within the jurisdiction of a specific set of public safety agencies—police, sheriff, firefighters, ambulance/rescue service, and so on. If you completed the risk assessment surveys in Chapter 5, "Pulling Together the Facts," you've probably already been in contact with the agencies that have jurisdiction over your area. If not, now's the time to find out whose jurisdiction you're in.

If you just purchased your home, your real estate agent should be able to supply that information to you. Otherwise, you can look in the Community/Local Government blue pages at the front of your phone book, or contact the nearest state police office or local government center—either place should be able to help you track down this information.

Not-So-Anonymous Tip

You can also get information on local agencies on the Internet. If your county, city, or town has its own Web site (many do), it probably contains contact information for local government agencies—and sometimes even maps showing jurisdiction and district lines. If you can't find a Web address for a county or city site in your local newspaper somewhere, go to your favorite search engine and search by entering your county/city name and the words "local government," "emergency services," "public agencies," or other key terms. You should turn up an online source for the information you're looking for.

When you've identified and located your own special agencies, you can get down to the business of gathering some important information on them.

Local, County, and State Police Agencies

If you live outside any city or corporation limits, your policing will be the responsibility of the county sheriff and deputies. In most areas, the county maintains sheriff's branches in lots of small towns throughout the county, as well as in the county seat. If you don't have many towns in your county, call your county sheriff's office to find out where the nearest branch is located.

If you live within the town or city limits, you are most likely under the jurisdiction of a local police department. In large cities, you may have a local branch or station. Some police agencies even have set up satellite offices in housing complexes or shopping malls. In any event, here are the questions to ask about the local police service:

➤ What are staffing levels like?

➤ How many cars are usually on patrol during midnight to 8 A.M., 9 A.M. to 6 P.M., and so on? (In most departments, half of all the officers are assigned to patrol.)

➤ What is the average response time to emergency calls in your neighborhood?

➤ Do they do vacation checks on properties, if owners notify the agency that they'll be out of town?

➤ Do they have separate departments or *special units* to deal with various aspects of a crime, or will one or two people investigate, follow leads, process data, and so on?

➤ What types of community programs are in place, and how can you become involved in them?

Talk the Talk

Smaller communities tend to have police officers who do it all—investigation, patrol, community services, and so on. Police officers in larger cities are placed in **special units,** a term used to describe the officers' area of specialization.

Now, given the information that you've gathered, how would you rate your local police, sheriff, or state law enforcement agency?

Did the agency seem responsive and helpful? _____

(No = Low; Somewhat = Medium; Yes = High)

Is the agency quick to respond to calls? _____

(Takes more than 15 minutes = Low; Takes 10 to 15 minutes = Medium; Takes less than 10 minutes = High)

Is the agency staffed adequately to provide good 24-hour coverage in your area? _____

(No = Low; Usually = Medium; Yes = High)

If not, at what hours is the agency most vulnerable?

(Days/hours) _____

Did you note any particular areas of weakness (lack of investigative power, patrol staff, dispatch network, and so on)? _____

What's Cooking at Your Local Fire Station

It's reassuring to drive by a firehouse and see all the firefighters standing by, shooting hoops, or polishing up the fire truck. It's nice to know they're there, ready to respond to a call. But there's nothing reassuring about hearing sirens approach your neighborhood. You want to know that they're going to get to the fire and put it out—fast. Do you need to worry about what happens *after* your firefighters are called? You'll find out in this section.

Security Password

Depending upon the population (and comparative wealth) of your area, neighborhood, or town, you may be serviced by a volunteer (rather than civic-run) fire department. That doesn't mean that you're getting second-rate firefighting service, though. Volunteer fire departments can be incredibly effective and efficient at fighting fires. Volunteers get special training, and many of them may live right in your area and have special connections to and concerns for the people they serve. If your area is serviced by a VFD, make sure to attend the local fund-raising events so that you can get a good picture of the men and women who volunteer.

Sound the Alarm!

Your insurance agency will take your local fire department's ISO rating into consideration when calculating your rates. If you get a notice that your insurance rates have gone up, call your agent and ask if the area's ISO rating has changed. If you can't get an answer, call your local firefighting agency and ask what its ISO rating is and how long it has had it.

One good way to quickly rate your local fire service is to find out if it's already been rated—by the pros. The Insurance Services Office (ISO), a New York–based independent industry advisory organization, rates the firefighting abilities of firehouses all over the United States, based on the agencies' ability to receive reports of, respond to, and fight fires. The ISO rating goes from 1 to 10, with 1 indicating the best protection and 10 being none (the national average ISO rating is 4). If your insurance agency doesn't tell you what your area firefighting agency's ISO rating is, you can call your local fire department and ask (many large fire departments list their ISO rating on their Web sites).

If your firefighting agency hasn't received an ISO rating, you can do your own little survey and rate it yourself. Here are the types of issues that ISO ratings take into account:

➤ What type of emergency dispatch service does your fire service operate? How many lines go into it, and how many people are staffed and on those lines at all times?

➤ How many fire stations are in your area, and do they consider themselves to be well-equipped? (The ISO requires a standard of a station within five miles of every home as a minimum protection limit, but in some remote areas, that standard isn't very realistic.)

➤ How far are you from the nearest fire station?

➤ What is the station's average response time to your area?

➤ How good is your area's water supply? Is there an issue of water pressure not being adequate to fight a fire during times of peak use?

Determining just how long it takes the fire department to respond to calls in your neighborhood is all part of your risk assessment process.

So, in grading your fire service based on this information, you should know the answer to this question: Is your service likely to get and respond to your call quickly?

High: Good communication network, fire station located within a mile of your home, average response time to your area of less than 10 minutes

Medium: Communication network, fire station located within three miles of your home, average response time of less than 15 minutes

Low: Radio relay system set up with no staffed communication center, fire station located more than five miles from your home, average response time of more than 15 minutes

Security Password

You may be able to get a lot of information on your local fire department online. Most city fire departments maintain a Web site that lists information such as how many firehouses they have, the size of each territory they cover, how many firefighters they typically have on staff, and what types of equipment they have. The site should also list their ISO rating. You can search for the site at your favorite search engine (Yahoo!, Excite, Northern Light, and so on), using your city, county, and state names, and then refining your search from there.

Useful Utilities Information

Why do you need to gather information about your utility services? Mainly because you need to be able to contact them in case you have a fire or other emergency that requires you to have gas or electrical service to your home temporarily cut. And, if you have a serious utility outage, your ability to quickly report it and get it repaired may have a big impact on the potential damages that the outage can cause. The main things that you need to know about your utility services are these:

➤ How far are you from the offices/dispatch centers of your local utility services (gas, electricity, water)? _____

➤ Does the utility have an emergency repair contact number? _____

➤ What has been the average response time (over the past year or so) to repairs during major weather or other widespread causes of outage or supply disruption? _____

If you're new to the 'hood, talk to your neighbors to find out what experiences they've had with power outages and utility interruptions in the past. If services are interrupted frequently and it takes a long time for the utility people to get things back up and running, expect to get a full and detailed report. If services aren't often interrupted and the repairs are made quickly, folks probably won't have much to say about the issue.

Sound the Alarm!

If anyone in your family requires special equipment to manage a medical condition, the response time of your utility company to repair interruptions in service becomes even more critical. Make sure that your security plan covers this potential issue by including backup power supplies and a plan for relocating during long outages, if necessary.

No specific numbers govern this grade; just rank your utility services based on your assessment of their responsiveness to your questions and overall self-reported repair times.

High: The utility has responsive service.

Medium: The utility will get to you within a reasonable period of time.

Low: You'd better have a big supply of candles and firewood on hand during the winter.

The whole electricity supply scene has become a lot more confusing over the past couple of years. As deregulation sweeps the electrical supply industry, you may be able to choose (or may already be getting) power from sources outside your area—or even your state. As companies have to actually compete for your business, there's always the chance that they'll put better customer service and emergency repair practices in place. And they definitely should make someone available to answer your questions. If you're not sure where that glo-juice is coming from, check the contact information on your bill to track down your electrical supplier. If you want to find out if alternative suppliers are available in your area, check online at www.greenmountain.com to see if your state has deregulated the electricity supply.

The loss of electrical power or telephone communication rips a big hole in your security net. That's why the response time of your utility repair service plays a big role in how secure your security plan really is.

Emergency Help Is on the Way

It goes without saying that you stand a better chance of surviving a medical emergency if you have a quick response to your call for help and if you have adequate medical help available within a reasonable distance from your home. To gauge just how good your emergency medical response and treatment prognosis might be, here are the questions you should ask:

➤ How far from my home is the nearest:

Ambulance dispatch center _____

Hospital _____

Emergency medical center _____

➤ What is the average response time to ambulance requests in my area? _____

➤ Does my nearby hospital emergency room seem to be well-staffed and adequately equipped? _____

➤ What services does the hospital offer? _____

➤ Is there a poison center nearby? If so, what are its services?

_____

_____

Again, you don't need to assign specific rankings to these categories. The hospital should have a public relations assistant who can give you information to answer the preceding questions, and from that information you should be able to determine your level of confidence in the emergency medical services in your area. So, roughly, you could classify the services like this:

High: Response time is five minutes or under, and the nearby hospital, medical center, and poison control center seem to be well-run and well-prepared to deal with most emergencies.

Medium: Response time is seven minutes or under, and the hospital emergency room handles most emergencies but has a good reputation for transferring patients to other facilities, if necessary. A poison control center and emergency medical center are available but not nearby.

Low: Response time to your area varies widely but can be more than 15 minutes. The local emergency room is poorly staffed or stretched beyond its capacity, and anything other than most basic injuries or illnesses requires transfer. Other nearby facilities are overworked and understaffed as well, so emergency medical situations are unlikely to be dealt with promptly.

The information you've gathered and assessed in this chapter has moved you farther on down the road to creating your own customized home security plan.

The Least You Need to Know

➤ Your first job in grading your local public service agencies is to find out whose jurisdiction you're in. Contact your local or county government offices if you can't track down the agencies through the phone book.

➤ You base a big part of your local law enforcement agency assessment on its communications system, staffing, and response time.

➤ Your local firefighting agency may have an ISO rating, based on its ability to receive reports of, respond to, and fight fires. If it doesn't, you can rate it yourself.

➤ If your utilities are interrupted following a home emergency or weather disaster, your home (and you folks who live in it) could suffer some nasty damages. To a certain degree, your home security involves how quickly your utility companies will respond to your calls for help.

➤ To really gauge how good your security plan handles medical emergencies, you'll need to know how quickly an ambulance will reach you and how good the service will be in the emergency room that you visit.

Chapter 7

What Your Assessment Reveals

In This Chapter

➤ What crimes and accidents do you face?

➤ What are the risks?

➤ How bad will it be?

➤ Your personal list of must-fix security issues

So, it's all there before you in black and white, right? You've called the cops; spoken with your neighbors; taken a good, long look in the mirror; and gathered all the information you need for your risk assessment. Now, all you have to do is shake it all down to get the answer to the *real* question: What am I fighting with this security plan?

That's exactly the question you're going to answer in this chapter. All the forms and questionnaires that you've filled out to this point are designed to help you quantify things that are really pretty difficult to, well, quantify—things such as the quality of your local law enforcement agency or whether your home is going to be attractive to criminals. The point of this part of the book is to get you to think really hard about the way you live, work, landscape, and decorate, and how all those things create or eliminate security risks. Now you've done that, and I'm going to show you how to translate the information you've gathered into a "must-fix" list of security issues your plan will address.

Putting a Face on Your Security Risks

You've gathered a lot of information to help you determine what kinds of security risks you're facing. First, let's look at the neighborhood assessment.

Your Neighborhood Risks

Checking back over the information that you gathered in the "How Safe Is Your Neighborhood?" section of Chapter 5, "Pulling Together the Facts," fill in the following assessment details. Based on the number of No responses in the "Look Around Your Neighborhood" section, your general observations reveal the risk level of your neighborhood:

0–3 No responses	Low risk
4–5 No responses	Medium risk
6 or more No responses	High risk

Based on the number of No responses in the "Check the Police Blotter, and Chat Over the Fence" section of Chapter 5, you found that your neighborhood risk for these incidents is at the following levels. (For each of these items, if the police or neighbors report one occurrence, that item's risk assessment is medium; more than one occurrence puts the assessment at high risk.)

	Neighbors	Police
Vandalism	___	___
Robbery	___	___
Break-in	___	___
Assault	___	___
Theft	___	___
Murder	___	___
Rape	___	___
Other _____	___	___

Review the results of your risk assessment in the "Look at the Police Blotter, and Chat Over the Fence" section of Chapter 5. Based on the information that you recorded there, list here the five most commonly reported, recorded, or perceived risks in your neighborhood. Review the "Patterns" subsection; list any patterns that neighbors, police, or insurance agents reported for any of these top five risks (day, time, method, victim/object):

Example:

1. Breaking and entering: midweek daytime, back-door kick-in; electronics and jewelry

Your Top Five Neighborhood Risks

1. _____
2. _____
3. _____
4. _____
5. _____

Security Password

Despite everything you've seen in TV and films, most home burglars aren't cunning intellectuals-gone-wrong who carry a complex set of break-in tools hidden away in their wristwatches. Most burglars get into homes through garage doors because those tend to have the weakest locks (and many times are left unlocked anyway). Most burglars who *do* use tools to break in use screwdrivers, hammers, pry bars, channel-lock pliers, and so on. In other words, these are tools many of us keep in the garage, making that an even more attractive target for would-be break-in artists.

Your Home or Apartment Risk Assessment

Based on the total number of No responses in the "The Great Outdoors" section of Chapter 5, assign a risk level of High, Medium, or Low that reflects the security snafus of your home's placement, landscaping, and construction:

General placement (0 = Low; 1 = Medium; 2 = High)   _____

Landscaping/Lighting (0–1 = Low; 2–3 = Medium; 4 or more = High)   _____

Construction (0–2 = Low; 3 = Medium; 4 or more = High)   _____

Locks/Entrances (0–2 = Low; 3–5 = Medium; 6 or more = High)   _____

Based on the total number of No responses in the "Down on the Farm" section of Chapter 5, what is your farm risk assessment level?

0–2	Low	_____
3–6	Medium	_____
7 or more	High	_____

Based on the No responses in the "Inside Your Castle" section of Chapter 5, list your humble pad's level of susceptibility to these risks:

Fire risks (1 or more = High)   _____

Crime risks (0–1= Low; 2–3 = Medium; 4 or more = High)   _____

Accident risks (0–1 = Low; 2–3 = Medium; 4 or more = High)   _____

Given this assessment, list the five greatest weaknesses in the security setup of your home, its placement, construction, and physical details, and describe the related No answer.

Security Password

If someone deliberately uses force against a homeowner to get into his or her house, that crime is officially known as home invasion (a term that you may have associated with visiting relatives or your son's ska band).

Examples:

1. **High risk for crime:** Outdoor lighting inadequate; doorways and parking area not lit

2. **High risk for crime:** No locks or grilles on basement windows, no secure lock between garage and house

3. **High risk for fire:** No fire extinguisher in kitchen

The Five Risks That Your Home Is Most Susceptible To

1. _____

2. _____

3. _____

4. _____

5. _____

Your Lifestyle, Baby!

We're getting there! Now it's time to sort out just how risky your day-to-day habits *really* are. Take a look at the "How Safe Is Your Lifestyle?" section of Chapter 5, and then fill in the responses here.

Based on your No responses in each of the following areas, your lifestyle risk assessment looks like this:

Around the house (0–3 = Low; 4–5 = Medium; 6 or more = High)   _____

With your neighbors (0–3 = Low; 4 = Medium; 5 = High)   _____

In daily habits (0–2 = Low; 3 = Medium; 4 or more = High)   _____

In fire safety (0–1 = Low; 2 = Medium; 3 or more = High)   _____

In your car (0–2 = Low; 3 = Medium; 4 = High)   _____

Security Password

Carbon monoxide poisoning is the leading cause of poisoning deaths in the United States. It's a sneaky killer, too; you can't taste, smell, or see it. And once carbon monoxide gets into your system, you don't think clearly, so the chance that you'll notice that you're becoming "groggy" are relatively slim. All of these factors make prevention the first goal for protecting yourself against carbon monoxide poisoning. Make sure that your security plan takes this issue into account.

Based on your total number of No responses in the Lifestyles section, your lifestyle places you at this general level of risk:

8 and under   Low risk

9–14   Medium risk

15 and over   High risk

Now, based on this, what would you say are the five greatest threats to your security that result from your personal habits, routines, and lifestyle?

Example:

1. **Some security weaknesses in daily habits/safety networking with neighbors:** I travel a lot without telling police/neighbors the house will be empty.

2. **Around the house:** I allow unsupervised workers in my house.

3. **Daily habits:** I carry large sums of cash.

The Five Riskiest Personal Habits/Behaviors/Lifestyle Choices

1. _____
2. _____
3. _____
4. _____
5. _____

The National Insurance Crime Bureau suggests that you use a layered approach when deciding on how sophisticated your personal anti–car-theft program should be. Much as I've done in this chapter, the NICB advises you to assign points depending on your circumstances:

1. Add the listed number of points if you live in or near a city with a population:

Over 250,000	8
250,000 to 100,001	6
100,000 to 50,001	4
50,000 to 10,000	2
Under 10,000	0
Total points	_____

2. Add these points, based on your vehicle style:

Sports car	5
Luxury car	4
Sport-utility	4
Sedan	3
Passenger van	1
Station wagon	0
Total points	_____

3. Vehicle age

0 to 5 years	1
6 to 8 years	2
9+ years	0
Total points	_____

4. Add 1 point if you live near an international port or border.

   Total points   _____

The NICB recommends protection "layers"; the number of layers you use is based on your total points.

0–4 points   Use Layer 1.

Common-sense deterrents: Lock your car, remove keys, park in lighted areas, and so on

5–10 points   Add Layer 2.

Visible or audible deterrents: Steering wheel locks, steering column collars, tire locks, decals, audible alarms, decals, and so on

11–14 points   Add Layer 3.

Visible immobilizer: Smart keys, kill switches, and starter, ignition, or fuel disablers

15–16 points   Add Layer 4.

Tracking systems: Microchip and transponder system used to track the location of a vehicle.

You learn more about each of these techniques in later chapters of the book.

What Are My Risks?

Okay, now you know what neighborhood risks you face, what your home's weaknesses are, and what areas of your lifestyle put you at risk. How do they match up?

For example, if your neighborhood has a high risk assessment for vandalism, and one of your home's most susceptible areas is its lack of good outdoor lighting, the chances are relatively good that you'll suffer some kind of vandalism at your home. If you travel a lot and don't have any kind of buddy system worked out with your neighbor, you're an easy victim for a break-in, even in a neighborhood that has a low or medium break-in risk assessment. If you don't tell the police that you'll be gone, you don't cancel your deliveries during your absence, and your habits never vary in any way while you're at home, your chances of being hit with a break-in are much higher.

Crime Clock

According to the National Center for Victims of Crime, 78 rapes occur every hour in the United States.

This part of the assessment requires that you really look over the top five lists in this chapter and also study the specific Yes and No responses that you gave in each risk area in Chapter 5.

Adding Up Crime Risks and Susceptibilities

Based on your assessment of the neighborhood crime risks, your home's security weaknesses, and the riskier aspects of your lifestyle, list here the five to seven crimes that you are most at risk of suffering (list all applicable/known details, such as date, time, method, and so on):

1. _____
2. _____
3. _____
4. _____
5. _____
6. _____
7. _____

Adding Up Fire Risks and Susceptibilities

Based on your assessment of the neighborhood history, your home's history, your home's fire security weaknesses, the risks of your lifestyle, and your family members' ages, list here the five to seven fire-related risks that most threaten you:

1. _____
2. _____
3. _____
4. _____
5. _____
6. _____
7. _____

Adding Up Your Susceptibility to Accidents

Based on your assessment of your home's security weaknesses and the risks of your lifestyle, list here the five to seven accident risks you are most likely to suffer:

1. _____
2. _____
3. _____
4. _____
5. _____

6. _____

7. _____

Security Password

According to the Federal Bureau of Investigation (the good old FBI) the majority of crimes in 1995 occurred in the South; the fewest took place in the Northeast. As it happens, the Northeast had the highest cop-per-citizen ratio in the United States, with 2.7 officers for every 1,000 people (the national average is 2.1 per 1,000). Keep that in mind when you're calculating the staffing of your own local constabulary.

How Much Can You Lose?

So, if you know what bad things you're susceptible to, your next step is to figure out just how bad the aftermath of those bad things might be (was it bad, the way I said that?). Anyway, this part is pretty simple. It mainly requires that you look at two things:

➤ How much do you stand to lose in a worst-case scenario?

➤ How much can you count on your public service agencies to contain the loss (in other words, can the local police, fire, and ambulance/medical service help you end up with a best-, or at least better-case, scenario)?

What's the Worst That Could Happen?

Working from the crime, fire, and susceptibility lists that you completed in the preceding section, record next to each listed item the potential loss that the incident could cost you. For example, if you're susceptible to a break-in during the day when you're at work, you could conceivably lose all of your possessions. Car theft would cost you the replacement cost for your vehicle, along with any other related costs of inconvenience. Loss of replaceable possessions, of course, is eased a bit by most insurance coverage.

But don't forget the irreplaceable items that you might lose in a house fire—that makes the personal loss much higher. And, of course, the loss resulting from murder or assault isn't *really* covered by any amount of insurance. If you have small children or an elderly parent living with you, the potential losses from a house fire skyrocket.

How Good Are the Rescuers?

Now, remember back in Chapter 6, "Grade Your Public Safety Agencies," where you were casting judgment on all of those helpful local servants? Well, go back there right now, and let's just tally up their scores.

In the "Local, County, and State Police Agencies" section of Chapter 6, you gave your local law enforcement agency these marks:

Helpfulness   _____

Responsiveness   _____

Staffing levels   _____

Weaknesses   _____

Vulnerable times _____

Security Password

You may not have to go out of your way at all to be the victim of a crime. According to the FBI, in 1997, there were nearly 11,000 hate crimes reported in the United States, most of them being crimes of intimidation. Sixty-three percent of those crimes were motivated by race hatred, 14 percent by religious intolerance, and another 12 percent by homophobia.

In the "What's Cooking at Your Local Fire Station" section of Chapter 6, your local fire department got these scores:

Communications/response time _____

Equipment/manpower rank   _____

In the "Emergency Help Is on the Way" section of Chapter 6, your local ambulance service got this response time ranking: _____

In that same section, your medical center/emergency room got this ranking: _____

And in the "Useful Utilities Information" section of Chapter 6, your local utility services got this response time ranking: _____

Adding It All Up

Now you know what crimes, accidents, and other security risks you're most likely to face. You also have given your personal assessment of just how high the losses from these incidents are likely to be. And you also have determined (roughly) what level of help you're likely to get from your local public safety groups if one of these incidents should occur. With all of this information before you, you should now be able to rank your most likely security risks in order of the gravity of harm that each one is capable of inflicting on you, your family, and your home.

Bam! Your List of Must-Fix Security Issues Is Ready

Congratulations! You've reached the end of the most important part of this book. With the information from earlier chapters, coupled with the investigation and that assessment you did in Chapters 5 and 6, you now should have a list of the crimes, accidents, and other security risks that you are most likely to face and their potential damage. You now have an accurate idea of exactly what security risks your system must address. And you know which risks warrant the greatest investment in your security plan, too.

For example, from your assessment, you have learned that vehicle theft in your part of town is more prevalent than burglary. You don't have an expensive car. But you do have an expensive coin collection that you want to protect. For the most part, you'll put most of your security efforts toward reducing the risks of incidents that are most likely to occur. However, don't forget to weigh and balance the likelihood of a particular loss against the gravity of the loss if it occurred.

Now that you've completed your assessment, you can better gauge how much of your time, money, and other resources you may need to spend on security. As I said before, this assessment isn't scientific, and it's even somewhat subjective. But I guarantee that if you went through the entire assessment process, you laid the foundation for an effective security plan *and* you learned a lot about your neighborhood and public safety agencies in the bargain.

The Least You Need to Know

➤ You've assessed how your home or apartment's placement, landscaping, and construction may compromise your security; your ranking of them shows where your greatest security weaknesses lie.

➤ Based on your assessment of your daily habits and lifestyle, you now know which security risks they expose you to; with that information, you can design a security plan that protects you from yourself!

➤ The information you've gathered tells you which risks you're most susceptible to. To list your top security issues, though, you also have to take into account the potential losses of any crime, accident, or other incident.

➤ With your list of "must-fix" security issues, you're now ready to put together a security plan that will give you the protection you need—and you know where you most need to invest your security time *and* dime.

Part 3

Home Security Doesn't Have to Break the Bank

You've done a good job of sorting out the holes you have to patch up in your security net. But how are you going to choose between all of the security options out there right now—and then how are you going to pay for whatever system you choose? I mean, those deathray-equipped robots may well scare off the kids who have been blowing up your mailbox, but you don't want to go too far, now do you?

In this part of the book, you're going to learn how to choose the system that's right for your security needs and how to manage the costs of your system (whatever it may involve). So forget about the attack robots and get ready to do some savvy security shopping!

Calculating Your Security Budget

All of us would like to have the most effective and sophisticated security system available, but practically speaking, that's just not, well, practical. Say that you live in an apartment building, for example; chances are slim that you're going to feel like investing in a high-cost alarm system, outdoor lighting, better locks for the entrances, and a new sprinkler system for the stairwells. But you may be able to get the landlord to give you more smoke detectors, install brighter lights in your stairway, or add stronger strikeplates to your doors. And you might be able to put any number of affordable security boosters in place to make even a temporary home a bit less risky.

In this chapter, whether you live on a farm, in a small town, in a row house, or in your first studio apartment, I'll show you how to determine just how much security system you need—and how much you can and should spend to put it in place.

Options for Reducing or Eliminating the Risks You Face

You probably know of a number of different types of security systems, from barking dogs to car alarms, to motion detectors and full-blown hard-wired alarm setups. But home security systems have gone through a lot of changes in the past few years.

If you think of a burglar alarm as a siren that wails if someone tries to open the door, you may be surprised by the systems available today. Fire, heat, motion, and sound detectors are part of many home security systems. Sensors may trigger alarms that link to a central communication system, to the police, and even into your own desktop or laptop computer at work.

Some systems can be installed by most homeowners in a weekend; in fact, lots of effective security equipment is really pretty simple to install. That includes those cutting-edge security camera systems. Just about anyone can put a surveillance camera in a doorbell or a peephole, to monitor just who's knocking at the door. If you really need to go undercover, you can even hide a camera in a lamp or a smoke detector to keep an eye on what's happening in your home during your absence.

Given all the recent changes in home security technology, it might be a good idea to take a minute to review a sampling of some of the security options you have to choose from. Allow me to take you on a brief tour.

Sound the Alarm!

Solid-wall privacy fences and thick shrubbery offer some defense against intruders, but they also prevent anyone passing by, your neighbors, or police/watch group patrols from seeing your house and yard. Unless you absolutely need the privacy, consider using a woven metal or palisade fence instead of a solid fence around your home.

Stay on Your Side of the Fence, Please

From solid-board construction privacy fencing to woven metal topped by razor wire, erecting some sort of barricade around your property can make it more difficult for nefarious types to invade your space. Some of the more high-tech solutions in perimeter fencing involve fiber-optic sensor fencing that sounds an alarm and contacts a patrolling security unit (that would run you between $100 to $250 per linear foot). Middle-of-the-road solutions include welded steel palisade fencing or electrically charged metal fencing. Chain-link fencing and thorny shrubs offer lower-tech but still effective fencing solutions.

Palisade fencing looks better than chain link, and it's certainly less forbidding than razor wire! Open fencing like this (or even a little less grand than this) lets neighbors, police, or passersby see anyone suspicious hanging around outside your windows or doorways.

The Classics: Locks, Bolts, Pins, and Titanium

Improved locks and guards on your windows, doors, and all attic, basement, and garage entrances can make your little fortress much safer. Deadbolt locks and strikeplates can definitely upgrade your home security, and you can add them for less than $25 per door. You can hire a professional locksmithing service to come in and update all of your locks, but if you have the time, you should be able to install most locks yourself.

A number of products (and simple techniques) are available for making your windows harder to access, too. Window stops (to prevent windows from opening more than a few inches), sliding door stop bars, and storm-glazing are a few types of security barriers that you can easily install in your home's "windows of opportunity."

And don't forget those outbuildings and sheds, either! You can buy titanium padlocks for exterior buildings and sheds to help keep your stored goods stored—and to help prevent would-be criminals from gaining access to your own tools and using them to break into your home.

Not-So-Anonymous Tip

Never hand over your house keys with your car keys to a parking attendant; it takes little time to make duplicate keys. If your keys have a number code stamped into them, have a duplicate made *without the code numbers* and keep the coded key safely hidden. With the key manufacturer's code number, anyone can get a duplicate key made anytime—without having the original key itself.

A mere $25 worth of hardware can turn a not-so-secure lock into a Ft. Knox–worthy lock. Heavier, larger strikeplates and longer screws make this lock much harder to kick in or pick.

Unfortunately, some of the things people do to their homes in the name of security actually end up making their houses *less* safe. For example, window and door grilles look like they make a home harder to break into, but they don't—a good burglar can get those security bars off in a flash. But those bars make getting *out* of the house much more difficult; they could cost your life in case of a fire (the exception to this rule is basement window grilles, which are useful deterrents in basements that aren't used as living areas).

The same is true of double-cylinder deadbolt locks (the kind that you have to open with a key, even on the inside). In the panic and confusion of a fire, you could die before finding the key. Because of this, many communities' fire codes prohibit the installation of double-cylinder locks on exterior doors. Make sure that you take all of your security concerns and local regulations into account when you install any security measure.

Alarm Systems and Other Hoopla

Your options are many here (for that very reason, we offer an entire chapter on choosing and using intruder and fire alarms). Your first choice may be between a *wired* or a *wireless* alarm system. Wireless alarm systems are usually easy to install yourself, require less physical alteration to your home, and offer most of the features you can find on hard-wired systems (but, like anything else, the better the system, the more it costs). Door and window sensors run approximately $20 each.

Sound the Alarm!

Many jurisdictions have ordinances against programming alarm telephone-dialers to dial 911. But you can program your dialer to call the seven-digit telephone number of the police department.

Most of us have bought a smoke alarm at one point or another, so you may know that you can get them for as little as $5 each. And carbon monoxide detectors can be found for less than $20. But many monitored security systems also include smoke and carbon monoxide detectors. Monitored systems will trigger an audible alarm and contact the programmed numbers whenever detectable levels of smoke or CO enter your home. Some monitored systems even trigger when the house temperature falls below a certain point, to prevent freeze damage during a homeowner's absence.

To fend off bad guys, you can use a *local alarm*, which sounds within the premises when triggered by someone going through a door or window, or by motion around or within the house. Audible alarms run anywhere from $30 to $50 each. These systems can be effective, but you have to depend on the neighbors or someone passing by to hear the alarm and call the police (your local ordinances may determine how long the alarm can sound and how loud it can be, though, so check to see if this type of system is even feasible for you). Many people use audible alarms to supplement the alarm systems in really large houses, or when they want alarms to be heard in outbuildings or guest houses.

Another inexpensive way to protect an individual door or entryway is by installing a "wedge" alarm. These battery-operated wedges cost about $20 and simply slip under your door. When the door opens, a loud alarm sounds (you can take this security system on the road with you, too).

The telephone dialer is one example of a *self-monitored system*. When the system is triggered, the dialer automatically dials four telephone numbers that you've programmed into the unit. When the call is answered, the system plays a prerecorded message for help.

A *continually monitored alarm* system is somewhat more reliable than a telephone dialer because it will trigger even if your phone lines go down. When the alarm is triggered, an audible alarm sounds, and the security service's monitoring center dispatches police to your home.

You'll have to check with your local vendors to get exact prices on the system of your choice, but in general, you can buy a wireless security system that guards two windows and a hallway for about $150, with additional window and door monitors costing less than $20. If you want to install your own monitored security system, you can buy the basic setup for around $130, with extra door and window monitors running $20 and less. The monitoring service charges its own monthly fee, which varies from area to area.

Talk the Talk

A **monitored** system is a security system that relays an alert for human intervention when a system alarm is triggered. Some monitored systems simply call programmed telephone numbers to alert specific people or agencies to a triggered alarm; other monitored systems send signals to security agencies where employees respond.

Security Password

Did you know that many wireless security systems can be activated and deactivated by remote control? You can keep the remote right there on your key chain and turn the system on or off with a single push of a button as you walk to or from your door. The remote can turn your lights on and off, too, and it can notify you by pager when the system has been activated or deactivated.

To get a professionally installed and monitored burglar and fire alarm system for a 2,500-square-foot home, you should expect to pay between $1,000 and $5,000 for the installation, and a monitoring fee of $30 to $50 per month.

You'll learn more about security alarm systems in Part 4, "Bells and Whistles: Using Alarms Systems." In that part, you learn how to choose a system, find a service, or wire up your own Ft. Knox.

Not-So-Anonymous Tip

Infrared sensors are even better than traditional motion detectors because they're triggered by body heat (of the 98.6° human variety) and therefore are less likely to go off if your cat chases a mouse across the living room floor.

For a Really Moving Security Experience

Motion detectors can go far in discouraging crimes before they happen. When these detectors sense any motion or vibration in the room, they sound an alarm, turn on a light, or contact a pager number—or do any combination of those things. In most cases, this kind of activity sends would-be intruders running. These systems don't have to be complex or expensive. For around $50, you can install a simple motion detector in any room; add another $15 bucks or so, and you can throw in a lamp activator that will make the lamps flash on and off when the motion detector is triggered.

Lights and/or a loud alarm usually are enough to scare off a criminal looking for an easy mark. But a mean, barking dog may be even more discouraging to a would-be crook. For around $50, you can buy a motion detector that triggers a ferocious barking sound whenever anything moves inside your home. (These wireless systems come complete with their own installation instructions, which we talk more about later in the book.)

A motion detector will set off a racket any time it senses anything moving in a protected area. You can even get motion detectors that turn your lights on and off—and bark like a dog!

If you want your robotic attack dog to bark on your command, you can buy one that has a key-chain remote that you can keep by your bed at night. If you wake up at night and think you've heard a noise in or near your home, you can trigger the remote to start up the electronic barking! Throw in another $20 or $25, and you can add on an outdoor motion detector that will bark and then turn on the lights indoors—is that great or what?

You don't need to adopt an electronic dog to get good protection from a motion detector, though. Even a $20 motion-detecting light over your back door could end up saving you thousands of dollars (and a lot of sleepless nights) by deterring a would-be thief. Lots of people combine motion detectors with surveillance cameras, and we'll talk about that in just a minute.

Somebody's Watching You

You probably have a security monitor camera focused on you several times a day. From highway intersections to ATMs to the local stop-and-rob (that's the convenience store, to some of you), security cameras are doing their job to help deter and gather evidence of crimes. When it comes to using monitoring cameras in private homes, we used to think that was a practice followed only by Greek shipping tycoons, Hollywood celebs, and maybe a few XXX movie producers. But today, you'd be surprised at how many average Joes (and Jo-leens) use security cameras to monitor the goings-on in and around their homes.

Home surveillance systems can be as simple or complex as you want them to be. Color and black-and-white outdoor cameras run anywhere from $100 to $400 each. Standard indoor surveillance cameras cost around $150 each, compact miniature cameras (which are less than an inch square) can be had for $80 to $100, and pinhole cameras (some of which can see through an opening no larger than 1/8 inch in diameter) cost up to $200 each.

Add another $200 for transmitters and receivers (that's for wireless surveillance systems), plus the $150–$200 cost of a monitor, and you're all set.

Of course, you can juice up this system quite a bit. Outdoor motion-triggered weather-proof cameras cost around $250. For about the same price, you can hide a covert camera inside an indoor motion detector.

Not-So-Anonymous Tip

Wireless systems are a boon to folks who live in older homes. You can install them without having to bury wiring and make other structural changes. Wireless systems offer just about any security feature that you'd find in a hard-wired system, and the technology just keeps getting better.

Sound the Alarm!

In case you were planning to add hidden protection to your bathroom, you should know that some jurisdictions prohibit the covert (hidden) videotaping of persons in areas like bathrooms, where there is a heightened expectation of privacy.

Smoke get in your eyes? This smoke detector does double-duty with its hidden surveillance camera tucked away inside.

If you don't want someone to see that you're seeing them (got that?), you can use one of many different types of surveillance camera cover-ups. You can buy a mantel or wall clock with a camera right inside ($200–$400), an alarm clock with a hidden camera ($200–$500), a desk lamp ($250–$550), or even a smoke detector with a camera buried in its belly ($200–$500). Just remember one thing—that good old camera will be watching *you*, too!

In Part 5, "I've Got an Eye on You, Babe! Setting Up Home Surveillance," I'm going to give you an eyeful of information about choosing and installing a surveillance system.

Step Away from the Car!

Last but not least, let's take a look at the typical cost of some auto-theft prevention devices. These devices range in complexity from a simple steering-wheel lock to a steering-wheel-to-pedal locking device, and cost between $25 and $50.

Car alarms are becoming much more sophisticated as car thieves get better at overcoming them. For less than $15, you can buy an alarm that fits into your cassette tape player and that can be deactivated only with a key. If anyone breaks into your car, an incredibly loud alarm sounds. Some car alarms also have a feature that disables the car, by interrupting either power or the gasoline flow. You can find one of these systems for around $75.

For an installation fee, a per-month satellite fee, and additional charges based on numbers of commands, you can have your car tracked by satellite, using Geographic Positioning System (GPS) technology. Now, this isn't a cheap solution, but if you *really* want to track down your car (or simply disable the engine, if your son tries to drive it to San Diego for the Phish-fest), you can do it with a satellite track and command system.

You'll learn a lot more keeping your car secure in Chapter 21, "I ❤ My Car: Guarding Against Vehicle Theft."

In Your Own Estimation

To start estimating the cost of the system *you* want to use, you need to return to your list of security priorities. Jot down next to those priorities the types of systems that you believe would best address the type and level of security risks on your list.

As you're considering security system options, make sure you match the level of protection the system is likely to offer with the level of risk you assigned to that particular security issue. As I said earlier, you don't need a howitzer to knock off an ant, but on the other hand, a new padlock garage door probably won't protect you from a high risk of home break-in.

Price Check

When you have a fairly good idea of what type of system (or systems) you want and need to install, you can begin looking more seriously into the cost. I've given you some rough ideas about costs for different types (and levels) of home security, but you'll want to do more research on your own, too.

To estimate the cost of any system, don't forget to add up the total number of devices (cameras, motion detectors, smoke detectors, and so on) that you will need to protect all the appropriate rooms in your house. And also remember to add in any monthly fees for off-site monitoring or services.

> **Not-So-Anonymous Tip**
>
> You'll find some good online sources for security products, and most sites also list installation and price information. (Appendix B, "Resources," lists Web addresses for several security system vendors.) You also should call local providers for estimates, check out the displays at your local home improvement store, and talk to people you know about their security systems.

Your local hardware or home improvement store will undoubtedly have a wide variety of smoke detectors, anti–auto-theft devices, security and fire alarm systems, and so on. Spend some time browsing the shelves to get an idea of the do-it-yourself price of home security.

Don't Forget the Savings!

As you're calculating the cost of a security system, you also need to factor in a few cost *savings* that some systems will bring you. For example, what about your insurance premium? Check with your agent to see if you rate a lowered premium if you install an approved type of security device. This discount could apply to both your home and your auto insurance rates.

And in some of your security priorities, the potential losses include those that are priceless. If you're looking for a system to ward off a potentially fatal accident or crime, you won't want to scrimp on the price. Everyone has limits to what they can afford, but this isn't a time to go with the cheapest solution. Finally, take a moment to figure in that incalculable "peace of mind" bonus that I mentioned earlier.

Security Password

According to research published in the *Journal of Law and Economics,* some experts estimate that the per-capita cost of crime is more than $4,000 for every person living in the United States. Believe it or not, this estimate includes costs for everything from the value of a murder victim's life to the cost of time spent locking doors and looking for keys. So, I guess that means that even if you never buy a security system at all, you're already going to end up spending a few thousand dollars on security, one way or another. Might as well get something for that money, huh?

To find some online sources for home security products and prices, check out Appendix B.

Security in the Balance

Now that you've thought about some potential fixes for your security loopholes and have gathered an estimate of the costs for those fixes, you need to figure out whether the benefit outweighs the cost. That's really pretty easy to do.

How high is the potential for the risk? How high did you rank the potential loss, or gravity of harm, for the risk? Compare those two ratings to the cost of reducing or eliminating the risk, and you should be able to determine whether the fix is worth the cost.

For example, let's say that you've been experiencing mailbox vandalism; you assigned that risk a high probability ranking but a low gravity of harm. The cost of fighting this risk by installing a reinforced concrete mailbox or high-tech surveillance system probably isn't offset by the risk's low gravity of harm. Doing nothing to combat this risk will cost you maybe $50 plus your time each time you replace a destroyed mailbox.

How much can you afford to spend, and how much can you afford to lose? The information that you've gathered in your risk assessment, along with the products and pricing information that you've pulled together in this chapter, should help you answer that question nicely. But before you spend a penny on any system, take a moment to read through the next few chapters for the fundamental security upgrades that you need to put in place first—they're cheap, they're easy, and they make any other systems that you add on more effective.

The Least You Need to Know

➤ You can choose from among a wide variety of security systems, in terms of technologies, complexity, and cost.

➤ When you're calculating the cost of a home security system, you need to be sure to figure in any monthly service fees, monitoring expenses, and other post-installation charges.

➤ You can install many security systems yourself, even relatively high-tech systems such as surveillance cameras and motion detectors.

➤ You may be able to save money by adding a security system, if your insurance company gives premium adjustments for clients who beef up security on their home or car.

➤ Some security risks aren't likely enough or potentially damaging enough to warrant high-cost, high-tech fixes. You need to match the cost to the cure.

➤ Don't forget to factor in the value you place on your peace of mind when weighing the costs and benefits of any security system.

Chapter 9

Fast, Easy, Cheap Crime-Fighting Basics

> ### In This Chapter
>
> ➤ Security "layering" starts here!
>
> ➤ Low-cost neighborhood crime busters
>
> ➤ Security savings begin at home
>
> ➤ I'm cheap—but safe!
>
> ➤ Miscellaneous crime-fighting miracles

I admit it—trimming hedges and installing a light over your front door don't have the cachet of hooking up a spy camera to catch that brat next door in the act of tagging your garage. But I've gotta tell you something: No matter how much sophisticated security gadgetry you surround yourself with, you won't really be protected if you don't begin with a layer of safety basics.

These security basics are a good idea for a very simple reason: You can't turn over the responsibility for your security to a machine, device, or security system monitor. Putting a good security system in place means *thinking* about potential dangers and doing what you can to ward them off. Toward that goal, I'm going to walk you through some very basic checklists of minimum-security safeguards and practices for reducing the risk of crime in your home.

Your First Layer of Security

No preaching or long-winded explanations here—this stuff is (as I keep saying) very simple and basic. Read through the list; check off anything you've already got covered or can implement immediately. As you make other changes, check the appropriate issues off the list.

After you've satisfied yourself that you've completed (or noted) as many of these items as you need to, you'll be ready to reassess your security status before moving on to the big-league security systems installations that I discuss in following chapters. And who knows, you may have so reduced or eliminated certain risks that you don't need further layers in that particular part of your security blanket!

Neighborhood Security Shape-up

Here are a few of the "good things" that you can do to make your neighborhood safer for you—and for everyone else, too! Remember, you can't be safe in your home if you're not safe in your 'hood.

Got it covered? ✓ it off!

If you live in a city or in an apartment:

❏ You know at least one or two families in your neighborhood/apartment building.

❏ You keep your hallways and entryways clear of trash.

❏ You report vandalism immediately.

❏ You keep an eye on strangers hanging around your building, and you report loiterers to management.

❏ You're involved in Neighborhood Watch or other community policing activities in your area.

❏ You don't prop open laundry room doors or alleyway entrances; you make sure that all outside doors close and lock behind you.

❏ You don't buzz people into the building unless you are confident that you know who they are; you refer them to the manager.

You learn how to set up a Neighborhood Watch program in Chapter 13, "Stir It Up: Start a Neighborhood Crime Watch."

Not-So-Anonymous Tip

Want to know a profile of a typical home break-in? Well, sometime during the day, while the homeowner is at work, someone forces open a door (usually a back door or an inside garage door). As soon as the burglars get in, they go around and open all the other doors, in case someone comes home and the crooks need to vamoose fast. Then they go straight for the master bedroom and look for money, jewelry, guns, and cameras. On the way out, they'll grab the TV, computers, camcorders, and any other small electronics that they can lay their hands on. In 15 minutes or so, they're out the door.

If you live in town:

- ❑ You've set up a buddy system with at least one neighbor.
- ❑ You keep your property clear of trash and junk.
- ❑ You report broken or out-of-order streetlights.
- ❑ You join the Neighborhood Watch program in your area (or start one).
- ❑ You spend time outside your property and walk through the neighborhood when you can.
- ❑ You've asked your local council to keep sidewalks in good repair, to keep the neighborhood looking good, and to encourage people to be active and visible within it.

Security Password

Neighborhood Watch programs have made a huge impact in controlling crime in areas across the country. A lot of people think they're going to have to become a twenty-first–century Barney Fife to be in the program, but it's really pretty simple. You don't have to patrol the neighborhood or chase down bandits—you don't even have to be a homeowner. You just have to keep an eye on things in your neighborhood and let others know when you see something suspicious.

If you live in the country:

❏ You have motion-sensitive lighting for all farm-yards and outbuilding exteriors.

❏ You have strong locks securing all outbuilding entrances.

❏ You keep gates and fences in good order.

❏ You've posted "No Trespassing" signs where appropriate.

❏ You keep locked gates across all access roads on your property.

❏ You inspect your property on a regular basis, to detect signs of intrusion.

❏ You know your nearest neighbor and have set up a buddy system for emergency assistance.

Sound the Alarm!

Consider using tamperproof and break-resistant globes on all outside lighting. If someone can throw a rock through your outdoor light to disable it, they can throw your yard, farm lots, and outbuildings into darkness in a matter of seconds.

Don't think that good security has to break your bank account. You learn how to set up cheap motion detectors and other outdoor security gadgets in Chapter 18, "Smile, You're on Hidden Camera!"

Minimum (Cost) Security at Home

The things you'll see in this list are inexpensive (some are even free) and are relatively simple ways to ward off crime in your home. Try to check off every item on this list.

Got it covered? ✓ it off!

Outside your house:

❏ Shrubs and hedges are trimmed back to avoid giving crooks a hiding place.

❏ Tree limbs are trimmed back to prevent people from using them to access the second story of your home.

❏ Every entryway is lighted.

❏ Outdoor lights are on at night or are connected to motion-sensitive switches.

❏ Exterior lights are high enough to prevent people from tampering with them.

❏ Ladders are put away, and outdoor sheds are locked with secure padlocks.

❏ House numbers are large and easy to see from the street.

❏ Bicycles are stored away and locked out of sight every night.

Outdoor lighting has gone high-tech in recent years. Security strobes are a new kind of outdoor security lighting that are connected with an alarm system. When the security alarm goes off, an outdoor light flashes to tell police or neighbors exactly where the alarm is located. (These strobes have no connection with Jimi Hendrix, although they may keep company with the Doors.)

No matter how little you like to "regiment" your shrubbery, it's just plain dangerous to let it get so high that it gives burglars a hiding place.

That's better! There's still plenty of greenery around the house, but no cozy nooks for burglars to hide in.

Sound the Alarm!

Double-cylinder deadbolt locks are doubly secure (they require a key on both sides), but they can be unsafe in case of a house fire. Although the key may be on a nearby table or stand, it's easy to drop or lose a key in the smoke and panic of a house fire. To combat that, many folks leave their keys in the inside lock; at that point, though, you're really compromising the value of the system in the first place. Some local fire and/or building codes prohibit the use of double-cylinder deadbolt locks on exterior residential doors. A panic-proof lock with a built-in turning mechanism is a better answer—just make sure that no glass panel is close enough to allow someone to break in and turn the lock.

This outdoor strobe light is connected to a security alarm; it flashes when the alarm sounds to guide police to the property. Although it's not particularly expensive (less than $30) or difficult to install, even the sight of this system could scare away a crook.

Check the doors:

- ❏ All doors are solid hardwood or metal and have secure, tamperproof locks.
- ❏ All lock bolts extend at least one inch into a secure strikeplate.
- ❏ Door hinges are exposed on the inside, not the outside.
- ❏ All mail slots have been sealed up.
- ❏ All outside entrances are fitted with 180° peepholes.
- ❏ Glass panels near locks are fitted with security glass.
- ❏ The door connecting the house and garage has a secure deadbolt lock.
- ❏ All sliding doors have sturdy locks *and* prop rods.
- ❏ The garage door has a secure lock that isn't connected to the automatic door opener.
- ❏ All doors are locked at night and whenever you leave the property.
- ❏ You know *everyone* who has a key to your house.
- ❏ Roof openings, old coal chutes, and exhaust vents are lockable (and kept locked).
- ❏ All outdoor storage sheds lock with a secure, tamperproof padlock.

Even that good old mini-barn needs a secure lock; why tempt thieves to poke around in your sheds, where they might find tools that will help them break into your house? Use padlocks that resist tampering or cutting.

Check the windows:

❑ All windows are fitted with secure locks and storm glazing.

❑ Windows have dowels or stop pins to allow them to open only a few inches.

❑ Basement windows are fitted with strong locks and security glass.

❑ Window air-conditioning units are bolted into the window framework.

Not-So-Anonymous Tip

If you want extra security on double-hung sash-type windows, you can make your own window stop rods from one-inch dowels. Cut the dowels to extend between the top of your lower sash and the upper part of your window frame. The window can't be opened until the dowel is taken out (from the inside, of course). Lots of folks have used prop rods to keep windows open; this one will help keep your window shut!

Inside your home:

❑ Emergency phone numbers are kept posted near the phone.

❑ You have a strong lock on your bedroom doors.

❑ You have a phone and a flashlight in each bedroom.

❑ You have a safe deposit box where you keep extremely valuable jewelry or large amounts of money (rather than in your home).

❑ You check all references of domestic workers.

❑ You don't let baby sitters entertain in your home.

❑ You don't keep valuables where they can be seen from the street.

❑ You keep blinds and curtains shut at night.

❑ You leave a radio or TV playing when you leave for short periods of time.

❑ You have a barking dog, or at least a "Beware of Dog" sign; you keep a huge dog bowl near your back door.

❑ Using a cheap engraving tool, you've engraved valuables with an identifying name/number.

Talk the Talk

Dupe numbers are the manufacturer's identifying numbers stamped on keys. These numbers identify the cut pattern of the key, so they can be used to duplicate a key without copying an original. Keep these keys at home or with you at all times—don't hand them over to service attendants or parking valets. You don't want those numbers to get around!

Check your car:

❏ You keep your car locked when it's parked (even in your garage).

❏ You leave duplicate car keys with service attendants (rather than the originals with the *dupe numbers* stamped on them).

❏ You keep copies of all your registration and insurance information at home, as well as in the car.

❏ You park in well-lighted areas whenever possible.

Don't ever underestimate the ingenuity of the criminal world. As more and more high-tech gadgetry becomes available, crooks find ways to use it in perfecting their craft. Code-grabbers, for example, are electronic devices that can pick up and remember a code transmission when you use your remote garage door opener. The captured code will then open your garage door, and the thief is in!

I'm Cheap—but Safe!

Most of the safety stuff in this list doesn't cost a thing—for the most part, this is just a list of safe behaviors. You can put these measures in action just by forming some good habits (for a change). When you've checked off each of these items, you can stand in front of the mirror and say, "I'm good, I'm smart, and, gosh darn it, I'm secure."

Got it covered? ✓ it off!

Staying safe:

❏ You never give out personal information to telephone solicitors.

❏ You never invite strangers into your home.

❏ You ask to see references and identification for all workers that you hire.

❏ You never allow workers to be in the house when you aren't there.

❏ You keep your house and car keys on detachable rings, and you never give your house keys to parking attendants or valets.

❏ You rekeyed your house when you moved in.

❏ When someone rings the doorbell, you yell, "I'll get it!" even if you're the only one at home.

❏ You arrange direct deposit for regular checks, when you can.

❏ You arrange with a neighbor to pick up your mail and newspapers while you're gone and to come in once a day to open and close drapes and turn lights on or off.

❏ You arrange to have snow cleared from your driveway when you're gone.

❏ You tell the police (or building manager) when you'll be away for extended periods.

❏ You vary your routines to prevent anyone from using your schedule to plan a crime.

In Chapter 11, "Be Your Own Bodyguard," you learn many more low-cost methods of taking the risk out of your daily life.

And While You're at It ...!

Before you move on, I just had to throw in a few last-minute miscellaneous crime-fighting ideas. None of these will require a trip to the bank, but they're all good practices:

➤ Adjust the tracks of sliding patio doors so they can't be pushed out of their tracks.

➤ Be sure that some outdoor lights are placed high enough so thieves cannot simply un-screw the bulbs.

➤ Place lights in opposite corners instead of center areas to eliminate dark spots.

➤ Never leave messages on answering machines indicating that you'll be out of town.

➤ Don't leave property unattended in your yard; it's an easy target for a crime of oppor-tunity, and you don't want to lure criminals into your property.

➤ Turn off or unplug electric garage door open-ers when you leave for a long trip or vacation. Thieves can use "code-grabbers" to gain ac-cess to unprotected, older-model electric garage doors.

Not-So-Anonymous Tip

Newer-model garage-door openers have encryptors to de-feat code-grabbers. Most large electronics stores carry encryptors for your current opener, so you can update your security without installing a new garage-door opener.

The Least You Need to Know

➤ Effective security systems depend on a firm foundation of basic crime-fighting practices.

➤ A crime-safe home needs a crime-safe neighborhood; every action you take to reduce and prevent crime in your neighborhood helps make your home a safer place to live.

➤ You can make your home a less-inviting target for crime by keeping it well-lighted, maintaining unobstructed views of the doors and entryways, and using strong locks on windows and doors—a certain amount of caution and common sense won't hurt, either.

➤ Your daily habits play a huge role in determining whether you'll be a victim of crime. Blend some security-smart habits into your current lifestyle.

Chapter 10

Low-Cost Commonsense Fire Safety Techniques

In This Chapter

➤ Fireproofing your hearth and home

➤ Appreciating the great detectors

➤ Planning the great escape

➤ A few other hot ideas

As I said back in the last chapter, the most sophisticated security system needs to rest on a foundation of basic safe practices. That applies to fire security systems, too. In later chapters, you'll learn about choosing and installing systems with smoke and fire sensors, sprinkler systems, and other pretty nifty fire safety features. But that stuff is only half-magic without the basic tools and practices that you learn about in this chapter.

None of the things that I talk about here require a huge investment of your time and money, but they'll up the value of your home security system by leaps and bounds. So chill for a minute as you burn your way through these fire-safety checklists. The more you check, the more you save!

The Fireproof Hearth and Home

Think your sweet little pad is as fire-safe as it can be? Well, I hope you're right! But just in case, take a minute to check through this list of fire-safe techniques and tools for keeping the home fires *from* burning.

Got it covered? ✓ it off!

❏ Your house numbers or E911 numbers (numbers assigned by local fire/police agencies for quick identification of rural locations) are visible from the street.

❏ All matches and lighters (and hazardous chemicals, for that matter) are kept where children can't get to them.

❏ There is a fire extinguisher in the kitchen, and at least two people in the house know how to use it.

Not-So-Anonymous Tip

Fire extinguishers come in a lot of different forms. Make sure that yours are tested and labeled by the Factory Mutual Research or Underwriters Laboratories. Fire extinguishers are classified according to what kinds of things they'll put out:

➤ Class A handles ordinary combustibles, such as fabric, wood, furniture, walls, carpets, and so on.

➤ Class B handles flammable liquids, such as grease, fat, gasoline, oil and oil paints, paint thinner, and so on.

➤ Class C handles electrical equipment, such as appliances, power tools, small motors, and so on.

It's never a bad idea to have more than one class of extinguisher—and, if possible, you should have an extinguisher in the basement, in the kitchen, and in an upstairs bedroom or hallway.

❏ If you live in an older home, you've had the wiring checked for safety.

❏ You don't overload electrical sockets or circuits.

❏ When the circuit breaker trips or a fuse blows, you find the cause and fix it (by taking some appliances off the circuit, repairing faulty wiring, and so on).

❏ All electrical cords and plugs have been checked to make sure that they aren't frayed, cracked, or scorched.

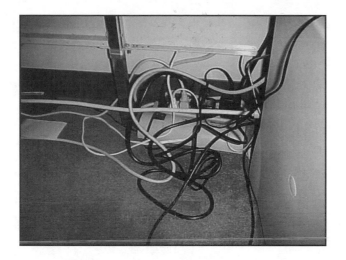

Look familiar? If you don't have to power a small village from one electrical outlet, please don't. Although extension cords and plug extenders seem cheaper than re-wiring your home, they won't seem nearly so economical when your wiring fails and a fire breaks out.

❏ You make sure that all the vents on your TV, VCR, stereo equipment, and appliances are open and free from dust. (I know, that dust thing's a tricky one. Just keep at it.)

❏ You clean the lint trap on your dryer with each load, and you check the exhaust pipe occasionally to remove built-up lint that has blown into it.

❏ You regularly clean and service your furnace and all portable heating devices.

❏ You never put portable heaters in hallways or doorways, and you *always* keep them away from draperies, furniture, and papers.

❏ You never add fuel to a portable heater while it's on or still hot.

❏ You have your fireplace chimney cleaned regularly.

❏ You use a screen and chimney fire arrestor in your fireplace.

A simple chimney cap or spark arrestor won't be expensive to buy and install, but it can save a lot of money if it prevents a wayward fireplace spark from lighting up your life.

❏ You keep trees trimmed back at least 10 feet from your chimneys, and you keep brush trimmed back 100 feet from your home.

❏ You know how to put out a cooking fire.

❏ Curtains, towels, and other combustibles are kept away from the cooking area.

❏ No one leaves the stove unattended for long periods of time when it's on.

❏ You clean the stove's vent hood filter regularly, to prevent it from becoming a major grease jam.

❏ You make absolutely sure that no one in your house smokes in bed.

❏ You never smoke when you're handling gasoline.

❏ Every smoker in your family follows the motto "If you have to put it down, put it out."

❏ You don't keep piles of newspapers, empty cardboard boxes, and other stacks of flammable rubbish around your home.

❏ You sleep with your bedroom doors closed.

Sound the Alarm!

I know that it always looks cool when folks in the movies kick back in bed with a ciggie, but smoking in bed is just plain stupid. More than 4,000 people die every year in house fires, and close to 30,000 are injured. And the number-one cause of fatal house fires is careless smoking. If you connect the dots, I think you'll see that smoking in bed just shouldn't be in the picture.

Security Password

Most fires occur at night when people are asleep. You should have a smoke detector in each bedroom, but if you don't, make sure that you have one in your stairwells and hallways near the bedrooms.

The Great Detectors

Smoke detectors are cheap, easy to use, simple to install, and real lifesavers. Here are a few "best practices" for the care and feeding of these beasts—and their gas-sniffing cousins, carbon monoxide detectors.

Carbon monoxide detectors are still an evolving technology, so to speak. There has been a lot of debate among safety groups, the National Gas Association, and several testing agencies as to just how effective the little devils really are. Many problems stem from the fact that nearby traffic or power plants can up the CO levels outside, which naturally can then up the CO levels *inside*. A number of false carbon monoxide alarms can keep any fire-fighting agency stretched beyond its limits. However, most firefighters and public safety groups agree that every house should have at least one CO detector.

If you thought that the only source of silent and deadly gas was your Uncle Morrie, you're wrong. Learn more about carbon monoxide poisoning threats in the home in Chapter 2, "Principles of Protection."

Got it covered? ✓ it off!

❏ Smoke detectors are located in central areas around your house and are mounted high on the wall or ceiling.

❏ Everyone in your home knows how to recognize the sound of the smoke detector.

❏ None of your smoke detectors is near the doors, windows, or vents.

❏ You clean smoke detectors twice a year and check their batteries every month or so.

❏ You have battery-powered smoke detectors, not just those that go down when the power fails.

❏ You have at least one carbon monoxide (CO) detector in your home, and you check it regularly.

❏ You know what the CO alarm sounds like and what to do if it triggers (open windows, get outside, call 911).

❏ All chimneys and heating element exhaust vents are kept clean and clear.

❏ You don't let your car run in a closed garage.

❏ You've had every alteration to your gas lines or exhaust systems checked by a professional.

Maintaining smoke and CO detectors in your home is just about the best security investment you can make. Put them up and check them regularly, so you don't get caught with your detectors down.

Sound the Alarm!

Anyone can die of carbon monoxide poisoning, but children and people with heart and lung problems are the most vulnerable. One of the deadliest qualities of CO poisoning is that it makes your thinking "foggy," which can prevent you from realizing that you're suffering the symptoms of exposure (headache, dizziness, weakness, nausea, shortness of breath, rapid heartbeat, loss of hearing, blurry vision, and even cardiac arrest and coma).

Sound the Alarm!

Toxic smoke can completely fill a house in less than three minutes. Sleeping with your door closed may slow the spread of smoke to your room and give you extra time to escape.

Planning Your Great Escape

If you always wanted to get away from it all, now's the time to make your plan. Firefighters agree that one of the most important things you can do to keep your family safe is to teach everyone what to do in case of fire. If you live in an apartment building, you have the benefit of lighted exit signs and fire-walled escape corridors. But wherever you live, planning what to do in case of a fire is essential to any good security plan.

Not-So-Anonymous Tip

You can do an official escape plan pretty easily. Just draw up a rough floor plan of your house or apartment. Use a colored pen (blue, for example) to note doors, windows, big pieces of furniture, and fire extinguishers. Then use a red pen to draw a couple of escape routes from each room. Draw a plan for each floor, and then go over it with your kids a couple of times a year.

Got it covered? ✓ it off!

❏ Everyone in your family knows where to meet outside in case of a fire, and how and when to call 911.

❏ Everyone in your family knows at least two ways to get out of every room.

❏ All upstairs rooms have roll-up or fold-up ladders or other escape avenues.

❏ Everyone in your family knows that, if a fire breaks out, they should feel all doors before opening them.

❏ Everyone knows to drop and crawl to move through smoke (about 12 inches of breathable air will rest on the floor).

❏ You participate in the Tot Finder and Pet Finder programs in your area.

❏ Your kids know not to hide if a fire breaks out, and they know not to go back inside for any reason.

If you think putting all of these basic fire-safety practices in place takes too much time, you should try recovering from the effects of not having them when you need them. No matter what types of systems you "layer" on top of this fire-safety foundation, the practices you've learned in this chapter are your most important step toward protecting your house and property from the dangers of a house fire.

The Least You Need to Know

➤ Fire safety is a fundamental part of your home security plan, and a good fire safety system includes basic fire-smart tools and practices.

➤ Regular servicing and maintenance of stoves, chimneys, heaters, and electrical equipment is essential to fire prevention.

➤ Everyone in your home should know certain rules for fire-safe behavior: how to recognize alarms, when and how to call 911, and how to use fire extinguishers.

➤ Smoke detectors are incredibly important in protecting you and your family from injury or death in a fire; check and clean them regularly.

➤ Get an escape plan together: Whether you live in an apartment, house, or mobile home, everyone in your family needs to know at least two ways to get out of every room—and where to meet once they're outside.

Chapter 11

Be Your Own Bodyguard

> ### In This Chapter
>
> ➤ Acquiring day-to-day security smarts
>
> ➤ Home-alone security
>
> ➤ When a baby sitter calls
>
> ➤ Home-away-from-home security

Maybe you don't envision yourself as a black-belted living weapon, karate-chopping your way from the parking lot into the grocery store. Even so, you have to be concerned about your personal security if you want to put together a strong home-security plan. You can up your security quotient without ever raising a hand (or a foot) in anger, simply by following a few rules of personal safety.

As I did in previous chapters in this part of the book, I'm going to present you with a checklist of personal security practices. As you check off practices that you already follow, congratulate yourself—each one is a lesson that you won't have to learn the hard way. Where you don't follow a practice, realistically assess just how hard it would be to adopt that practice, and compare that to how much you could lose if you *don't* adopt it. Your goal should be to have at least 75 percent of these items checked (100 percent would be even better, of course).

Everyday Security Smarts

Other chapters in this book have presented ideas for keeping your home secure, but how do you protect *you*—whether you're working in the yard, walking or running for exercise, driving to work, shopping, or doing any number of other mundane daily activities? You may think that you don't have the time or the need to analyze your personal security habits, but if you want to put together an effective security plan, you have to include your day-to-day personal safety concerns. If you leave many of these items unchecked, you could use a personal security makeover.

Got it covered? ✓ it off!

❏ You always stay alert and aware of what you're doing and what's going on around you.

❏ You walk calmly, confidently, and with purpose so that you don't have the appearance of a tentative, frightened victim-in-waiting.

❏ You vary your habits so that you don't run or walk the same route(s) every day.

❏ You walk in well-lighted streets and as far away from shrubs, recessed doorways, and other dark, hiding places as possible.

❏ You have studied some form of self-defense.

Not-So-Anonymous Tip

Don't bother being polite! If you are scared that someone is following you, turn around and say in your loudest and most intimidating voice, "Leave me alone!" If someone is following you when you're in your car, don't drive home or try to lose them with fast, erratic driving maneuvers (you aren't a stunt driver, are you?). Drive to the nearest open, well-lighted business or police station, and lay on the horn.

❏ You carry your wallet in an inside coat pocket or a front trouser pocket; if you carry a purse, you carry it in front of you, with the opening facing your body.

❏ You don't flash a lot of money or jewelry in public places.

❏ If you work late, you have a co-worker or a security guard walk you to your car.

❏ You keep your key in your hand as you approach your apartment, house, or car door.

❏ When you ride public transportation, you sit close to the driver and remain awake and alert.

❏ You keep your car doors locked when you drive.

❏ When stopping at a red light, you stop your car at the point where you can just see the rear tires of the car in front of you touch the road. This gives you some room to move your vehicle if someone tries to enter it while you're stopped.

❏ You park in well-lighted and well-traveled areas.

❏ You always have your keys ready when approaching your parked vehicle.

❏ You look under your car as you approach it to see if anyone is hiding there.

❏ You check the back seat of your car before you get in it, and you lock the door immediately after you get in.

❏ You don't keep your home address on anything in your car.

❏ You keep your garage-door opener on you, rather than in your car.

❏ You never leave your vehicle running, either in your driveway or away from home.

❏ You try to shop with others rather than by yourself.

❏ When shopping, you always have at least one hand and arm free.

❏ You don't take risks with strangers, including giving strangers a ride, letting them into your home, or allowing them to convince you to follow them somewhere for any reason.

Not-So-Anonymous Tip

In spite of how much other people's cell-phoning annoys us, a mobile phone can be a real lifesaver. Whatever people *really* do with their cell phones, nearly everyone who owns one says it's "for safety." Whether you're stranded on a lonely road with a flat tire or need directions through a strange part of the city at night, the immediate, portable access to assistance that a cell phone provides can reduce both your risk and your worry.

Security Password

Who knew shopping could be so dangerous? But it can, so you need to exercise as much caution as possible on your shopping trips. Look out for predators in the parking lot. Park near the building in a well-lighted area, and look around before you get out of the car, to be sure it's safe. If you have a large number of packages, ask store security to watch them at the door while you go get your car. Scan the area around your car as you're walking toward it, and then get in the car quickly and lock the door. If anyone looks or acts suspicious, turn around and go back into the store.

Not-So-Anonymous Tip

One good way to be prepared and protected is to practice strategic visualization (like defensive driving but with out gasoline). Look around and determine what threats exist in the area where you're walking, parking, and so on. Talk to yourself about it. "If I go that way, I'll have to pass that dark parking lot. It's the shortest way, but I don't like those two dark spots over there. Think I'll cross the street here and walk one more block over."

Make sure you're thinking ahead: "What's this parking lot going to look like when I get back to my car later this evening? I don't see any street lights—oh, look, there's a 24-hour grocery just across the street. I'll park there."

A Word About Self-Defense

Good personal security practices share one thing: If they don't work, at least they don't make the situation worse. For example, when you lock your door at night before you go to sleep, you aren't guaranteeing that someone can't get into your house. But the lock *may* foil a burglar's attempt, and it certainly doesn't put you at any greater risk.

Other strategies, such as active self-defense, have the possibility of backfiring. Although knowing self-defense techniques can boost your personal security "system," you need to consider it a last resort after all other personal security efforts have failed.

Remember, for self-defense strategies to work, they have to immediately incapacitate the attacker long enough for you to make an escape. Delivering a debilitating karate chop to someone's Adam's apple or jabbing their eyes out isn't quite as simple as it looks in the *Austin Powers* films. You wouldn't try to fight off a grizzly bear with a flyswatter; in the same vein, it may not be a good idea to try to fend off an attacker with the less-than-deadly "windmill" punch you learned in second grade. And keep in mind that if you pull a gun on someone, you'd better be justified, ready, and very well-trained to use it.

Finally, never forget that most self-defense techniques require lots of training and months or years of practice to be effective. And self-defense usually isn't a practical strategy for kids, elderly people, or folks with physical limitations. I'm not trying to discourage anyone from learning self-defense techniques here; I just want you to approach the idea of using this form of personal protection with open eyes.

Home-Alone Security

It doesn't matter whether you're an adult, a teenager, or a young kid—if you find yourself alone in your home, you need to follow some basic safety practices. And if your kids are loveable latch-key–ites, they have to get with the personal-security program as well.

One really important security tool everyone has at his or her disposal is an instinctive "gut response" to potential danger. When you're on your own, your internal alarm system can be your best friend. For example, if a stranger knocks at the door and you're frightened or suspicious, you need to TYI (Trust Your Instincts). Stay alert, listen to your "gut," and if you sense danger, practice these anti–home-invasion techniques:

➤ Call someone, say that you're worried about the person at your door, and remain on the phone until the situation is over.

➤ Decide whether to reply or answer the door. Your best strategy may be not to answer.

➤ If you have a cordless phone, bring it with you to the door, if you decide to answer it. Lay down the phone, and don't hang up with your friend. Your friend can overhear what's going on and summon help if needed. If the friend is close by—perhaps a neighbor—you may want to have that person come by the house.

➤ Before you answer the door, look through that peephole that I told you to install. Size up the situation, and, again, TYI. If the person (or people) at the door look threatening to you, ask the person you have on the phone to call the police.

➤ If you decide to answer the door, yell loud enough so that the person outside can hear, "I'll get it, John." You want the visitor to think someone else is in the house—and, not to be a sexist, most would-be assailants believe a man is more of a threat than a woman.

➤ If you have a panic alarm key-chain switch, have it ready. Use it at the first sign of danger.

Just because you're alone doesn't mean you have to be an "easy mark" for crime. Ready to test your solo savvy? Then, in the style to which you have become accustomed in this book, check away to see where you and yours stand on home-alone security preparedness!

Got it covered? ✓ it off!

❏ You have a set of "house rules" and have them posted where the kids can read them.

❏ Everyone in your household knows how and when to call 911.

❏ You have a fully stocked first-aid kit, and everyone in the house knows where it's kept.

❏ You've established regular check-in routines for your stay-at-home family members while you are away; they check in with you or you check in with them at regular times.

❏ You have a well-established policy for your kids on cooking or using any heat-generating appliance when no adults are at home.

❏ You have locked up anything in your home that you don't want your children to have access to (medications, guns, alcohol, and so on).

❏ Your stay-at-home family members have your work numbers, as well as the name and number of an at-home neighbor or responsible adult who lives nearby.

❏ Your children follow the same route home from school every day and check in with you immediately when they arrive home.

❏ Everyone in your family knows how to answer the phone and door when they are alone in the house (that is, always behave as if someone is with them in the home, never tell callers that other family members are absent, and so on).

❏ Everyone in the family knows to ask for identification from anyone who knocks at the door.

Sound the Alarm!

If you have an elderly parent or young children at home, fire safety needs to take a top priority in your home-security plan. Make sure that your smoke detectors are working, that everyone knows how to get out of the house during a fire, and that you've taken every reasonable precaution to avoid the chance of a fire breaking out while you're away.

❏ Everyone in your family knows that they aren't to go into the house if they return home to find the door open, a window broken, or other signs that an intruder could be inside.

❏ You know your kids' schedules, and they know yours, so no one has to worry about the others' whereabouts.

❏ You keep a cell phone with you.

❏ Elderly family members have an emergency call button for contacting help if they fall or can't get to the phone for any reason.

❏ You keep the walkways and traffic areas in your home clear of extension cords and electrical wires.

❏ All runners and area rugs are slip-resistant.

❏ You've installed grab bars near the tub and the toilet.

To learn more about fire safety, see Chapter 10, "Low-Cost Commonsense Fire Safety Techniques."

Not-So-Anonymous Tip

Role-play with your kids to see how they'd respond to emergencies or potentially danger-ous situations during your absence. By stepping through some "what if" exercises together, you'll get an idea of how well-prepared they are to be alone, and they'll have an oppor-tunity to learn the *right* techniques for dealing with the unexpected.

Your children should know how to use the fire extinguisher, what to tell callers, when and how to call 911, how to get in touch with you, who in the neighborhood to turn to for help, and how to do basic first aid. Make a game of it, but act out as many different types of emergencies as you think necessary to be sure that your kids are prepared to be on their own at home.

Mind the Baby Sitter!

If you have a baby sitter in your home, you're turning over the reins to that person for your family's safety and the well-being of your home. And the baby sitter is how old? Not to worry—baby-sitting is one of the world's oldest professions (I said *one* of them), and it doesn't have to leave you with the jitters. Take a minute to make sure you're following these basic "Baby Sitter Bootcamp" rules for keeping things under control while you're away, and you can spend some quality time *away* from the kids.

Got it covered? ✓ it off!

❑ You give your baby sitter a list of contact phone numbers and information that includes the following:

> Your location and schedule
>
> Your phone/cell phone/beeper number
>
> Your home address and phone number
>
> The local emergency number (911 or other)
>
> The names, ages, and weights of your children
>
> The phone number of a poison control center
>
> The name and phone number of nearby neighbors

❏ You have a posted list of house rules that the baby sitter has read and understands.

❏ Your baby sitter knows where to find a flashlight and knows what to do if there is a power outage.

❏ Your baby sitter knows how to use your security system.

❏ You lock all doors and windows before leaving, and you show the baby sitter how the locks work.

❏ Your baby sitter knows specifically whether he or she is allowed to take the children anywhere outside the home.

❏ Your baby sitter knows that no guests are allowed during your absence.

❏ Your baby sitter knows how to get the children out of the house in case of fire.

❏ You leave a second vehicle (if you have one available) parked in the drive when you go out for the evening, to give the illusion that adults are at home.

❏ Your baby sitter knows to get someone on the phone before he or she even thinks about answering the door.

Not-So-Anonymous Tip

Like any other person you hire, your baby sitter needs to turn over references to you—and you should check them out. Just because someone looks like the nice kid next door, you can't assume that the person *is* nice. You should be prepared to talk with the baby sitter's parents, too, because they may want to check *your* references. This is a good sign, and it gives you an important chance to find out more about the background of your potential sitter.

Home-Away-from-Home Security

You may spend more time in your car and on the road than you do in your home. Your home security plan should protect you while you're traveling—for business or pleasure—just as it does while you're in your favorite easy chair. Here are the basics for keeping your life on the road safe and secure.

Before You Leave

Planning for a trip takes a lot of effort. But don't think your planning's over when you've made your hotel reservations. Make sure you can check off the items in this list before you wave good-bye.

Got it covered? ✓ it off!

❏ You let someone you trust in your office or neighborhood know when you're leaving, where you'll be, and when you'll return.

❏ If you'll be gone a long time, you arrange for a trusted neighbor or the police to do periodic checks on your house, and you have a neighbor or house-sitter collect your mail, turn lights on and off, park in your drive, open and close blinds and curtains, and so on.

❏ If you have no "buddy system" in place, you cancel the mail and newspapers, and you set light timers to various schedules around the house.

❏ You arrange for someone to mow your lawn or handle snow removal while you're gone.

❏ You unplug heat-producing appliances (toasters, coffee pots, irons, curling irons, and so on) before you leave.

❏ If you're traveling to an exotic location, you pre-arrange contact times with someone at home, and you register with the consulate as soon as you arrive at your destination.

❏ You familiarize yourself with the location to which you're traveling before you leave so that you know where you need to go once you arrive.

❏ You take notarized photocopies of your passport with you when you travel abroad.

Security Password

Globalization of our economy means that a lot of us are vacationing and doing business in countries that are under a lot of internal turmoil. Before you travel to any remote part of the world, make sure that you study up on the customs and local political scene so that you can prepare yourself to travel safely. Remember how quickly things change. Don't rely on old information; use the Internet to check up on the international news from the area so that you know exactly what you're getting into. And don't forget those medical requirements, either; make sure that your shots are up to date and that you know exactly what kind of visas and clearance you'll need to travel into the country and across its borders.

On the Road (or in the Air)

Once you hit the road, you still need to keep security in mind. While you're rambling on, make sure you keep the items in this list "checkable."

Got it covered? ✓ it off!

❏ You always lock your luggage, and you never let it out of your sight while it's in your possession. When you leave it with a bellman or a porter, you get a receipt.

❏ You never get into a taxi with someone other than the driver already in it; you never let the driver stop to pick up someone you don't know.

❏ Even in strange cities, you always walk as though you know where you are and where you're going.

❏ You always travel with an identification card that includes medical allergies/conditions, emergency contact number, and so on.

❏ In your hotel, you always look for the fire exit nearest your room.

❏ You keep the safety lock in place at all times when you are in your hotel room.

❏ You leave valuables in the hotel safe (abroad, you take a notarized photocopy of your passport with you and leave the original in the safe).

❏ When you register at a hotel, you don't say your name loudly, and you never answer the phone with your name.

❏ You carry a rubber door wedge in your luggage and use it to wedge shut the door to your room during the night.

❏ You always request a room on an upper floor, if possible.

❏ You use your "Do Not Disturb" sign whenever you are in the room.

❏ When you arrive at your hotel room, you prop open the door with your luggage until you have inspected the room's hiding places.

❏ At night, you ask the bellman for an escort and use valet parking, if you're alone.

When you're driving, leave a bit of breathing room between your car and the one ahead. Tailgating is a major road-rage trigger. Pulling up too close at stoplights can box you in--and it gives you little or no room to maneuver if someone tries to enter your car while you're stopped.

To Rage, or Not to Rage? That's a Question?

Are you a "road-rager"? According to the American Automobile Association (AAA), between 1990 and 1996, there were 10,037 reported incidents of aggressive driving in the United States, resulting in 218 murders and 12,610 injuries! That makes road rage a real personal security issue. The number-one reported complaint that ignites the road-rage fuse is one driver who won't let another one pass.

Although it may not fit with the "winner-take-all" mentality of modern life, you have real benefits to gain by avoiding road rage—and here's how to do it:

➤ Practice the golden rule: Treat others the way you would like to be treated. I know how annoying it is to see someone speed by a whole line of merging traffic, ignoring merge signs to rush up and clog the entire system by trying to cram in at the front of the line. No way you're letting him in, right? Wrong—what'll it cost to let the jerk over? Do you think he'll learn his lesson if you don't? Give the fool a break and forget about it.

➤ Don't be the jerk who's enraging everyone else on the road. Use your turn signals and check the mirror before you change lanes; don't tailgate, put on makeup, read the newspaper, or gab on your wireless phone while zooming along at 20 mph or more over the posted speed limit.

➤ When you know that you have a killer commute in front of you, be prepared—to be calm, that is. Listen to soft and soothing music, books on tape, or low-key talk radio while driving. Give yourself plenty of time, and take construction delays in stride. Important note: Freaking out rarely reduces travel time.

➤ All of us have made some bone-headed maneuver behind the wheel at some point in our driving career. The next time you start to react to the bonehead in the car beside you, remember your last driving mistake, and feel humble. When a driver pulls something really stupid, it could just be a mistake rather than a driving philosophy.

➤ Rage begets rage. Don't flip off the other driver, throw up your hands in disgust, or try to fix that driver with your steely glare. The other driver probably doesn't care, or he or she might care and decide to start a steely glare contest that results in a 20-car pileup (with you and the other driver at the bottom).

Security Password

Some major metropolitan areas, such as Washington, D.C., have enacted road rage laws. If you're reported or observed to have been driving too aggressively, the cops can nail your lane-swapping, tailgating little fanny with stiff fines or even a license suspension. So when you're behind the wheel, be cool, my friend—be cooooooool.

➤ Avoid making eye contact with an angry driver.

➤ Don't retaliate. Never underestimate the other guy's capacity for inflicting injury. That small, mousey-looking guy might just have a gun.

➤ If an enraged driver attempts to follow you, you can bet that you don't want to pull over and have a chat. Don't drive home; go straight to the nearest police station. If you have a wireless phone, call the police. If you're on the road, look for a police car and try to signal for assistance.

➤ Never try to outrun or outdrive a road-rager. The risk of having an accident is too great. If you must stop at a traffic light or a stop sign, avoid eye contact with the other driver, keep your doors locked, and if the other driver gets out of his or her car and moves toward you, start blowing your horn and carefully pull away.

Your personal security is your business. You don't have to be a kick-boxer, a trained assassin, a stunt-driver, or a masked crime-fighter to cover your back with some sound safety practices. Think about what you're doing, stay alert to what's going on around you, and direct your efforts toward avoiding security snafus rather than recovering from them. It's the smart way to be your own bodyguard!

The Least You Need to Know

➤ Being alert and aware of what's going on around you is the cheapest and most effective form of personal security you can use.

➤ If you have young children or elderly family members at home, make sure that they know how to take care of themselves during your absence. Post rules for the kids, talk with the adults, and practice "what-if" scenarios to discuss what they'd do in case of an intruder, fire, or other emergency.

➤ If you hire a baby sitter, your home-security plan is only as sound as that person's ability to follow it. Post all the essential information so that the sitter can reach you, a responsible neighbor, and the local emergency service (911 or otherwise), if necessary.

➤ When you're traveling, take your security sense with you. Bone up on your destination so that you know where you're going once you arrive. Keep someone at home informed of your location at all times, and don't leave your home neglected, quiet, and dark during your absence.

➤ Don't be a victim—or a perpetrator—of road rage. Drive defensively, but don't make it a crusade.

Chapter 12

Your Name Here
_____:
Branding Your Stuff

In This Chapter

➤ Deciding what to record

➤ Mug shots of your loved ones (possessions, that is)

➤ Branded! Marking and engraving

➤ Making a list, checking it twice

➤ You're one-of-a-kind!

In a previous chapter, I asked you how you would estimate your losses if a house fire or burglary wiped out nearly everything you own. This isn't just a hypothetical question. If you lose property to theft or fire, you don't stand much chance of getting it back or being compensated for it if you can't describe it exactly or prove that you ever owned it.

Your insurance company has nagged you for years to photograph and engrave your possessions. Now, I'm asking you to do it—for your own good. In many cases, an engraved identity mark on a piece of goods will actually deter someone from stealing it. If someone does steal your stuff, an engraved ID will up the chances that it's recovered—and that you get it back. And that photo record will encourage Mr. Insurance Agent to cough up the bucks to replace your _entire_ surround-sound system instead of slipping you a used close-and-play if your system gets torched in a fire. Now, warm up your camera and get that motor tool in motion. We're gonna do some branding, baby!

So, What Do You Want to Record?

When you're deciding what to include in your marking and recording frenzy, think about the value of the items and how easy or difficult it would be for you to replace them. Stuff that ranks high in either area is a good candidate for engraving or photographing. Also, you should mark or photograph any item that you think someone would try to *fence* as stolen property. Your mark makes that item a lot less worth stealing—and a lot more difficult to unload.

I can't identify everything in your home that you need to record or mark, but I can give you a general list of things that I think should be included in your ID program.

Here are some of the things you should engrave, mark, or indelibly label *and* photograph:

➤ Televisions

➤ Radios

➤ Stereos (this means the amplifier, CD player, speakers, and everything else)

➤ Household appliances

➤ Sporting goods (bicycles, scuba equipment, fishing equipment, and so on)

➤ Cameras, camcorders, telescopes, microscopes, and binoculars

➤ Tools

➤ Power equipment (including tools, lawn mowers, tillers, and so on)

➤ Valuable clocks

➤ Guns

➤ Musical instruments

➤ Computers and equipment (monitors, CPUs, laptops, printers, and so on)

Here are some things you should photograph—if you can find an inconspicuous way to mark them, too, that's even better:

➤ Jewelry and watches

➤ Furs and expensive clothing (you can stitch identifying marks in the seams, inside pockets, or in other hidden spots)

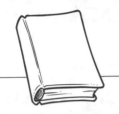

Talk the Talk

In case you sleep through most police or detective programs on television, the term **fence** means to sell stolen goods to someone who may or may not know that the stuff is hot (now, I'm not going to define that term, cause I bet you know what it means even if you did sleep through every episode of *Columbo*).

Security Password

Police monitor pawnshop records, flea markets, and classified ads searching for stolen property matches. Sometimes, thieves will even set up booths at flea markets or hold garage sales to dispose of stolen property. For the police to recover property from these sales, they must be able to identify it as being stolen.

➤ Antiques

➤ Artwork

➤ Oriental rugs

➤ Silver

One of the most important things you can do to record your possessions is to make sure that you write down the make, model number, and identification number of any appliance or other electrical device you buy. Lots of people toss away those registration cards that come with just about any electrical appliance sold today, but that record is good for more than just verifying your warranty information. Records like those can also help trace your hot property if it "goes missing" from home. So register your purchases, and keep your own list of identifying information as well.

Take a Picture, Why Don'tcha?

If you've spent much time cruising around on any online auction site, you've probably seen just how important photographs are for really describing any object. Especially if you own antiques, Oriental rugs, paintings, or other artwork, you need a photographic record that clearly identifies each piece.

A photographic record will be invaluable to you whether your possessions are destroyed or stolen. The insurance company can use your record to verify your losses, and the police will definitely use your record as they attempt to track down your stolen goods.

You can have a professional appraiser prepare a photographic record and inventory and valuation of your stuff for you. Or, you can do it yourself by photographing your possessions and documenting the value (both what you paid for the pieces and any market prices you can find for comparable items).

Security Password

Your automobiles, appliances, and many other items will already have a vehicle identification number (VIN) or registration number assigned to them. You need to keep records of all of those numbers *in addition* to the photographic records you make. You should feel free to add your own identifying mark to the items as well, in case the registration mark is ground off or obliterated.

Not-So-Anonymous Tip

Before you shoot and process 15 rolls of film, you should guarantee that your lighting is adequate. If you have any doubts about the lighting, shoot a test roll under a number of different lighting conditions (recording which lighting each photo captures), and use the results to choose the best lighting setup.

Taking the Photos

You can take your photographs with any form of camera—a self-developing camera, a 35mm camera, or a digital camera will work just fine. If you're photographing stereo equipment, expensive tools, or coins, black-and-white film is fine. Antiques, furniture, rugs, artwork, and so on should be photographed in color. Don't forget a few basic tips for these snaps:

Sound the Alarm!

Bad lighting can make a photo worthless (unless you really think that a silhouette is the best way to capture that mink coat). Don't photograph things against bright back-lighting, and make sure you set your camera's light meter to the amount of light reflected from the object you're photographing—not on the amount of light hitting the camera.

➤ Include some sort of measuring device (a yardstick or a 12-inch rule, a coin, or another "universal" object) in the photo to record the relative size of the object, where appropriate.

➤ Take full-view shots, but also take close-ups of any feature that affects the value of a piece (for example, a signature, a maker's mark, a date, or a serial number).

➤ As you're photographing, you should keep a written photo log that lists the film roll and photo number, and a description of each photo. That way, you'll know what you're missing if some of the photos don't come out.

When you get your photographs back from the developer, check each of them against your list, and make sure that you have all of the photographs you took. Reshoot any that are missing. Then write on each figure the identifying number that you assigned to it on your photo log with a short description of the subject.

Make a photo log to record each roll of film and each photograph you take. That log is an essential part of your photographic record. Your photo numbers should be in sequence from roll to roll; record each photo log number on the appropriate photo when it comes back from processing.

Photo Log Dining Room	Date 6/10/01

Film roll # 2   Film type, speed/ASA EKT. 400 36 Exp.

Photo#	Description	Price/Value
37	GRANDFATHER CLOCK ReG.# 9736410B	$5700
38	OIL PAINTING landscape, "MARSHALL, 1917"	$1500
39	Close-up of painter's mark	—
40	SPODE TEASET PoT, 2cups, Sauc.	$725
41	SPODE Label close-up	—
42	Silver Flatware DReweRy Bros Marquessa	$800
43	DINING TABLE TELLCITY, 1940's	$1700

Sound the Alarm!

Choose your weapons carefully when deciding which camera format to use in creating your photographic record. If your photos aren't right, you'll have wasted a lot of time and money. Self-developing cameras give you instant results, but they're not great for capturing close-up details. Digital cameras are wonderful—they give you instant results, and you can zap the photos around the country instantly via e-mail. But they're not great for capturing minute details, either. The 35mm cameras give you the best detail; you can get the film processed in an hour, too, so you don't have to wait forever to see the results. Make sure that you choose your camera format carefully.

Putting Together Your Photo Record

What good are all of those lovely photos if you don't know how much the stuff is worth? Along with the photographic record, you should collect and record information regarding the value of the pieces you've photographed. Receipts or other records of the amount you paid are good, but lots of things you own may go up in value every year. If you have recent appraisals or estimates of items you own, store these with the photo log and photos.

Make a copy of your photo log, and then store the original, along with the photographs and estimates, in your safe-deposit box at the bank or in a safe, fireproof location in your home. Keep the negatives or disks in a separate location, in keeping with that "spread the risk around" strategy that I told you about in Chapter 4, "Calculating Your Risks."

Not-So-Anonymous Tip

When you run across magazine articles, newspaper pieces, or even online sales information regarding the value or sale price of an item identical to or even similar to something that you own, clip it out and stash it in a drawer. Periodically round up the clippings and store them with your photographic record; this information will help you verify the value of antiques, art, and one-of-a-kind wonders.

Security Password

Keep records of your property's registration numbers, in addition to marking your property with your ID. The police can enter the registration numbers of your stolen goods into the National Crime Information Center (NCIC) computer and then track the stuff if it shows up on the market. If crooks scratch out or chisel off registration numbers and markings, the police can often raise an image of the obliterated marks.

Beware, the Mark of ME!

Your local law enforcement group may already have a property identification program (for example, Operation Identification), complete with engraving tools, instructions, and recording forms, already in place. If so, just give your local cops a buzz, and they'll tell you what you have to do to get started.

If your area doesn't have an identification program going, you can start your own exclusive little club.

One of the most common methods for marking property is to use an electronic engraving pen to etch an identifying number somewhere on the item. You hold these tools like a pen, and the tip of the tool vibrates as you write the number. For heavier metal objects, such as outdoor lawn equipment, boat trailers, and so on, you can weld on an identifying number or use metal stamps to stamp the number into the metal body of the object.

You can use an engraving pen (top) or a permanent ink marker (bottom) to put your own serial or ID number on your property. Engraved numbers are much harder to alter, remove, or cover up than those made with permanent ink.

Whatever method you use, follow these tips:

➤ Use a personal registration number other than your Social Security number. It was previously recommended that you use your Social Security number, but people are stealing those numbers themselves these days. Mark your property with some combination of your birth date and your initials, or your driver's license number or some other identifier that you can make uniquely yours.

➤ Follow the directions that come with the engraver. In case you've already thrown those away, the basic rules are to keep the engraving tool straight up, not slanted, when writing with it. Most tools have a depth adjuster that helps you crank up the power if you're engraving on a hard surface.

➤ Put the number or mark in two places, if possible; one should be clearly visible so that the would-be thief knows he's stealing branded property that will be hard to unload. The other one should be hidden so that if the thief finds a way to obliterate the first mark, your other mark is still there.

➤ Be sure to make a record of your marked property, along with the identifying marks that you've given each piece. Put the record in a safe place.

Sound the Alarm!

Lots of people use a permanent ink marker to ID their property, but this method isn't as effective as stamping, engraving, or welding on your number. Inked numbers are easy to alter, erase, and cover up.

Security Password

If you carry a laptop, you really should take the time to engrave an ID on it. Some insurance industry groups estimate that nearly 400,000 laptops (containing data and software worth well over $15 billion dollars) are stolen every year.

John Smith, Des Moines, 99-1234

When choosing a serial number, use some combination of your name, initials, city name, and a sequential number. Your Social Security or driver's license number make it easier for the police to trace the property back to you, but they give thieves important personal information about you.

Not–So–Anonymous Tip

You don't have to use a long number alone to mark your goods. If you have any other kind of identifying mark, such as a logo or a stamp, use it. Or, if the item itself has a little "beauty mark," such as a unique bit of damage or repair, record that mark in your log. Anything you can use to identify something as yours puts you one step ahead of Joe Criminal.

Make Those Lists!

I don't want to beat this into the ground or anything, but I would like to show you some ideas for recording the vital statistics for your valuables. I've shown you one arrangement for a photo log—here are a couple of other records you might keep.

You'll need a good form for recording the VIN, registration numbers, and other vital IDs for your car, motorcycle, camper, boat, bike, or what-have-you. This is one version, with some identifying notes for a car:

Make/Year/Model	Color/ID Marks	License #	Serial # or VIN	Cost
Toyota 1998 Camry	Dark green/ tan interior cigarette burn on carpet near passenger door	18G4381	187435555555	$15,000

And don't forget to keep the same kind of record for your credit cards, too:

Card Type	Bank/Origin	Acct Name	Acct#

The important thing about any list you keep is to record any important identifying information for your property, and then *put the list in a safe place.* These lists really need to be kept in copies; one in a fire-safe place in your home and the other in a safe-deposit box or with a trusted friend or relative. That way, you're covered in almost any event.

The Least You Need to Know

➤ Your records and property identification marks can help prevent your property from being stolen, or help you get it back or replace it if it is stolen or destroyed.

➤ You need to take photographs of your property, but you also need to log those photos and keep the log in a safe place.

➤ Property identification marks can be numbers, combinations of numbers and initials, or any identifying logo, stamp, or design. Even noted repairs and damage can help identify stolen property.

Chapter 13

Stir It Up: Start a Neighborhood Crime Watch

In This Chapter

➤ Starting a Neighborhood Watch program

➤ What are we watching?

➤ Keeping the group alive

In case I didn't mention this in just about every previous chapter in this book, let me tell you right now that your neighbors are among the most important crime-fighting tools you can use. (And I'm not assuming here that you live between Louis Freeh and Jean-Claude Van Damme, either.) I know that living in anonymity among your fellow man—and woman—has its appeal, but if danger comes to call, you sure will appreciate a nearby helping hand.

My all-time favorite author (and fellow Hoosier) Kurt Vonnegut has often written of his admiration for our nation's volunteer fire departments, and his reasoning extends to community policing groups, too. He has rightly pointed out that in a culture where the nuclear family has been blown apart and extended families communicate over satellites instead of Sunday dinner, these volunteer groups give us the helping hand that we used to get from our nearby kith and kin. Support, protection, aid—that's just what Neighborhood Watch groups provide.

And, unlike real family members, your fellow neighborhood watchers probably won't feel compelled to tell you to keep your hair out of your eyes or stand up straight!

Count the Ways Neighborhood Watch Helps *You*

Neighborhood Watch programs are groups of people who watch for and report suspicious people or activities in the area where they live. Depending on the interests of the program members, the group can also organize periodic educational events, public service training, or property identification programs. The members of each group determine the shape and focus of its activities.

Security Password

If you want to get involved in an existing watch program in your neighborhood, contact the local police or law enforcement agency. Or, call the number listed on the Neighborhood Watch sign in your area.

Not-So-Anonymous Tip

The Neighborhood Watch program can be adapted to almost any group or geographic area—for example, you could form a boat watch, a business watch, an apartment watch, a crop watch, or a park watch group. Whatever the focus, the purpose remains the same: people banding together to help keep things safe and secure.

Nearly every police program in the United States encourages and supports Neighborhood Watch programs—and with good reason. Not only does community policing cut down on crime, but it also helps neighbors resolve issues that need intervention, but not necessarily from the long arm of the law.

Here are just some of the reasons that you want to start or join one of these groups:

➤ By belonging to a Neighborhood Watch group, you know what's going on in your neighborhood and are among the first to know when crimes occur near you.

➤ Neighborhood Watch groups are *proven* to be effective in preventing crime. Your participation will repay you by making your neighborhood—and your home—a safer, better place to live.

➤ Your neighbor can be a cornerstone of your home security plan. Being an active member of a Neighborhood Watch program guarantees that both the police and your neighbors will pitch in to keep your home secure.

➤ The Neighborhood Watch program educates its members about security measures that work—and don't work.

➤ Neighborhood Watch programs can be a good forum (and tool) for dealing with nuisance issues, such as barking dogs, loud parties, abandoned vehicles, neglected properties, and other things that attract crime and make a neighborhood less appealing to live in.

Being a member of the Neighborhood Watch program doesn't require that you grab a six-gun, saddle up your horse, and join a posse. And no painful initiation practices or secret handshakes are required! Here are other things that a Neighborhood Watch group *isn't*:

➤ It's not a vehicle for vigilante justice. Members don't track down criminals, interrupt burglaries in progress, or chase down fleeing suspects. They just watch for problems and report them to the police.

➤ It's not a cult. In spite of my "extended family" analogy, Neighborhood Watch programs don't require that you turn over huge portions of your life and privacy to your neighbors. Members simply get to know who lives in the neighborhood so that they know who's a resident and who's just visiting, passing through, or hanging around waiting to steal your VCR.

➤ It isn't a 24-7 commitment. You go to a few meetings and then keep your eyes open during your normal activities in the 'hood.

➤ It's not just for "town fathers"; anyone—young, old, man, woman, homeowner, or renter—can join.

Get Things Going

Your neighborhood might be a city block, the last street on the west end of a small town, or the 80 square miles owned by you and your three closest neighbors. Whatever geographic boundaries make up your neighborhood, if you decide to form a watch group, you'll want the participation of as many of its residents as possible.

In essence, here are the steps to starting your watch group:

1. Contact the local police department to find out what information it has and whether a watch group already exists in your area. Your local law-enforcement group may have a watch-group starter kit or other important information just waiting for you.

Sound the Alarm!

Don't try to cover too much with one group. Most law enforcement agencies recommend that a Neighborhood Watch group encompass no more than 25 or 30 houses so that members have no trouble identifying each other.

2. Talk to your neighbors about the neighborhood's security. Let them know you're interested in forming a Neighborhood Watch group, and gauge their interest in participating. Exchange names and phone numbers.

3. Plan a date (at least a few weeks in advance) for your first meeting (good times may be around 7 or 7:30 P.M. Monday through Thursday). Coordinate with your local law enforcement agency—someone probably will be sent to attend and speak at your first meeting.

4. Post signs and flyers around your neighborhood announcing the meeting, and send an announcement to the local paper.

5. Two or three days before the meeting, stop by to remind people of it. Invite them to attend and to bring a list of any security issues or neighborhood concerns they would like the group to address.

Not-So-Anonymous Tip

If you want to get people to attend your launch meeting, you'd better assure them of a few things. First, let them know that they won't have to attend a bunch of meetings to participate in the group. Second, reassure them that members will *not* risk their safety by participating in the program. Third, state clearly that the police will *still* do the policing, while the watchers will *simply* watch and report.

Your First Meeting

These meetings can be as formal or as informal as the group wants them to be. But your first Neighborhood Watch meeting needs to get down to business and make real headway into establishing the group and its role.

If you've organized the meeting, you should introduce yourself and then briefly talk about the basic goal of the Neighborhood Watch program. If a police officer or other community representative is there (in most cases, someone from law enforcement will attend your first meeting), introduce that person and let him or her present the watch program basics. If you're on your own, here are some topics you should cover:

➤ The goal of the watch group is to reduce crime by keeping an eye on the comings, goings, and activities within the neighborhood.

➤ Discuss crime/security problems you've noted in the neighborhood, and ask others to contribute their concerns, too.

➤ Offer some effective ways that people can prevent crime and keep the neighborhood safe (this book is full of that information).

➤ Discuss what types of suspicious behavior people should watch for (I'll talk about that in a minute).

➤ Tell people the numbers they should call to report a crime or suspicious activity.

Have a sign-up sheet near the door, or pass a clipboard with a sign-up sheet around the group. Ask people to indicate whether they'll participate, as well as if and when they'd like to have another meeting.

Things to Watch For

Your local police may give you lots of tips on what and who to keep an eye on as part of your Neighborhood Watch activities. In general, though, here are the types of things that you want to be alert to:

➤ People going door to door, especially if one remains out front while another goes to the back of a residence

➤ People who don't live in the neighborhood going into the back or side yards of homes

➤ Nonresidents carrying property down the street or to a waiting vehicle

➤ Strangers loitering in front of businesses or homes, or running through the neighborhood

➤ Lots of people coming and going from a residence on a regular basis, especially late at night or at odd hours

➤ Nonresidents tampering with doors or windows of a home or with any part of a vehicle

➤ Vehicles moving slowly through the neighborhood at night, especially with headlights out

➤ Nonresidents sitting in parked cars for long periods of time

➤ Strangers loading property into a car or truck

➤ People conducting business (exchanging money and so on) from a parked car

➤ Abandoned vehicles

➤ Any signs of forced entry, or open or broken doors and windows

Security Password

Many Neighborhood Watch groups elect a "block captain," usually the person responsible for calling meetings, contacting outside agencies for extra information or special assistance, welcoming new residents into the program, and so on. In your first meeting, ask the group if they're interested in having a captain, and if so, when they'd like to elect that person. The sign-up sheet could include a blank for nominations.

Sound the Alarm!

I can't say it often enough: *Contact the police if you hear or see something suspicious in your neighborhood.* In many cases, you won't be able to apprehend a crook or wrestle a gun from a murderer. The most effective thing you can do if you suspect that a crime has taken place is to get law enforcement help immediately.

➤ Large accumulations of goods in and around the property (people may be storing stolen goods right there in your neighborhood)

➤ Unusual noises: screams, gunshots, fighting, or dogs barking incessantly

Now, just about any of these people or situations could be perfectly harmless and reasonably explained—but they just as easily could be signaling a crime or a serious neighborhood problem. Your group should watch for these things and report them immediately to the police.

Keep the Ball Rolling

If your Neighborhood Watch program is really successful, you may find that things become so safe that people stop seeing a need for the group. Here are some ways that you can keep folks interested and active in the Neighborhood Watch program in your area:

➤ Hold periodic block parties or street festivals. These are great vehicles for keeping folks friendly and familiar with each other, and they help provide the glue that keeps the community together—and united.

➤ Have a speaker come to a member's home to talk about setting up a home security system, wiring up outdoor lighting, installing video monitoring systems, drawing up a fire escape plan, or other home security and neighborhood issues and ideas.

➤ Organize a progressive dinner or potluck supper for your neighborhood.

➤ In warm weather, host a pool party or a picnic, or set up your own outdoor "movie theater."

➤ Sponsor neighborhood clean-ups; the better kept your neighborhood is, the less appealing it becomes to criminals.

➤ Start an after-school watch program or elder watch to help guard the youngest and oldest members of your community from crime.

The more cohesive and "neighborly" your neighborhood is, the harder it will be for criminals to walk in and claim your turf for their own.

Not-So-Anonymous Tip

Just because someone is unable to leave the home easily doesn't mean that he or she can't play an important role in community policing. "Window watchers" can keep an eye on things right from the comfort of their windows (just like Jimmy and Grace did in Hitchcock's classic *Rear Window*). These watchers can help make sure that kids walk home from school safely, that neighbors' mailboxes aren't being tampered with, and that no one is loitering around on a corner with evil in his or her heart.

The Least You Need to Know

➤ A Neighborhood Watch program can make your neighborhood a safer and better place to live, raise property values, and help protect you and your family.

➤ Neighborhood Watch programs are cheap, easy, and low-maintenance crime-busting measures.

➤ Your local police or law enforcement agency will probably help you start and maintain a watch program.

➤ Being in a Neighborhood Watch program doesn't require that you risk your life, sacrifice your privacy, or give up your free time.

Chapter 14

What's Left to Do?

In This Chapter

➤ Review your crime prevention list

➤ Review your fire prevention list

➤ Reorganize and prioritize remaining needs

I must say, you've done wonders with your home—security, that is. In case you've lost track, you've taken a huge bite out of the potential for security problems in your pad.

You're in a very different "security space" than the one you occupied when you started this book—or even when you created your "must-fix" list of security risks. If you've instituted some of the basic security measures that I talked about in the preceding chapters of this part, your list of remaining issues and priorities may have changed considerably.

So before we get into the major security investments and installation segment of the book, let's take a few moments to brush up your list of security issues and priorities. Then you can concentrate on bringing out the big dogs to tackle the security problems that your fast, easy, cheap fixes couldn't eliminate.

The Way We Were

Let's take just a moment to look back over where you've been in your quest for ultimate home security:

➤ You assessed the risks you face for crime, fire, and accidents in your home.

➤ You estimated which of the risks are the most likely to occur and could be the most costly.

➤ Based on all of this information, you created a prioritized list of crime, fire, and accident risks that your security plan *must* address.

➤ You surveyed a number of potential options for eliminating or reducing your security risks.

➤ You learned the basic crime, fire, and accident security measures that you can put in place with little investment of time, energy, or money.

Security Password

Some police units divide crimes into specific categories:

Crimes of opportunity

Asset-targeting (professional burglary)

Home invasion assault/robbery

Stalking

Terrorism

The type of job you do, your associates and co-workers (and those of your family members), the assets you keep in your home, and the amount of publicity you, your family, or your belongings receive all play a role in determining which type of crime you're most likely to experience. Your fast, easy, cheap fixes will definitely reduce the potential for crimes of opportunity and even asset-targeting crimes, but you may need to think about some more-involved solutions if you're at risk for some of the other types of crime on this list.

Now whip out that prioritized list of "must fix" security issues that you created in Chapter 7, "What Your Assessment Reveals." You probably recall that this list is prioritized by several factors:

➤ The risks for crime, fire, and accidents that you are most susceptible to

➤ The help that you can realistically expect to receive from your local public safety and medical agencies

➤ The potential cost (gravity of harm) of each incident

So, just for example, let's say that your list of crime risks looks something like this:

Top Crime Security Issues I Gotta Fix

1. Make sure that the kids are safe during the after-school hours before I get home from work.

2. Make windows and doors more secure against daytime break-ins.

3. Eliminate "hiding places" and dark areas around the outside of the house.

4. Protect the house while I'm traveling.

5. Protect my business papers, laptop, and other on-the-road essentials I carry in the car.

… and so on.

Not-So-Anonymous Tip

Did you know that you can make your neighborhood safer, cleaner, and healthier by making it friendlier to nonvehicular traffic? I'm talking about walking and biking, of course. A community where people are out and about is better in a multitude of ways: Activity discourages criminals from preying on deserted areas; the chances of getting help fast in an emergency are greater when people are out in the neighborhood as opposed to driving through; upgraded sidewalks, bike paths, and better speed limit enforcement make your neighborhood more attractive to new residents; less car traffic cuts down on noise and pollution; and walking is great exercise—you're encouraging a healthier lifestyle when you encourage walking. Making your community more "walkable" is a good step toward upgrading your home security.

Now, jot down a list of the fast, easy, cheap crime-security fixes that you put in place in Chapter 9, "Fast, Easy, Cheap Crime-Fighting Basics." That list could look something like this:

1. Met two of my neighbors and discussed a "watch" exchange with them. May lead to Neighborhood Watch group.

2. Replaced locks on outside doors with more security deadbolts.

3. Trimmed the shrubs under my front windows

4. Added back and side porch lights, and replaced the burned-out bulb on the front porch.

5. Talked with the kids about safety.

Now compare what you've done with your list of "must-fix" crime issues. Talking with the neighbors is the first step in making your property safer both day and night, so that one is an important first step to making a big impact on every security issue on your list. Trimming the shrubs and adding lights helped make your house less accessible at night, but you've really just scratched the surface on eliminating those risks. Talking with your kids helps get them thinking about security, and again, that's an important first step.

Sound the Alarm!

If you decide to use a Neighborhood Watch group as part of your home security plan, make sure to follow through to get the maximum pay-off of an effective program. Once the program is rolling, don't drop the ball. Neighborhood Watch signs posted around your street will go only so far toward deterring crime. Would-be criminals are quick to spot a neighborhood that no one's watching.

Lighting up your sheds and outbuildings makes a big difference in the "crime curb appeal" of your home. If you put an outdoor light on your dark, well-hidden outbuildings, you've eliminated at least some of the risk of nighttime break-ins around your home.

Meanwhile, there's more to be done in each of these areas—not to mention the fact that you haven't done anything about the whole issue of car security. So, your revised crime to-do list might look like this:

1. Institute a firm plan with neighbors for watching each other's property; make plans for the first Neighborhood Watch meeting.
2. Install a door/window security system.
3. Set up a "check-in" routine with the kids, and teach them how and when to activate and deactivate the security system.
4. Install motion detectors for outdoor lighting, with an alarm option.
5. Put in a car security system.

Now, that wasn't so difficult, was it? Chances are good that you've whittled your list of remaining crime-prevention tasks to a manageable number. Now, on to the rest of your security make-over.

How Hot Are Your Fire Security Fixes?

So how are you set for fire safety? Well, take a look at your "must-fix" list, and then review the basics that you've already put in place. Everyone's fire-risks list will be a bit different because this one is really affected by the type of house you live in, the ages of the folks who live in it, and the proximity, equipment, staffing levels, and skill of the nearest fire-fighting unit. For example, if you lives in a relatively modern two-story home, one elderly parent lives with you, and the nearest fire department is more than seven miles away, you might have these concerns:

1. Upgrade the warning system to get up and out of the house fast.
2. Set up an escape plan that everyone can follow.
3. Make best use/placement of extinguishers to try to contain blazes until the VFD gets here.

Now, in response to these needs, you may have put the following "basic fixes" in place:

1. Added two new smoke alarms
2. Installed a drop ladder from my mom's bedroom window and showed her how to use it
3. Put another fire extinguisher in the upstairs hallway

You've definitely helped reduce your risks of losing it all in a fire, but you still have a bad situation brewing if your mom is home alone and a fire breaks out. What are the chances that she'll be able to use the extinguisher, or keep her cool and get out of the house if she starts a cooking fire while you're at work? In light of that, your new fire-security fixes list might look like this:

1. Add a monitored fire-alarm security system.
2. Get estimates on a home sprinkler system.

Like I said, your list of fire-safety concerns is unique, and you've probably taken some basic steps toward reducing and eliminating some of the risks that it contains. Re-prioritize your list of must-do fire-safety fixes in light of the changes you've already instituted, and then read on to learn how to turn the fire hose on those that remain.

Security Password

According to the National Crime Prevention Council, nearly 70 percent of those surveyed in a 1999 national crime attitudes survey said that fear of crime hadn't caused them to change their conduct over the preceding year, but fear did make them change some crime-prevention strategies around their home. For example, 52 percent of respondents reported that they were locking doors more frequently, 51 percent said they trusted strangers less, 39 percent were avoiding certain areas of the community, 19 percent were going out less, and 10 percent were installing a home security system. If active, connected communities are the safest, and if we want to deter *as well as detect* crime, we need to add a good dose of community policing, neighbor-to-neighbor buddy systems, and neighborhood social activities into our security mix.

What Does Your New List Tell You?

Use the same process that I've just described to review the changes that you've put in place to address your personal safety issues and your accident potential, both in your home and on the road. If you've started parking in well-lighted spaces, close to the entrance of the mall, that's great! But are your threats great enough to warrant buying a cell phone and learning some basic self-defense techniques, in addition to those less-demanding fixes that you've already put in place?

No matter how many new locks, smoke alarms, and other fast, easy, cheap fixes you've put in place, your risk of crime and fire may be so great that you just have to go whole hog and install a monitored system.

Now put together the remaining crime, safety, and personal/accident security fixes that you absolutely have to put in place; reprioritize where the fixes you've already instituted have reduced (but not eliminated) risks. The list you have now tells you what major security steps you need to take to protect yourself, your family, and your home—and to gain that peace of mind factor that I spoke of earlier.

Ready to Take It to the Next Level?

Now, here's a little road map to help you find the information you need to take your home security plan to the next level:

➤ If you think you need a crime or fire security alarm system, read Chapter 15, "The Shocking Truth About Security Alarm Systems," and Chapter 16, "Choosing Your Alarms and Diversions."

➤ If you know that you want to install a monitored system, but you just need to know how, read Chapter 17, "Do-It-Yourself Alarm Systems."

➤ If you're thinking about putting in a surveillance system, read Chapter 18, "Smile, You're on Hidden Camera!" Read Chapter 19, "Installing That Eye in the Sky," if you want to install one, and then check out Chapter 20, "Here Comes the Judge!" to make sure you know what you legally can and *can't* monitor.

➤ If you want to install a car alarm, see Chapter 21, "I ♥ My Car: Guarding Against Vehicle Theft."

The Least You Need to Know

➤ You've put some basic security measures in place, so your prioritized list of security issues has changed.

➤ Your new list of crime security issues reflects security gaps that can't be filled with "quick-and-easy" fixes.

➤ After putting some basic low-cost fire-safety measures in place, the fire-safety threats that remain move to your final "must-fix" list of home security issues.

➤ Your final, prioritized list of crime, fire, and other "must-fix" security issues is your roadmap for creating the home security plan that will best protect your home, property, and family.

Part 4

Bells and Whistles: Using Alarm Systems

So you've decided to go with an alarm system, eh? Good choice! Alarm systems do a great job of detecting a crime in progress, and they might even deter a criminal from targeting your stuff in the first place. And alarm systems keep getting better all the time; new wireless alarm systems are relatively cheap and a real breeze to install.

In this part of the book, I'm going to tell you a bit about how alarm systems work so that you can be a smart shopper. Then I'll show you how to choose and install the security and/or fire alarm system of your dreams. You'll be shocked, amazed, and startled at how simple and effective these systems are to install and use. So, jump to it!

Chapter 15

The Shocking Truth About Security Alarms

In This Chapter

➤ The nuts and bolts of security systems

➤ Hard-wired or wireless—what's your pleasure?

➤ Monitoring means somebody is watching—and it might be you

➤ Don't forget these other safety hitters

Unless you choose the "surprise me" approach to important purchasing decisions, you really need to know how alarm systems work; you can't choose the right one if you don't know what you're choosing. Not only is the security system going to help protect your family, your home, and all your valuable stuff, but a good security system also can make a big difference in the value of your home.

And if you think it can't be that difficult to choose a system, let me just say that it's about as easy as finding the right kind of screws at the home-improvement Deathstar or picking up some panty hose at the EverythingMart. Where did all of this variety come from?

Although all alarm systems serve the same basic function—issuing some sort of warning that something is happening that ought not to be—they do it in a number of different ways. You can go with a wired or wireless; crime, fire, or crime and fire alarm; monitored or unmonitored system; motion-detecting; phone-dialing ... well, you get the idea. Let's just slow down and move through these systems one by one, check under the hood, and kick a few tires. After all, you don't want to come home with something that doesn't fit!

All in the Family: Alarm Basics

No matter how varied their technologies may be, all alarms have certain things in common. Both fire and burglar alarm systems are triggered by some event. In the case of fire alarms, heat or smoke are the typical triggers. Most residential burglar alarms are tripped when motion is detected, when an electrical circuit is broken or closed, or even when pressure is applied to an object.

Not-So-Anonymous Tip

Not only can a good home security system up the value of your property (lots of home buyers are drawn to a home with a good security system in place), but it also can save you up to 15 percent on your homeowner's insurance.

Security Password

In some rural areas, thieves have been known to use a vehicle and a rope to yank electric meters off the walls of houses to interrupt power and disable the security system. That's why battery back-up is a good idea with hard-wired systems.

After their trigger is tripped, alarms respond with some form of action: They let out a wail, they telephone for help, they turn on a set of sprinklers, they flash lights, they disable some system (as in a car alarm that shuts off gas to the car's engine), or they do a combination of these things.

Most alarms rely upon electricity, either through the power system or from batteries, or both (the exception being a residential sprinkler system, which is powered by your home's water supply and triggered by heat). The most effective systems use house current with a rechargeable battery backup. While the current is on, a small "trickle charge" keeps the batteries juiced up; when the house current is interrupted, the battery backup automatically takes over.

The Four Horsemen

Despite their diversity, you can classify most alarm systems into four categories:

1. Simple premises alarms are designed to sound an alarm to warn the home's occupants of a single type of danger. Examples include battery-operated smoke detectors, carbon monoxide detectors, and battery-operated door wedge alarms. These alarms are effective and inexpensive.

2. Local alarm systems sound a siren or a bell both inside and outside premises to warn occupants and those in the area that the system has been tripped. Although they spread the word outside the home, these alarms are more effective than simple premises systems only if someone outside the house hears and responds to the alarm (although the outside ringer could actually scare the intruder away).

3. Telephone dialer systems dial preprogrammed telephone numbers when the alarm is tripped. Professionally monitored systems dial the security service, which then contacts the police or fire department and the home's owner (some services even send a security officer to your home). Self-monitored systems call up to four separate numbers (for example, the owner's office and cell-phone numbers, a friend or co-owner, the local police, or a neighbor) and then play a prerecorded message requesting immediate assistance. Panic buttons also fit into this category of alarm.

4. Continually monitored security systems are the most effective, but also the most expensive. When your fire or burglar alarm is tripped, this system notifies your contracted security monitoring company, which in turn calls the police or fire department. Some security companies even send a security officer to check on your home.

I tell you how to choose a good security service in Chapter 16, "Choosing Your Alarms and Diversions."

Sound the Alarm!

Some communities have noise nuisance ordinances that limit the amount of time an alarm siren can sound. Burglars have been known to trip alarms and then sit back and wait to see if the alarm shuts down or if the police or a security agency respond.

The Parts Department

Smoke and carbon monoxide (CO) detectors usually are single, self-contained units, and their parts are few (and very basic). Usually, smoke and CO detectors consist of a battery, a connector, a case, and some sort of signaling device (bell, buzzer, and so on). Your job is to buy as many of them as you need to adequately warn your entire family of a smoke or CO emergency, to position them where they give maximum coverage, and to install and regularly test the batteries.

It's not so easy with other systems—well, it's not so simple, I should say. Although security systems have as many options and add-ons as your typical luxury car, here are the basic components that make up most of them:

➤ *Control panels* are the "brains" of the security system. The control panel receives the signal that the alarm has been tripped and activates the appropriate response (calling for help, sounding an alarm, and so on).

The control panel is the brains of most fire and crime security systems.

➤ *Security keypads* are your "keys" that turn the system on and off. You use the keypad by entering a code or a personal identification number to arm and disarm the system. (Some systems also provide you with a key switch.)

This keypad arms or disarms the system when you enter a code.

➤ *Sensors* are a vital part of security systems; reacting to motion, heat, sound, or the breaking of a magnetic contact, the sensors trigger the system. Typical sensors include magnetic contacts, motion detectors, and glass-break detectors.

➤ Interior alarms, exterior sirens, and visible alarm signals are the "voices" of most security systems. Sirens, buzzers, and bells are typical audible signals, and flashing lights are often used as visible signals. Interior signals may be located in individual sensor units or in separate locations around the house. Exterior sirens are sometimes mounted in a steel box and located under a home's eaves. A system's strobe light can be attached to a gable or another highly visible spot on the house to let police and neighbors know where the audible alarm is coming from.

Magnetic contacts are commonly used as sensors in security systems. When the door opens, the magnetic connection is broken, which triggers an alarm.

➤ Other common components include hand-held and keyless remote controls, lamp modules (these babies flash lamps on and off in alarm or provide timed lighting), and dialers (dialers telephone preprogrammed numbers when triggered and play a recorded message requesting help).

Some Sensational Add-Ons!

As I said, you can add on endlessly to almost any security system. For example, you can include surveillance cameras, sprinkler systems, or sensors that trigger an alarm when temperatures drop or water rises (racing stripes, bucket seats, and cup holders extra). Here are some of the add-ons you might want to consider for your security system:

➤ **Infrared motion detectors.** Passive infrared (PIR) motion sensors trip an alarm if they sense changes in infrared energy levels caused by someone moving around in a protected area. These detectors don't emit any energy on their own; they just "see" infrared energy emitted by people. They're a simple and cost-effective way to protect rooms, entryways, or other individual areas of a home.

Security Password

Magnetic contacts and glass-break sensors are commonly used to protect doors and windows. A magnetic contact consists of a magnetically triggered switch and a magnet. Typically, the magnet is attached to a door, and the switch is attached to a door frame; when the door opens, the alarm is tripped. Glass-break sensors trip the alarm when they hear the acoustic shock wave of breaking glass.

➤ **Panic switches or alarms.** In most cases, these alarms are manually activated switches that set off an alarm, activate a telephone dialer and message-delivery system, or otherwise bring aid to a bad situation. Panic alarms might take the form of wall-mounted switches or wireless handheld transmitters (like a garage door opener). Panic alarms are used in some "medical alert" systems, and some of them can be very sophisticated. For example, some transmitters are designed to be worn on a person's belt and send out a distress signal to a control panel if the person lies prone for longer than a preset period of time.

➤ **Residential sprinkler systems.** These sprinkler systems, plumbed into your home's water supply, are becoming more popular all the time. Typically, sprinklers are activated by heat. A water-release plate is melted by the rising heat of a fire and allows water to flow from the sprinklers over the "hot" area. These systems aren't cheap: If you build a sprinkler system into a new home, it probably will cost between $1 and $2 per square foot of coverage. Retrofitting a sprinkler system costs more—maybe even twice as much.

Security Password

Some statistics show that residential sprinkler systems can cut damage from a house fire by nearly 90 percent. Although these systems are slowly gaining popularity in private residential use, they've been used in commercial buildings for decades. The smoke alarm's warning that a fire has broken out—although critically important—may not guarantee that really young or elderly members of your household can get out alive. By stopping a fire before it spreads, a sprinkler system could make a real difference in their ability to survive a house fire.

A few other special types of alarms are worth mentioning. For example, *vehicle detection systems* use magnets (like the ones buried in the road to activate stop signals) to trip a chime or a doorbell, turn on lights, or even activate a video surveillance camera when a car enters your driveway. *Water-sensor alarms* use a float switch to trigger an alarm when water rises in your basement, and *temperature-sensor alarms* can warn you of freezing temperatures in areas where water pipes are located.

Now that you know the basic categories of alarm systems and their typical (and not-so-typical) features, let's get down to a closer look at how these systems work.

Hard-Wired or Wireless?

The ties that bind most security system components together are based on hard-wired or wireless technologies—or a combination of both. If you've purchased a phone in the past 10 years or so, you've already weighed the advantages and disadvantages of at least one form of hard-wired or wireless technologies. Many of the same pros and cons apply to these security system technologies, too.

Hard-wired systems use cable or wire to connect each of the components. This type of connection is very effective and not very susceptible to interference (although, as I said earlier, battery backup is the only way to keep your system ticking if the power goes out—or is disconnected). Lots of new homes are built with hard-wired security systems in place. The alarm system can be prewired just like the home's telephone jacks.

Sound the Alarm!

Don't think that a residential sprinkler system eliminates the need for smoke detectors and a good fire escape plan. Most sprinklers aren't smoke-activated, and smoke is responsible for a huge number of fire-related fatalities. A sprinkler system should be used only as an *addition* to the other fire safety measures that I talk about in this book.

Hard-wired systems are generally installed in either an open- or a closed-loop configuration (knowing these terms has value beyond that of impressing the salesperson at the home improvement center). *Open-loop* configurations are triggered when sensor connections are closed—in other words, the connections are open when all is well. Open a door, snap a magnetic switch up so that it connects to a magnet on the door frame, and you trip the alarm.

Most home alarm systems use a *closed-loop* configuration, in which the contacts are closed when nothing's happening. When the door is opened, the magnet separates from the magnetic switch, the circuit is interrupted, and the alarm sounds. Closed-loop configurations are considered the best because if the burglar tries to disarm the alarm by cutting the wiring before entering the door, the circuit breaks and the alarm sounds. See ya, bad boy!

Wireless technology integrates system components without using wires or cables (or belts, pulleys, chickens, or rubber cement). Wireless systems rely on radio waves that bounce between a sending unit and a receiving unit. These systems are more susceptible to interference, and (just like those wireless phones we all love) the range of each component is limited by distance and obstructions. You need to test wireless components at each location before you install them permanently.

The closed-loop configuration may be safer; it triggers if an intruder cuts the wire before opening the door or window.

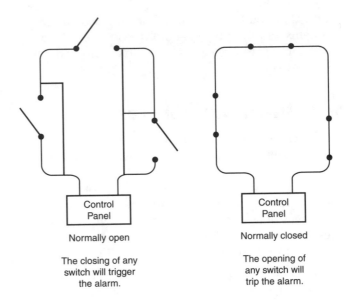

Control Panel

Normally open

The closing of any switch will trigger the alarm.

Control Panel

Normally closed

The opening of any switch will trip the alarm.

HE DID IT!

Not-So-Anonymous Tip

Wireless systems are really great if you're putting a system in an older home. You don't have to bury any wires or dig holes in your woodwork to hook everything together.

Telephone dialers come in both wired and wireless versions, too. (The wired versions use regular telephone lines.) Wireless dialers will defeat a smart burglar who tries to disarm your system by cutting your telephone line. Let 'em cut the lines—your telephone dialer works like a wireless car phone and calls for help anyway. On the other hand, not all locations are suited to wireless telephone systems, and their signal can be affected by bad weather.

Would You Like Monitoring with That?

A monitored security system is simply one that supplies some sort of guaranteed response (not just a reaction, like an alarm) to a system trigger. A trigger will cause a dialer to phone you or a security agency, or a trigger will cause a tone to sound on your laptop computer, at which time you can switch to a program that lets you see the activity being recorded by the Web-cam in your front entryway.

In other words, monitoring is really what separates the security *systems* from the security *alarms*. Now, that doesn't necessarily mean that a monitored security system includes a roomful of uniformed security officers watching a bank of TV monitors that display goings-on in every room of your home. But professionally monitored (versus self-monitored) systems usually contact a monitoring station, where the agency oversees or provides a response to the system trigger. The station operator determines what type of alarm has sounded and takes the appropriate action—by telephoning you and the proper police or fire agency, and, in some cases, by sending a security agent to your home.

Security Password

In the good old days, alarms were mechanical. That bell that jingles when you open a shopkeeper's door is a vestige of early home alarm systems. Another type of antique alarm system was rigged in the doormat; a step on the mat would shoot a puff of air down a tube to trip a door chime. Another type of door alarm worked on the same principle as "pull-the-string" talking dolls. The wind-up mechanism of the alarm was attached to the door, and its string pulled taut and connected to the wall. When the door was opened, the alarm sounded while the string retracted into the mechanism. While these systems were definitely low-tech, they were sophisticated enough to deal with the crimes—and criminals—of their time.

If you can't decide whether you need a monitored security system, don't despair. In Chapter 16, I help you decide which type of system is right for your security needs.

You're Ready to Design Your System

With that information under your belt, you're ready to move on to the decision-making stage of the security system game. In the next chapter, I'm going to help you decide which of these security systems is best for your home, sweet home.

The Least You Need to Know

➤ Home security systems involve sensors that trigger alarms when they sense smoke, heat, or movement, or when an electronic circuit opens or closes.

➤ Most security systems fall into one of four categories: simple premises alarm systems, local alarm systems, telephone dialer systems, and professionally monitored security systems.

➤ Hard-wired systems aren't subject to interference from obstacles or weakened by distance. Wireless systems offer most of the same features of hard-wired systems, but installing them is simpler.

➤ A closed-loop configuration security system will thwart a would-be thief who hopes to disable the system by cutting off the electricity because it will sound an alarm when the circuit breaks.

➤ Monitored security systems afford you the added security of having a guaranteed human response and follow-up to an alarm trigger.

➤ Motion detectors are great for guarding a single room or area; panic switches can be activated by the push of a button or by a number of other pre-programmed events or actions; residential sprinkler systems can snuff out a fire while it's still small and contained to a single area.

Chapter 16

Choosing Your Alarms and Diversions

In This Chapter

➤ Deciding what kind of coverage you need

➤ Protecting your inside and outside, and all zones in between

➤ Designing a security masterpiece

➤ Rating a security service

You've decided to install (or to have installed) a security system, so now you need to decide what type of system and components will work best for your property. You already know what you need to protect, but how are you going to protect it? Do you need to fend off intruders at every door, window, and mouse hole? Are you going to guard your house? Yard? Barn? Shed? Doghouse? All of it? Do you need a monitored security system? Should it protect you against crime? Fire? Crime and fire? Do you need motion detectors in every room? What about local alarms?

You'll answer these and other questions as you draw up a design for the perfect crime- and fire-fighting system for your baronial estate (that's your house or apartment). You'll determine what the strategic components of your system should include, where they should be located, and just how they'll be controlled.

But what if you're thinking of hiring a professional service? Well, then you're still not off the hook at this stage of the game. First of all, you need to be prepared to discuss their ideas for the security plan, so you should have an idea of what the plan should be and do. And you definitely need to know how to find, rate, and choose the best service: What kind of response time do they have, how much do they charge, how good are they at designing a system that's right for your home? By the time you hit the end of these pages, you'll be ready to make your list, check it twice, and separate the players from the also-rans.

Choosing Your Components

Let me start right off by saying that I assume you've followed the advice of previous chapters and already have taken care of the obvious first-level measures to beef up your security at home. You've installed better locks on your windows and outside doors; improved lighting around your entrances, outbuildings, and other dark areas; and trimmed back shrubbery and tree limbs to eliminate potential hiding places or second-story access to your home. You may already have installed dusk-to-dawn lights or motion-detected lighting outdoors, as well.

But if you're reading this chapter, you've decided that you need to go further than the basics to protect the perimeter of your home and property. In security system protection lingo, *perimeter* refers to the entrances to your home or apartment, including doors and windows, as well as outbuildings, yards, and drives.

Not-So-Anonymous Tip

Apartment dwellers can't just forget about outdoor security, either. Tenants have every right to ask their landlords for better outdoor lighting, safer landscaping, and other reasonable outdoor security precautions. In most cases, the closer to the ground your apartment entrance is, the stronger your outside security coverage should be. If you live on the tenth floor of a high-rise apartment building, you aren't going to have major concerns about someone entering from your balcony. But if you're on the third floor of a pre–World War II apartment building with outdoor stairways in the back, you're going to want ample outdoor lighting, locked gates protecting back entrances, reinforced door glass, peepholes, and strong door locks.

Whether you're buying a prepackaged security system and installing it yourself, or getting ready to hire a security service to do it for you, you need to take the time to decide what components your system needs (based on your research into your risks and so on) and what areas those components will cover.

If you're buying your own system, you'll undoubtedly need to buy extra components to match the system to your needs. Most prepackaged security systems come with a control panel, two or three window sensors, maybe a motion detector, and some sort of keypad or remote control. The following sections have important information to help you decide what other components your system requires.

Eliminating Windows (and Doors) of Opportunity

If you decide that you want to set up an intruder alarm system, your perimeter coverage is critical. For any such system to work effectively, you're going to need sensors or *triggers* on every entrance to your home (that includes the attached garage, if you have one).

What if you live in an apartment? Well, as I've already mentioned, your perimeter coverage needs to be stronger the closer you are to the ground. So, if you live on the first floor, you should plan to put sensors on every window and both the front and patio doors. If you're in a third floor (or higher) apartment, you probably don't need a sensor on the balcony door, unless people can climb from patio to patio on your building.

Talk the Talk

The term **trigger** is a high-security sounding name for any sensor that sets off an alarm or other programmed response when it detects motion, sound, smoke, water, or other elements or events.

Ever heard of a second-story man? Well, apartment buildings offer these high-wire crooks excellent opportunities to enter through balcony and patio doors. Make sure that you're ready "to catch a thief" at both ground-level and prime second-floor entryways.

Security Password

Most security system "packages" contain two or three door and window sensors. You can buy individual glass-break and magnetic contact sensors to beef up your entry-point protection.

If you live in a house, again, you probably need to protect all the windows that open and that are large enough for someone to climb through. If you don't have trees or other "easy access" items near the outside walls of your home, you may not need sensors on second-story windows. Although your costs go up with the number of sensors you install, don't scrimp on this area of coverage. A burglar needs only one way to get into a house; if you leave a door or window unprotected, you really waste the money you've spent on sensors elsewhere in the house.

Sound the Alarm!

Lots of folks think they don't have to worry about basement windows because they're small. Not true! Basement windows are frequently the entry point of choice for intruders. In most cases, the residents are far enough away from the basement windows that they won't hear one being tampered with or broken, and a burglar doesn't need to worry about stepping through the window and into someone's lap.

A good way to protect basement windows is to cover them with a security grille; do this *only* if the basement doesn't include sleeping or living areas. If a fire broke out, grilled windows could jeopardize the escape of anyone caught inside.

I Second That Motion Detection

Motion detectors are a great way to take your system's watchfulness to the next level. They're inexpensive to add on (usually less than $70) and are great for guarding hallways, doors, and main entryways. You also should consider putting one in your master bedroom (that's the place most crooks head for first after they get into a home). Most prepackaged systems come with one motion detector.

Do You Need an Exterior Alarm System?

If you live in the country and have no close neighbors, local alarm systems (that sound a siren inside and outside your home when an alarm is triggered) by themselves carry limited value. Even if you have neighbors but haven't included them in your security planning (a very bad move, I might add), you can't rely on a wailing siren to summon help. But local alarms with their loud outdoor alerts and modulated interior alarms can be effective add-ons to other intruder-alert systems.

For example, if you have a large farm property with several outbuildings, a loud outdoor alarm could give you early warning that someone is attempting to break into one of your buildings. And in any setting, a loud external alarm may scare a burglar into fleeing. Again, as part of a total security system that involves other kinds of sensors and alarms, local alarms can give you a good safety net against break-ins and home intrusions.

If you're considering a local alarm, you'll want to add one with sensors attached to outbuildings. You also might want to consider a driveway sensor (that triggers a door chime or video surveillance camera when someone pulls in the drive, steps on your doormat, or walks through the back yard).

Hooking up your minibarn or other storage shed to your alarm system is a good idea, especially if you store valuable tools or equipment in them. Hooking up outside buildings is incredibly easy with a wireless system, and it's not much more difficult to bury a line from your outbuildings to link them into your hard-wired security system.

Above and Beyond

Okay, now you're ready to fill in the "extras" list for your security system components. Do you need to blend residential fire sprinklers into your system? How about temperature or water sensors? Make a note of how many of them you'll need and where they should be located.

Not-So-Anonymous Tip

Not sure whether to "arm" the second-floor windows of your house? If you have a patio or balcony on the second floor, put a sensor on it (them). The majority of home break-ins are perpetrated by young men, who may be a bit more agile than you and me (hey, I don't want to generalize about you, but I'm not racing anyone up the rose trellis).

Sound the Alarm!

Be careful when considering loud exterior alarms—if they're too sensitive, placed in the wrong location, or triggered by the wrong thing, they can be problematic. Alarms that are triggered by motion or pressure in the driveway can be set off by a meter-reader, a mailman, or a paperboy. Many communities have penalties for homeowners who have repeated false alarms. Alarms that "cry wolf" can lull your watchful neighbors into complacency.

173

Crime Clock

Depending upon your location, you could be safest or most at risk during a specific hour, day, and month. In Columbus, Ohio, for example, a local TV news team did an analysis of local crime and discovered that most crimes occurred on the weekend, between the hours of 5 and 6 A.M., and that May, June, and October were the heaviest crime months of the year.

If a prepackaged system you're considering doesn't come with a panic-alarm switch, I recommend that you install one or more of them as extras to your system. As I said earlier in the book, personal alarms can be simple, freestanding devices or can be part of a local or monitored system. These alarms give shut-ins, the elderly, baby sitters, and others added protection and peace of mind.

Security by Design

To design a good security system against crime and fire, you really need to draw up a floor plan of your house, showing each room and its access to other rooms, and indicating all doors, windows, and entrances (you'll need a separate floor plan for each floor, too—no cheating!). Not only will this plan help you determine how many sensors you need and where to put them, but it also can help you locate motion detectors, smoke detectors, and alarms for maximum protection. In addition, it can help you decide where to keep the control panel, which rooms need light-control modules, and so on.

You don't have to be Frank Lloyd Wright to draw up a helpful floor plan of your house. You'll use it to help determine how many sensors you need in your security system—it'll also help you when you're planning the locations and types of components your system should have.

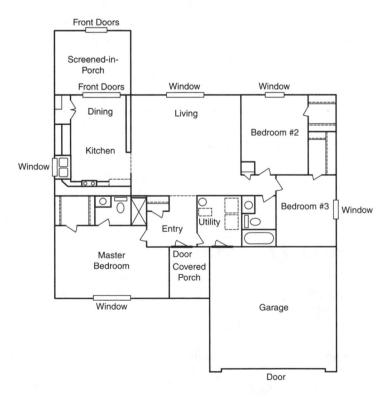

A Zoned Defense

When you're shopping for a security system package, you'll notice that the control panels can be set up to cover a range of zones. Setting up your security system by zones helps you get the coverage you need from your system, when and where you need it. Although a security zone can be a specific area, room, or group of rooms, a zone also could include a specific type of sensor throughout your home, all sensors in any one room, a single sensor, or any combination of those elements. And any one component or area can be included in multiple zones.

Rather than confuse you even more, let me show you how this zone thing works. For example, you can design your security system to have only the exterior doors activated (Zone 1) while the interior motion detector is deactivated (Zone 2). That gives you intruder protection, but it lets you move around inside while you're home and "in for the night."

Or, let's say that your bedroom is upstairs. When you go to bed, you want the sliding door and window sensors in your bedroom deactivated (Zone 3), and you want the motion detector in your bedroom and upstairs hallway turned off, too (Zone 4). You want everything else in your security system on high alert. You simply deactivate Zones 4 and 5, and the rest of your system is armed and ready for action.

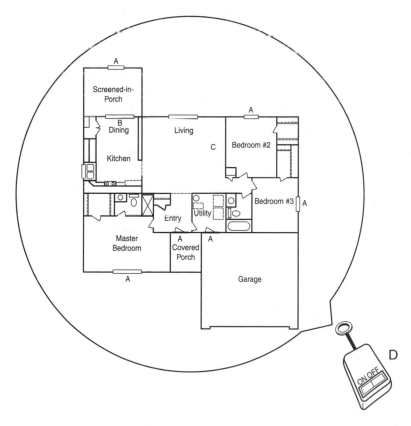

This home's security system is set up in four zones. Notice that the picture window in the living room isn't included in Zone A (accessible windows/exterior doors). It doesn't open, so no sensor is needed; and the motion detector would pick up anyone who entered by cutting through the glass.

Take a look at the figure to see an example of a four-zone security plan. Here, Zone A includes all accessible exterior windows and doors. Zone B includes only the door connecting the dining area and screened-in porch, allowing people to go in and out to the porch while the other exterior doors are armed. Zone C includes only the motion detector in the living room, which is off while people are at home. Zone D is a key-chain panic remote that activates and deactivates everything. (Panic alarms should always be in their own separate zone.)

Get Out Your Floor Plan

The control panel that you purchase limits the number of zones that you can have. That makes this preplanning stage critical; you have to plan how many zones you'll need before you buy the control panel, or you may end up with one that's just not adequate. Your biggest zone-planning tool is that handy little floor plan I talked about just a minute ago. By looking it over, and then thinking about how and when you use each area of your house, you should have a pretty good idea about the number of zones that's best for your system's design.

There's more to your designing chores than just putting in the window and door sensors, motion sensors, and control panel, though. If you decide to add extra panic buttons to accommodate someone who's sick or elderly, where are you going to put them, and do they need to be connected to audible alarms, a dialer, or both?

Not-So-Anonymous Tip

Locate a keypad or other control close enough to an entrance so that you can get to it quickly to disarm the system when you enter. Most systems (self-installed, monitored, and professionally installed) have a specific time period to arm or disarm the system after a door or window is opened or closed. Make sure you locate the control where it's possible to stay within that time frame.

While you're at it, sketch in the locations of the low-tech solutions that you added in Chapters 9, "Fast, Easy, Cheap Crime-Fighting Basics," and 10, "Low-Cost Commonsense Fire Safety Techniques." At the very minimum, a home should have at least one simple smoke detector on every level of the house. Also, a home should have at least one fire extinguisher located in or near the kitchen. A fire alarm component can easily be included with a local telephone or monitored system (and it should be on its own zone). I highly recommend including at least one smoke/heat sensor with any local telephone dialer or monitored system.

When you buy your system, take that floor plan with you. It will help you be certain that you're getting all the components you need—and that the system you're buying will fit the dimensions of your home. Don't you hate returning things when they don't fit?

Not-So-Anonymous Tip

Add the room dimensions to your floor plan; those will help you whether you're buying a wireless or a hard-wired system. For a wireless system, you can take the plan with you and check to make sure that the system you're buying has a range that will suit the dimensions of your home. If you're buying a hard-wired system, a sales representative at the home-improvement store should be able to use the room dimensions to help calculate the amount of wire you'll need to connect all the system components to the console.

Calling in the Pros

You can get professional help with your security planning, installation, and maintenance in a couple of different ways. Many self-installed home security packages, for example, include a monitoring service. You install the package and program your control panel, and then the company handles the response to alarms. Monitoring services are a nice halfway measure between total do-it-yourself security (which is perfectly adequate, in many situations) and a full-boat professionally installed and managed system.

If you decide to go with a professional security system installation and management service, you'll need to compare its system layout recommendations to the security plan that you've already sketched out for your property. Beyond the installation phase, though, the process of comparing and choosing a full-service installation is the same as that of choosing a monitoring service to cover your self-installed system. To make a call for either service, you need to compare these factors:

➤ **Reputation.** These folks are going to have the key to your castle, so to speak, so you need to check their references before you sign any contract. They should willingly tell you how long they've been in business and how many customers they have in your neighborhood. I recommend that you ask the police, the Better Business Bureau, and other consumer advocates to recommend a local monitoring company or to share with you any ratings they've given to a company you're considering. Check for local licensing requirements and be sure the company you select meets all government standards.

➤ **Response protocol.** Ask the company to specifically lay out for you—step by step—exactly what happens when an alarm is tripped. What is the company's average response time? How many numbers are called? Does the company call

177

Security Password

Find out how security monitoring companies handle false alarms. Many companies will call your home when an alarm is tripped. If you answer and tell the operator that you tripped the alarm by accident, you're asked to give a code word (one that you worked out in advance). If you do, the company doesn't call the police. This reduces your risk of fines in jurisdictions where false alarms are regulated.

Talk the Talk

In security system parlance, a **time delay** is the amount of time that you have to lock the door behind you after you've activated the alarm, and the time you have to deactivate the alarm after you've entered your house.

you or the police first? How many times will someone attempt to reach you? Does the company send an agent to your home? Is 24-7 monitoring service available, and what are the staffing levels?

➤ **Services.** So what will the company do for you if its system stops working? How often does it test system components, and does the company service any system components it sells? You need to know if you're buying *service* with this service.

➤ **False alarms.** What is the ratio of false to true alarms for a company-installed system? Does the monitoring or full-service company penalize you for false alarms? You need to know the company's specific policy on determining when an alarm is false and what false-alarm protocol it has in place.

➤ **Rates.** Of course, you want to know what the company charges. Prices vary depending upon where you live, the type of system you have installed, and the service itself. As a touchstone only, $25–$50 per month is a typical charge for a contracted monitoring service. A professionally installed system for a 2,500-square-foot home could cost anywhere between $800 and $4,000. Many companies charge between $70 and $80 per window or door.

Knowing your system is the best way to reduce false alarms. Work out a *time delay* that best suits your situation. Locate your key lock or touch pad in an area close to where you generally enter or exit. You may want to locate a touch pad just inside the door or even on the exterior side of the door. Be sure that your touch pad has an antitampering switch that will automatically activate the alarm, in case someone tries to remove or damage the touch pad.

Going with a professional security service is never the cheapest solution. You'll save around $1,000 (at least) by installing your own security system. And you can avoid monthly monitory fees by using a telephone dialer—but if you do, be sure that you follow all state and local ordinances (some places won't let you put 911 on a dialer, for example), and select contact people who are reliable and likely to be there when called.

That said, don't look on home security as a bargain-basement affair. If you don't feel comfortable in do-it-yourself mode on this one, go with the pros. If you feel like you can set it up yourself (and I'm going to show you how to do just that in the next chapter), put those extra security dollars into more sensors, better alarms, and maybe a fire sprinkler over the stove. See, no need to worry about leftover money! For a more detailed look at security system costs (both per component and for services), see Chapter 8, "Calculating Your Security Budget."

The Least You Need to Know

➤ Whether you hire a security firm to install a system for you or plan to carry out the entire installation yourself, you need to decide what types of components you want the system to contain and where those components should be located.

➤ When arming doors, windows, and other points of entry, don't limit protection to the ground floor. Second-story and basement windows and doors are frequent targets for break-in artists.

➤ Outdoor sirens and alarms can be a great addition to a security system for a farm or other property where the owner stores valuable equipment in sheds or other outbuildings.

➤ Draw up a floor plan (or floor plans if you have a multi-story property) that shows the layout of your rooms, the locations of windows and doors, and the proposed locations for security system components.

➤ Use the floor plan to arrange your system in zones, so that you can arm and disarm system components in logical groups.

➤ When you're choosing a professional security service, make sure that you check their reputation, response protocol, services offered, false-alarm ratio, and rates.

Chapter 17

Do-It-Yourself Alarm Systems

In This Chapter

➤ Security systems don't just happen—use your design!

➤ Untangling a wireless installation

➤ Weaving the web for your hard-wired system

➤ If your system's troubled, try a little troubleshooting

The hour of truth is at hand! When you've chosen and purchased the alarm system of your dreams (your wide-awake, realistic dreams, at least), you're ready to do some serious burglar-control damage and hook that baby up. The system you purchased undoubtedly came with its own instructions, which you know you have to follow. (You do know that, right? Go get that instruction booklet out of the trash, right now!) But in this chapter, I'm going to go through the process with you and give you some good general guidelines for working your way through the maze of those simple, foolproof instructions that never seem to work.

Your security system installation will undoubtedly be unique in some way. You've chosen your own configuration of components—your system may be wireless, hard-wired, or a combination of both. You may be laying all the wire for your hard-wired system yourself, or your home may have been wired for a security system when it was built, leaving nothing but the "hooking up" part of the installation to you. This chapter holds information that should help, no matter how "special" you and your installation may be.

Because hard-wired and wireless systems share many of the same components (control panel, window and door sensors, motion detectors, sirens, telephone dialers, and panic alarms), I'll begin this chapter by taking a look at the system installation itself, beginning with the wireless flavor. But before you install a thing, take a moment to get your layout in place.

Using Your System Design

In the previous chapter, I encouraged you to draw a floor plan, showing the locations of all of the components you wanted to include in your security system. Now's the time to grab that floor plan (or floor plans, if you have a multistory house) and finalize it, if you haven't already done so.

In the following sections, you learn about what limitations affect the location of components in hard-wired and wireless systems. If you're installing a wireless system, you can use your floor plan(s) to be sure that everything is located within the "range" of the system console. In a hard-wired system, the floor plan will help you figure out how much wiring you'll need to connect all the components. In either case, you need to use the plan to lay out all the system components.

Here are the components that a typical security system will include:

➤ **Control panel.** The "brains" of your system, the control panel will have a terminal strip to which you hook up the other components.

➤ **Keypad or touch pad.** Used to arm and disarm your system, the keypad sometimes has a panic alarm code.

➤ **Motion sensor.** This sensor is used to detect motion within the sensor's range.

➤ **Door and window sensors.** These sensors are used to detect when a window or door is opened.

➤ **Glass-break sensors.** These sensors are used to detect when glass is broken.

➤ **Smoke and fire sensors.** These sensors are used to detect heat and smoke.

➤ **Telephone dialer or security service.** This service is used to summon help.

➤ **Siren and strobe.** These tools are used to attract attention to the home.

➤ **Panic button.** This is used to activate the system upon command.

Getting in the Zone

Before you get busy, let's talk zones for a moment. Remember that each zone in your setup is like a separate alarm system, but all zones are connected to the same control panel. You tell the control panel which zones are to be activated—one, two, six, all, or none. The zones let you customize the system's protection to match the way you are using your home.

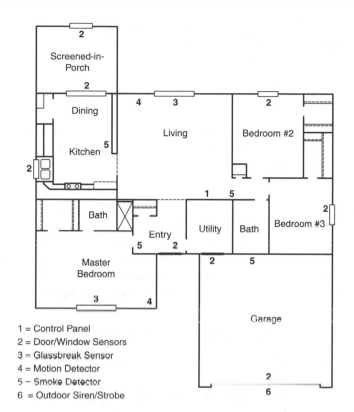

On this floor plan, I've marked the control panel and 17 other components that will be included in the security system. The picture windows in the bedroom and living room don't open, so they're equipped with glass-break sensors.

1 = Control Panel
2 = Door/Window Sensors
3 = Glassbreak Sensor
4 = Motion Detector
5 = Smoke Detector
6 = Outdoor Siren/Strobe

The number of independent zones you have is limited only by the capacity of the system's control panel. As you're installing your system, you'll need to make certain that you're following your plan's layout for the locations and the zone affiliation for each component. For example, a lot of people put motion sensors on their own zone, and all components for each level of the home on separate zones. Lay out your zones based on the way you plan to use your home, and then follow your layout in placing and connecting each component.

Okay, with your system plan in hand and your zones all nicely carved out, it's time to start putting this system in place.

Untangling the Wireless Installation

If you can set up your TV, VCR, and home entertainment center, then you can probably install your own alarm system. This is particularly true of wireless systems. Your biggest challenge in installing a wireless system will lie in locating the console where it will operate most effectively.

Unlike a hard-wired system, the wireless system relies on the successful transmission and reception of radio waves, so you have to make sure you get your console or control panel located in a spot where it can accurately send and receive signals to all its little co-worker components. With your system design floor plan(s) and a few tools, you're ready to begin setting up your system.

A Few Basic Tools

Although you aren't going to need to run a complete wiring plan, solder the entire system together, or build an electric generator from scratch, you will need a few tools to install your wireless security system:

➤ A screwdriver

➤ A pair of needle-nose pliers

➤ A wire stripper

➤ Double-sided tape

➤ A good supply of batteries for remotes, sensors, motion detectors, and so on (check the instructions that came with your system for exact numbers and size)

➤ A ladder

➤ Maybe (depending upon where you mount the components) an electric drill and some drywall anchors

This is a list of basic tools. Your home or system might require an additional tool or two. For example, if you plan to install your control panel on a brick wall, you'll likely need a masonry bit for your drill.

Everything in Its Place: Siting the System Console

Your console or control panel is going to be both the "brains" and the command center of your security system. As such, you need to make sure that it's where you can easily see and access it. If anything goes wrong with your system, a warning light will flash on the console; if you don't locate the console in a place where you'll pass by it often, you aren't likely to see the warning.

The wireless console will have to communicate with the other components in your system—the door and window sensors, motion detectors, and remote controls. So, you need to place the control panel in a location that will be central (or accessible via radio waves) to each of those components. The instructions that came with your system will tell you how broad the console's range is—usually it's 100 feet or so.

Besides requiring radio-wave access to each component, the console also must connect to your home's power supply and phone lines, so make sure that you locate it near a phone jack and electrical outlet. And try to avoid plugging the console into the same power line that feeds the television or radio—otherwise, the security system could cause interference in those devices.

Sound the Alarm!

The system's range gives you some idea of how far from the sensors and switches you can locate the console, but distance isn't everything. If you've ever used a wireless phone, you know how structural elements inside (and outside) your home can interfere with the signal. You'll need to test each component in place and perhaps test the console in a number of locations before you bolt down any of the security system components.

When you've determined where each of your components should be located, you're ready to install the system. Again, you have a complete set of instructions for installing each element of your system. But to give you a general idea of the process, I'll step you through the basics of installing some of the more common security system components.

If you need help drawing up your floor plan, go back to Chapter 16, "Choosing Your Alarms and Diversions," and read the section called "Security by Design."

Installing the Console

Installing your wireless console will involve some variation of these basic steps:

1. Your console probably has a battery backup system (it should); install the batteries now.
2. Plug the console into an electrical outlet (make sure it's not one that you can turn on and off with a wall switch).
3. If your console has an antenna, extend it all the way.
4. Use the phone cord that came with your console to connect the console to a telephone jack.
5. Turn the console switch to On, Run, Install, or the setting recommended in your instruction manual.
6. Check to see if you have to set the tone to pulse or touchtone and, if so, set it appropriately.

As I said, your console installation may vary somewhat from the preceding steps, but the instructions you receive with it will cover any changes in the procedure.

Installing the Window/Door Sensors

Depending on the make and model of the sensor you purchase, door and window sensors generally come in three parts:

1. A back cover, which you'll attach to the wall using screws and drywall anchors
2. The sensor itself, which will slide onto the back cover
3. The sensor's magnetic switch and magnet

The sensor's magnetic switch is connected to the sensor by a wire. You mount the sensor on the wall and attach the magnetic switch to the door or window frame. You then attach the magnet to the door or window itself, directly in line with the magnetic switch.

When the sensor is activated, a circuit is set up in the magnetic field between the two switches. If the door or window is opened, the circuit is interrupted (opened) and an alarm is triggered.

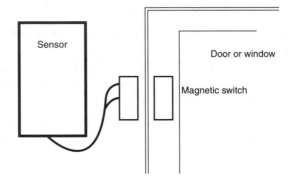

Sensor

Door or window

Magnetic switch

HE
DID IT!

Not-So-Anonymous Tip

Don't forget those zones you assigned each of your security system components to back in Chapter 16. To be sure that you know which sensor is in which zone, attach a sticky-paper dot to each sensor, and either color-code or label it to indicate to which zone you've assigned the sensor.

Most magnetic door and window sensors trigger an alarm when the magnetic connection between the magnetic switch and the magnet is interrupted, or opened. Most sensors give you the option of choosing to set them up as normally open or normally closed; Chapter 15 discussed the ins and outs of open and closed circuits, and recommended that you use normally closed settings. That way, if someone cuts the power to your sensor, the alarm is triggered.

Here are the basic steps for installing a magnetic window/door sensor (follow your own instructions, however):

1. Install batteries in the sensor, as required.
2. If you have an option, select the normally closed circuit position.

3. If you need to choose door or window sensor settings, do so now.

4. Use screws or double-stick tape to mount the sensor cover to the wall, and then slide the sensor onto it.

5. Use screws or double-stick tape to mount the magnetic switch on the door or window frame.

6. Use screws or double-stick tape to mount the magnet on the door or window.

7. Check the sensor by opening the door or window, or by using the sensor's Test button.

If you like to sleep with the windows open a bit, but you do not want to disarm the zone that contains these windows, you can have your cake and eat it by using a double-magnet setup on the windows in question. Place one magnet on the window aligned with the sensor on the window frame when the window is closed. Place another magnet a few inches below the first, where it will align with the sensor when the window is opened a few inches. You can get a breath of fresh air and still sleep soundly knowing that your security system is on the lookout.

Not-So-Anonymous Tip

Check your manufacturer's instructions, but many companies recommend that you mount the sensor high up, near the top of the window or door. Also, mount door sensors on the long side of the door, opposite the hinges.

Security Password

The sensor and one switch should already be connected with a wire; if the wire isn't long enough, you can use any suitable wire to extend the connection. If the wire is too long, cut it to the length you want, strip the ends, and then reconnect them to the magnetic switch.

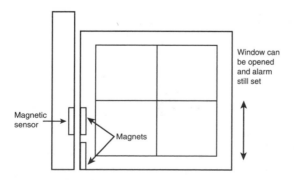

Window can be opened and alarm still set

Magnetic sensor

Magnets

By using two magnets with your magnetic window sensor, you can keep the window open a few inches while keeping that sensor armed and ready to report any movement of the window.

Sound the Alarm!

If you're mounting a magnetic sensor on a metal window or door frame, use a piece of wood or plastic to separate the magnetic switch from the metal frame. Check your manufacturer's instructions for the proper mounting instructions.

Installing a Wireless Motion Detector

Passive infrared (PIR) motion detectors work by sensing changes in temperature; they compare the background temperature with that of anything that moves across it within their range of "vision." Motion detectors can really upgrade your security system, but you need to place them carefully, or they won't be effective.

Most motion detectors include a swivel-mounting bracket that lets you change the side-to-side orientation of the detector to get the best coverage. The detector has a specific range that determines how many feet it can monitor. For example, a typical midrange motion detector will be able to "see" up to about 40 feet away and within a 90° span.

Most motion detectors work best if you place them so that anyone entering the room will cross the sensor rather than walk toward it. Make sure that the motion detectors are aimed horizontally across the room, not angled up or down.

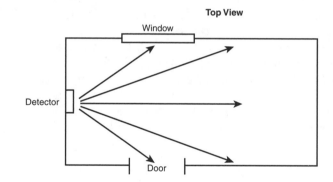

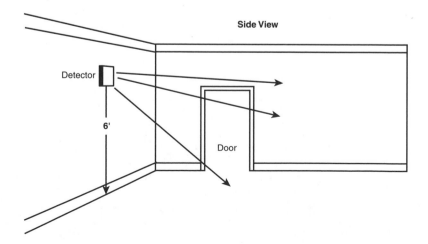

You can mount motion detectors on the wall or on a counter. Most manufacturers recommend that you mount the motion detector six or seven feet high, making sure that it's horizontal rather than angled down or up. And try to place and aim the motion detector so that anyone entering the area will walk *across* its "field of vision" rather than directly toward the detector (it's more likely that the detector will sense movement that way).

Here are the basic steps that your instructions probably include:

1. Mark the mounting location on the wall.
2. Install the necessary batteries, and label the monitor with a zone indicator.
3. Mount the detector using screws or double-sided tape.
4. Activate and test the detector using the manufacturer's instructions.

Motion detectors are an important component to your total security alarm system. They are a security safety net that will detect an intruder should the interloper be able to gain entry and avoid your perimeter security measures.

Installing Other Wireless Components

You won't have any trouble installing and setting up the other wireless components in your system. *Lamp modules,* for example, work much like light timers that many folks are already using in your home. The instructions that come with the module will walk you through the process. Do be sure that you don't hook up the lamp module to a lamp that can be controlled by a wall on/off switch. In most cases, you hook up the lamp module by turning the lamp's on/off switch to the "On" position, and then plugging the lamp into the lamp module. Then you plug the module into the wall switch.

Panic buttons and key-chain panic transmitters are common components of most wireless systems. Most panic buttons are single-unit transmitters that

Not-So-Anonymous Tip

Your motion detector may let you choose the "sensitivity" of its trigger. That's a helpful feature, for example, if you have pets that could trigger the alarm while you're gone. Check your manufacturer's instructions, and then set and test the sensitivity with different triggers until you reach the setting that's best for your "residents."

Not-So-Anonymous Tip

Don't forget to test every component of your system as you're installing it and after the entire system is in place. Follow your manufacturer's instructions completely, and make sure that everything's up and running properly before you put the system into regular use.

189

plug into a wall socket. If you push the button, an alarm sounds for a specified period of time, and (depending upon your system) the lights may flash on and off until the system is disarmed. Key-chain panic transmitters work like garage-door openers to trigger the alarm. Follow your manufacturer's instructions to program either of these components.

Panic switches are easy to install and operate. Key-chain alarms just need a good battery, and they're ready to go. Wall-mounted switches are usually installed just like a sensor—with double-faced tape or screws. Some panic switches look like doorbells, others are activated with a key, and still others have a keypad and are activated by pressing a combination of the star and pound buttons. If your panic button is designed with a pushbutton (like a doorbell), make sure that the switch is out of the reach of small children.

Hard-Wiring Made Easy

Hard-wiring a system is a little trickier than just sticking up those wireless components—but not a lot. You need to be comfortable working with some basic tools, and you need to be sure that you understand the installation instructions and are comfortable with all the processes before you begin.

And don't forget to check your local building codes to make sure that your system isn't governed by minimum construction and performance standards—some jurisdictions have them for hard-wired security systems. In most cases, though, the codes apply to businesses rather than do-it-yourselfer home projects, especially if the installation won't radically change the structure of your home.

Sound the Alarm!

Many jurisdictions set operation standards with respect to personal alarm systems. In other words, many places have rules that you can't program certain numbers—such as 911—into your automatic dialer. Lots of areas restrict how loud your outdoor sirens can be, too, and how long they can ring. And some areas require that all hard-wired alarm systems be installed by a professional security service. Check out the regs before you buy your system or launch into your project. You want to know sooner rather than later if your dream system might be a regulatory nightmare.

Everyone's wiring experience is unique—some folks may be wiring a new home, and others will be wiring an existing structure—but the general process of installing a hard-wired security system involves these basic steps:

1. Use the security floor plan that you drew to determine the locations of all your components and to divide them into zones.

2. Mark the locations of all components on the walls, door frames, and window frames of your home.

3. Lay in the wiring.

4. Install the control panel and other components.

5. Connect all components into the control panel.

6. Test the system.

In Chapter 16, I gave you an estimate on how much you can save by installing your own security system. Money aside, though, you need to be honest with yourself when deciding if you're up to the task. If you're just not mechanically inclined, rethink trying to install a hard-wired system on your own. Many do-it-yourselfers have actually paid more in lost time, money, and escalating frustration by taking on jobs that a professional should do.

Get Your Tools Ready

Before you start the hard-wiring project, collect these tools and supplies:

➤ Wire strippers

➤ Needle-nose pliers

➤ *End-cuts*

➤ Soldering gun

➤ Screwdrivers, screwdriver/drill (cordless is very handy)

➤ Ladder

➤ Wire staples, drywall anchors, screws, and electrical tape

Talk the Talk

End-cuts are wire cutters that allow you to cut excess wire right next to a connection. It's important not to leave bits of wire sticking out from under a connector because that excess wire can touch something and short out your entire security system.

The toolkit's a little heftier when it comes to hardwiring a security system. Here's the stuff I recommend you have ready.

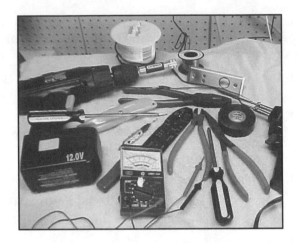

I also suggest that you buy or borrow a volt-ohm meter. You can probably pick one up for around $25 at most hardware or electronic stores. You'll use the volt-ohm meter to check the connection continuity (being sure that the connection is continuous throughout) of the line and magnetic switches.

Work from Your System Design Floor Plan

Get out your floor plan and check it over to make sure that it meshes with the system you're about to install. By now you have already determined how many zones you want in your house and what perimeter and interior sensors you want. Double-check to be sure that the control panel you purchased can accommodate all the zones that you want to set up.

Make sure that your floor plan shows where you're going to put your touch pad or keypad, panic switch, and control panel. Also indicate (if you've decided to use them) where you're going to put interior motion sensors, an outside siren, and any other components. Remember, this plan is your system blueprint.

Wire It Up!

If you're prewiring a new house (putting in the wiring before the drywall goes up) be sure to discuss the system wiring with your general contractor. He or she will likely give you advice on how to mark each area where a switch or sensor is going to be placed and how much lead wire to leave exposed at each connection. You don't want the ugly surprise of discovering that all your prewired component sites were drywalled over during your absence.

If you're hard-wiring an older home, now's the time to decide how you're going to run the wires from your components to the control panel. For both aesthetics and security, you should do your best to hide the wires. Maybe you can fish a line between the walls, either from the attic, the basement, or a crawlspace.

Or, you may be able to run the line behind your home's trim work. To do that, you'll have to pop off the trim, lay the wire, and then apply the trim back over the top of the wire. The trick here is to be absolutely certain not to run a nail or a staple through the wire when you're putting the trim back up. If you go this route, you really have to be careful with every stage. Don't crow-bar the trim off like it's made of steel—the trim will crack and splinter, and leave you with an irreparable mess. And in the best of scenarios, you should have touch-up paint or stain available to hide scratches.

If none of these sound like a good alternative, you could just staple the line as inconspicuously as possible to the floor trim. Use your judgment as to what will look right and be inconspicuous enough to avoid interference from an intruder.

Check Your Wiring, as You Go

Get out your volt-ohm meter to check the wiring to each sensor switch. The meter is simple to use:

1. After you've run your alarm wire line from the area of the control panel to the location of the first switch, twist the bare wire ends of one end of the wire together to form a "short."

2. Set the meter to the ohm function, and touch the probes to the bare wires. If the circuit is complete, the meter will show zero ohms.

3. Connect the switch to the door frame or window frame. Temporarily connect the previously twisted wire ends to the switch, completing the circuit.

Not-So-Anonymous Tip

Some places in your home may be more difficult to hard-wire than others. You may want to consider using a combination of hard-wired and wireless technology. If you decide that this "combo" setup is best for you, make sure to buy a control panel that can accommodate both or, alternatively, select a wireless control panel that can be used in combination with the main hard-wired control panel.

Not-So-Anonymous Tip

Remember, I recommend that you use normally closed circuits; those give you the most protection against an intruder who cuts the electrical lines to disarm your system. The interrupted circuit will trigger an alarm.

4. Close the door or window, and then touch the probes of the meter to the opposite end of the line. If the switches you are using are normally open, then the ohm meter should show an infinite resistance to current, meaning that the switch is open.

5. Now open the door or window; if the switch is working properly, the ohms will drop to zero, meaning that the switch is closed. (For normally closed switches, the ohms will be zero when the door or window is closed, and infinite when opened.)

Use the volt-ohm meter to check the continuity of your system's electrical circuits.

Check each switch and electrical line before you permanently connect anything. This check won't take more than a few minutes, and it'll prevent you from wasting time hooking up a component that doesn't work or running a long string of electrical wire that has a break in it.

Take a few minutes to check the switches and all your lengths of electrical wire before you hook anything up. You don't want to flush installation time down the drain on a broken line or a faulty component.

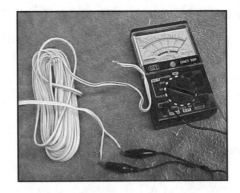

Wiring in the Sensor Switches

All the components in each zone of your system are hard-wired together, and then the entire zone is connected to the control panel. Depending on the configuration you choose, the switches in a zone will be connected in series or parallel circuits. Normally closed, or closed-loop, zones are wired in series. Normally open, or open-loop, zones are wired in parallel.

This is how it works: In a closed-loop zone, the system is at rest when current is running continuously through all the switches in the zone. If one of the switches opens and interrupts the flow of electricity through the circuit, the system is triggered.

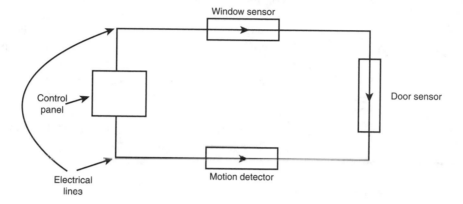

In a closed-loop zone, the current just keeps moving through the sensors and back to the control panel—unless someone opens a sensor and triggers the alarm.

In an open-loop zone, the system is at rest if *no* electricity is passing through the circuit. When someone opens a door or window or passes by a motion detector, the circuit is closed, allowing electricity to pass through the circuit and triggering the system. These systems have to be wired in parallel so that any circuit that closes will trigger the system.

When you wire up your house, the wires won't look like these neat little illustrations, but electrically they'll be wired just like they're shown in these drawings.

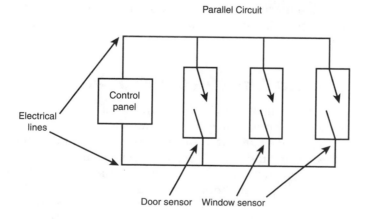

Parallel circuits operate in a way that's just the opposite of series circuits. If any sensor closes the circuit, the system is triggered. It's kind of like one of those road-trip puzzles you used to play as a child: Run your finger along the line to see how you can get from one end of the control panel to the other.

Sound the Alarm!

I can't say it too often (as you can see): Follow the manufacturer's instructions for connecting the control panel with other components.

As I mentioned before, your control panel will have a terminal strip, and all the wires leading from your alarm zones will connect to it.

The terminals will be numbered or otherwise identified for each of their respective purposes. Each terminal will include two hookups, to accommodate the two elements within each zone wire: one positive and one negative. You wire together all the components in the zone, and then you wire the zone to the corresponding terminals on the control panel. Although terminal strips vary from manufacturer to manufacturer, I've included my own post-impressionist drawing of a typical terminal strip.

Every zone gets two terminals, to connect the positive and negative cables within the wire leading from each zone.

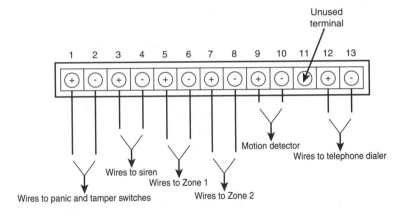

Remember each time you hookup a zone to follow the manufacturer's instructions on how to test each zone, be sure that it works before you make final installation.

Installing the Control Panel

Not-So-Anonymous Tip

I suggest that you solder the connections between the alarm wire and the switches before wrapping them in electrical tape, to ensure that the connections remain firm.

Unlike the wireless security system, a hard-wired–system console doesn't communicate with its components via radio transmission, so it needn't be within shouting distance of them, in some central location. But you do want to locate the console near an electrical outlet and phone jack. Because the hard-wired control panel isn't susceptible to interference, you don't need to locate it where you'll see it frequently to monitor for warning indicators. The indicator lights on the keypad or touch pad located near your entrance will warn you of any system triggers.

Before mounting the control panel, remove any panel "knockouts" to create openings where you'll feed wires to the panel. Ideally, the alarm wires will be fed from behind the panel—this is simple to arrange when you're prewiring the system, but it's not so easy if you're wiring an older house. In older homes, you may want to run the wires through a conduit from the floor or ceiling, depending on where they enter the room.

Line up the control panel box on the wall, and mark the location of the knockout areas and the predrilled screw holes in the panel's box casing. Set down the box, and then drill the holes in the wall. Use the appropriate kinds of screws or anchor bolts to attach the box to the wall.

Security Password

The type of "attachers" that you'll need to use are determined by the construction of the wall you're attaching the control panel to. For example, if you're attaching to drywall, use drywall anchors. Use masonry screws or anchors if your wall is made of stone or brick. And make sure before you start drilling that you won't tap into some hidden electrical, phone, or water lines.

Installing Magnetic Door/ Window Switches

Now you're ready to use the manufacturer's instructions to install the system components. I recommend that you start with the magnetic window/door switches.

Each magnetic door or window switch has two parts: a magnetic switch and a magnet. Both parts need to line up when the door or window is closed. When the magnet is in line with the magnetic switch, the switch is at "rest" in its normal position—either open or closed. You can attach magnetic door or window switches with double-backed tape or wood screws.

Most manufacturers recommend that you mount magnetic window/door switches on the frame near the top of the door or window.

The control console will likely have indicators that will let you know the status of the system. A simple console may just have a red and green indicator light. When the light is green, all the doors, windows, and sensors for that zone are closed. When the indicator light is red, that zone is armed, and opening a window or door after the time delay has elapsed on that zone will cause the alarm to trigger. More elaborate control panels will signal problems with a sensor or a switch and will flash a light during the time delay period.

Not-So-Anonymous Tip

Passive infrared motion detectors work by detecting heat moving against a steady background temperature. To prevent false alarms, avoid placing the motion detector near a heating or air-conditioning vent.

Security Password

Alarm keypads often have a simple code, usually two buttons touched at the same time that act as a panic alarm. If your keypads are designed this way, you're automatically installing a panic switch when you hook up your system keypads.

Installing a Motion Detector

You can place a motion detector or motion sensor in any room or area, but (as I told the wireless crowd earlier) you have to be careful to place them where they'll be effective. Generally, motion sensors work best when they're mounted on a wall, about six or seven feet up from the floor. The motion detector should be set parallel to the floor, not angled down or up. And you should try to place it so that anyone entering the room will cross through its path rather than approach the motion detector directly.

Check your detector's range to determine whether it has a big enough "field of vision" to handle the room or area you're protecting with it. Most motion detectors can detect motion up to a distance of about 40 feet, in a 90° field of vision. This is plenty of range for most homes. Motion detectors "see" both from side to side and up and down.

(To see my beautiful drawings of a good placement scheme for a motion detector, check the illustration in the earlier section "Installing a Wireless Motion Detector.")

Installing Panic Alarms

Hard-wired panic alarms are installed in much the same way as any other sensor or switch. To install a hard-wired panic switch, first select your location. As I said earlier, it should be in an area out of reach of small children (you know how kids love to push buttons). Attach an alarm line to each side of the switch's terminals, and run the line back to the control panel terminal strip. The terminal strip will be marked with letters or numbers that correspond to the manufacturer's instructions, which indicate the purpose of each terminal. Locate the terminals for the panic switch, and connect the remaining end of the wire accordingly.

Installing and Programming Your Telephone Dialer

There are a wide variety of telephone dialers, and your hookup process will depend on which variety you use. Most telephone dialers use landlines, but you can also purchase wireless telephone dialers that don't depend on telephone lines to call for help.

The dialers are easy to install. If you're using a landline model, you'll need a telephone jack. Plug the dialer into the telephone jack, and run the alarm wire from the dialer's terminal jacks to the appropriate control panel terminal screws.

Programming your dialer will be completely explained in your owner's manual, but in general, dialers work like answering machines in reverse. Make sense? No? Okay, you prerecord a message into your dialer, and then you program in the phone numbers to be dialed in an emergency. When the system is triggered, the dialer calls the numbers (in the sequence you specify) and then plays the message.

Installing Strobes, Sirens, and So On

As I stated earlier in the book, installing an outside siren or bell and a strobe light can be a really good idea. On houses, these should be installed on the street side and at a high point of the house, such as at the peak of a gable. For apartments, a good place to install an outside siren and strobe is about six to seven feet from the main entrance to your apartment; it should be protected inside a metal console. (You'll need to get the permission of your landlord to make this installation, of course.)

The actual installation is simple (not afraid of heights, are you?). Get out the ladder and make your way up to the roof or gable, or wherever you have decided that you will get the most street-side "notice" from your siren and strobe. Then follow these steps:

1. On the control panel terminal strip, find the terminal screws for the siren (again, your instruction manual will tell you which ones these are).

2. Run the line up to where you are going to place the siren and strobe.

Not-So-Anonymous Tip

In most cases, you'll hook the siren and strobe together in a parallel circuit, with one alarm wire running from the control panel to the siren and strobe. Most control panels have only one set of terminals for a siren, so by wiring the strobe and siren together at one end, you can hook them both up, and both will go off if the system is triggered.

Sound the Alarm!

Always remember to test the circuit for continuity. You don't
want to wire up an outside siren
and strobe system only to discover after the fact that there's
a break in the wiring or that a
switch doesn't work.

3. Attach the alarm wire to the siren terminal connection screws.

4. Run a piece of alarm wire from the siren terminal connection screws to the strobe's terminal
connection screws.

5. Attach the strobe and siren units to the house
using wood screws or masonry screws (depending on the surface you're attaching them to).

6. Secure the wire with electrical staples or other
device so that it's firmly anchored to the wall
of the building to which you've attached the
alarms.

If you took communication classes in school, you
learned how helpful audio-visual aids can be when
you're trying to make a point. Sirens and strobes are a
great way to get the attention of passers-by and direct the police or fire department to
your location. And all that noise and those flashing lights are sure to encourage any
burglar to beat a retreat.

A Little Troubleshooting on the Side

As I said earlier, before you put the final touches on your installation, make sure that
you follow the manufacturer's guidelines for testing and troubleshooting your system.
I'm going to give you a few troubleshooting tips of my own because you can never
have too much good advice, now can you?

You've put your system together, and something's not working. Here are some logical
next steps for locating the problem:

➤ **Check the power.** Do the control panel lights illuminate? For wireless systems,
do all the components have live batteries? Is proper voltage running to the
control panel?

➤ **Check the wiring.** Did you wire in series for normally closed circuits and parallel for normally opened circuits? Run a continuity test between each sensor and
the control panel.

➤ **Check the sensors.** If you used multiple sensors, test each one in progression
(that means you must disconnect all but the first sensor, test it, add the next
one, test it, and so on).

➤ **Check the voltage.** If the wiring configuration is correct, continuity is correct,
and power is present, check to see if the component has the proper amount of
voltage. The manufacturer sets the amount of voltage for the component. You

can test the terminals for proper voltage using a volt-ohm meter or a multi-meter. If the voltage isn't right, the component likely needs to be replaced or repaired by a professional.

➤ **Check the timing or other similarities in false alarms.** If you're having false alarms, try to determine if they're happening at the same time every day, or if they happen only when it storms, or look for other patterns that might lead you to uncover contributing factors.

Whether you choose hard-wired, wireless, or a combination, your system will be unique to your home and your needs. There are three "P's" to successfully installing a home security system: Preparation, Preparation, and Preparation. Carefully plan your home's security diagram. Be sure you select a system that meets your needs and your budget. Inventory the tools and parts needed for installation. And read and follow the manufacturer's installation and operation instructions.

The Least You Need to Know

➤ Your security system design is your blueprint for installation. Have it ready, with zones marked, before you begin installing your system.

➤ Wireless systems are a breeze to install, but you have to make sure that all your components are within the signal range of the control panel. Test everything in place before you screw or tape anything down.

➤ Hard-wired systems require more careful preplanning. Use your system plan to determine where components and the control panel will be located, and where to run wiring.

➤ All components within a zone are wired together, and then each zone has one wire (containing two strands) that connects to a positive and negative terminal on the control panel's terminal strip. Check the continuity of your wiring as you go.

➤ Although a hard-wired control panel doesn't have to be within "signaling" distance of the components, it does have to be hooked to a phone jack and an electrical outlet.

➤ Your system came with its own set of instructions and troubleshooting information. Use this chapter to supplement that information, not replace it.

Part 5

I've Got an Eye on You, Babe!
Setting Up Home Surveillance

Home surveillance systems aren't just for celebs and government spies. Surveillance technology has become much more simple (and less expensive) to install and use, so it's becoming popular with everyday folks like you and me. Surveillance systems can help you keep track of everything from what's going on in the kids' playroom to who's playing "knock-knock" at your front door. From nanny-cams to gateway eyes, I'll show you how to set up and use surveillance systems to help prevent crimes and accidents in your home and "on your watch."

Smile, You're on Hidden Camera!

Cracks about Big Brother aside, video surveillance has become a bit more affordable and a lot more effective than it was even five or six years ago—many homeowners are including it in their home security systems. Video surveillance can help you ward off trouble as it approaches (for example, if you have a camera monitoring your front door and walkway), and it can record infractions in action so that you can have a better shot at catching the folks who "done you wrong."

In this chapter, I give you an up-close look at what video surveillance can, can't, and *shouldn't* be used for. So don't change that dial!

Looking at Video Surveillance from Both Sides

So what are video surveillance systems (VSS), and what are they good for? Well, to begin with, a video surveillance system involves a video camera, a monitor of some sort, maybe a recording/playback device, and (often) a motion detector. The system captures, projects, and often records the activities within a given area. You've seen these things at work in stop-and-robs (I mean, convenience stores) for years now. And where would all of those *America's Funniest Security Cam Videos* programs be without VSS?

The system's purpose (in part) determines its setup. Generally, VSS is set up in one of two ways:

➤ **Overtly.** You want the possible thieves to know that the premises have video-tape surveillance. These systems have cameras placed in conspicuous locations and plenty of signs advertising the video system in place.

➤ **Covertly.** This involves hidden cameras. These systems are used to keep an eye on a housekeeper, a child caretaker, a home-repair person, or anyone in or on your property to make sure that they're not doing something that they shouldn't be.

Many systems include a combination of these methods. Some systems include an audio component so that the homeowner can hear (as well as see) what's taking place. Sometimes audio surveillance is used exclusive of video surveillance, and vice versa.

Security Password

One of the most common audio surveillance systems in use today are all those wireless baby intercoms. They work like walkie-talkies. You put the child down for a nap, set the wireless intercom next to the bed, and take the handset with you. If the baby awakes and starts crying, you hear it on your handset. These systems are also useful if you're taking care of an invalid; if the bedridden patient has a baby monitor nearby, help is available for the asking.

What Your Video Surveillance System Can Do for You

Why should you consider video surveillance technology in the first place? Well, not to repeat myself (which I try, try, try not to do), but remember that the three-part approach to deterring crime involves these three steps:

1. Reduce the opportunity for crimes to occur.
2. Increase the likelihood of criminals being caught.
3. Inflict firm consequences for infractions.

Video surveillance can help you in each of these three areas. After all, you can't be everywhere all the time. A video surveillance system (VSS) can be a real deterrent to crime if the would-be criminals know that they're being watched and videotaped. Covert video systems play a big role in catching and prosecuting criminals, too. Few pieces of evidence are quite as compelling as footage of our man "Robberick" climbing in your window and stuffing his pockets with your jewelry. The better your security system, the more peace of mind it brings you. Installing a video security setup gives a big boost to both.

Video systems are useful for keeping track of what's happening in and around your property. You can use them to monitor the "approaches" to your home, such as your driveway and entryways. You can use them as *nanny-cams* to keep tabs on what your kids are doing in their playroom, or to monitor an infant in its crib. You also can use surveillance to make sure that your cleaning service isn't taking you to the cleaners in more ways than one.

To learn about how to install a video surveillance system, see Chapter 19, "Installing That Eye in the Sky."

What Video Surveillance Can Do to You

As I've shown you, there are a number of good reasons to use video surveillance. But don't forget the downside of this type of security system, either. Here are some of the VSS pitfalls you should be aware of:

➤ A comprehensive VSS can be expensive.

➤ Hard-wired covert VSS requires some technical knowledge to install.

➤ Cameras can be stolen or damaged.

➤ A VSS requires ongoing maintenance.

➤ "Insiders" can tamper with the VSS to actually make the system work to their advantage.

➤ There might be legal challenges to a VSS in a court of law.

➤ When your home is wired up with video surveillance, it puts the entire household "on camera."

Talk the Talk

Nanny-cams are covert video surveillance systems that people set up to monitor their child's caretaker to make sure that he or she is remaining on the job, not entertaining unauthorized houseguests or using childcare tactics that the parents wouldn't approve of.

So there it is: While video surveillance is a very effective tool to deter and detect crime, it does have some pitfalls. When deciding whether or not video surveillance is a necessary part of your home security setup, make sure its benefits outweigh its potential problems.

Is Surveillance for You?

So how do you know which method of surveillance is best for your situation—or whether you want to use surveillance at all? Ask yourself these questions (I'll help you find the answers to these questions in this chapter):

1. What do you want the system to accomplish? Deter crime? Catch someone in the act of wrongdoing? Monitor the activities of infants or children?

Security Password

Keep legal and ethical issues in mind when considering whether to use a video or audio surveillance system. I'll discuss those a little later in this chapter.

2. Considering your goal, will video surveillance be effective? Will it need an audio component or the capability to record in limited lighting?

3. Can you afford the system you need?

4. Will you be able to maintain your system after it's in place?

5. Is the type of system you're considering socially acceptable and legal?

Draw up your list of goals to satisfy item 1 in the preceding list, and then use that list to determine the answer to the questions in item 2. Then read on to find the information you need to answer item 3.

Sound the Alarm!

Obstructions, distance between components, and other signal interference can all affect the range and reliability of wireless systems. Test your system before you permanently install the wireless components.

What's It Gonna Cost Me?

Now that you have set your video surveillance goals, let's take a look at what it might cost to set up your VSS. Wireless video surveillance systems are easy to use and install. Just like the wireless alarm systems, wireless audio and video systems rely on radio transmission between components to carry the signal. Wireless systems usually are portable, so you can easily move components to new locations, as necessary.

When pricing wireless or hard-wired systems, you'll quickly discover that, as with most things, the nicer the nice, the higher the price. If you want weatherproof cameras (for outside surveillance), night-vision, and "stealth" capabilities (this just means hidden units), you'll pay more.

Wireless Component Prices

You can find wireless system components in any price range, but here are a few sample components at prices that I found online when I was writing this book:

➤ A mini-wireless camera that lets you send color video and audio from an indoor or outdoor location to your TV or VCR (up to about 100 feet away) costs about $150. Now this isn't a cover system; although the camera is characterized as mini, it isn't disguised or hidden. If you want to make one of these relatively inexpensive cameras covert, you'll need to figure out a way to disguise or hide the camera on your own.

➤ A bit less basic surveillance kit, with up to three cameras, a motion-sensor trigger, and a TV/VCR hookup, costs around $200 (you provide your own TV and VCR).

Many basic wireless surveillance system kits come with a battery pack; these systems are typically set up near a threshold so that the homeowner can see who's at the door before answering it.

➤ Wireless black-and-white (or color, in some models, at a higher cost) surveillance cameras disguised as a clock radio, book, wall clock, or smoke detector cost between $250 and $500.

➤ A wireless videocassette recorder with a hidden black-and-white camera can be purchased for approximately $450.

A Brief Look at Hard-Wired Component Prices

Again, you can meet or beat the prices that I found in a number of places, but here are some representative components and their prices:

➤ A hard-wired color surveillance camera disguised as a smoke detector can be purchased for less than $220.

➤ A hard-wired black-and-white motion-sensor triggered camera costs about $130. Of course, as the name indicates, you'll have to run cable from the camera to your TV or VCR to hard-wire these cameras.

➤ You can find color hard-wired "pinhole" cameras for about $200, or black-and-white models for about $100. Pinhole cameras are those that can be mounted

behind a wall and that require a very small, almost invisible hole drilled through the wall to see the images. Professionals such as the police and security agencies often use pinhole cameras.

➤ Weatherproof black-and-white hard-wired surveillance cameras cost approximately $120 and up; color models start at about $180.

➤ Professional multispeed VCRs with time and date generators cost anywhere from $430 to $550.

➤ If you want to go superfly spy, you can buy a hidden video wristwatch and pager for between $400 and $450. You'll have to "wear a wire" to use it though, with connecting cabling to video input jacks.

You can find just about anything you need with respect to VSS to fit any budget. However, like anything else, the more elaborate the system, the more you can expect to pay.

Even Big Brother Needs an Attorney

No two ways about it, using VSS can be interpreted as an attempt to eavesdrop on unsuspecting people. A wide range of regulations govern surveillance, and if you consider using such a system, you're wise to become familiar with the regulations in your jurisdiction.

Unless you're working for the police, you don't need to be concerned about constitutional search-and-seizure issues involving video surveillance in your home. But you do need to be concerned with other covert surveillance regulations in your jurisdiction. In most jurisdictions, for example, you can legally wire up your private home and business for covert video surveillance for reasons of safety and security. But some states prohibit covert surveillance in areas of a business or other public place where people could expect to have privacy, such as a restroom or a dressing room.

And always remember that federal law expressly prohibits "the interception and disclosure of oral, wire, or electronic communication by using a device to intercept wire or wireless communications between people without a warrant." In other words, you can't listen to or tape other people's phone conversations unless you have a warrant, or unless you tell them beforehand that you're going to do it. This prohibition applies to private citizens like you and me, as well as the police. So if you think that your baby sitter is making 900-number calls from your telephone, you'd better think twice before you splice a recorder into your phone lines to record calls and catch the sitter in the act. Each and every call you record covertly can result in fines and other penalties.

Not-So-Anonymous Tip

Under federal law and many state laws, you may legally record a telephone conversation that you are having with another person covertly and without their consent. But this isn't true under all state laws (remember those calls between Monica Lewinsky and Linda Tripp?). Before you decide to become a secret agent, check the laws of your jurisdiction.

The Least You Need to Know

➤ Although it still isn't cheap or "no-brainer" technology, video surveillance has become affordable and simple enough that many homeowners are including it in their home security systems.

➤ You can use video surveillance systems (VSS) with or without audio to monitor the actions of people in your home or business.

➤ Video surveillance systems aren't cheap, but a basic system can be installed that will fit most security budgets. Installing and maintaining a VSS can require some expertise, too.

➤ Most jurisdictions have laws that govern covert video and audio surveillance.

Chapter 19

Installing That Eye in the Sky

In This Chapter

➤ Deciding whether you want to do it yourself

➤ Learning the lingo of VSS

➤ Installing a wireless watcher

➤ Recording what your watcher sees

➤ Looking ahead

Installing a video surveillance system isn't a walk in the park, but it isn't nuclear fission, either. In this chapter, I'll try to give you a good idea of just what's involved in this endeavor, along with enough information to help the more technically inclined among you to go it alone. If you don't think you want to tackle this installation on your own, this chapter will give you a great idea of exactly what's involved in the installation so that you know what you're hiring someone to do. That should help you determine what that work will be worth to you.

Security Password

This book is intended for home-owners, apartment dwellers, and small shop operators—not professional electronic or security personnel. I'm not going to give a dissertation on video system installation here, but I will talk about some basic technical terms and techniques you'll find helpful whether you're installing your own system or hiring a professional to do the installation for you.

Is This a Do-It-Yourself Project for *You?*

Installing a video surveillance system (VSS) may be a job for a professional, but that all depends on your own knowledge, skills, and comfort with setting up recording systems. If you're one of the many folks out there (hi, Mom!) who have cheerfully given up on learning to record programs with their VCRs, I'd say you should be shopping for a professional VSS installation service. On the other hand, if you're something of a video-cam buff, you've hooked up your home entertainment system, and you feel comfortable with basic wiring and electronic connections, go for it!

Keep in mind that you can buy a simple wireless VSS kit that will be really easy to install. But these kits present you with a very basic system. If you want or need some special components in your VSS, such as lots of perimeter coverage, hidden cameras, or other special devices, the installation becomes much, much trickier. Before you decide whether to hire out the installation or go it alone, take a minute to look at some VSS installation terms and potential concerns.

Sound the Alarm!

I'm going to explain how to install and set up a wireless system in this book; if you want to go with a hard-wired system, you can review the basic information that I provide for setting up a hard-wired security system in Chapter 17, "Do-It-Yourself Alarm Systems," and then extrapolate that information to the VSS installation. The system you buy will come with basic instructions; if you aren't really comfortable with setting up electrical systems, I recommend that you consult a professional to install a hard-wired surveillance system.

A VSS Installation Glossary

Just to talk about VSS technology and the installation process, I need to make sure that we're all on the same page with some basic VSS terms. One of the major components of any VSS is the camera. Here's a short list of some of the basic terms used to describe VSS cameras and their capabilities:

Field of view (FOV): This is the size of the area the camera will see at a set distance from the camera. The field of view is dependent on the *lens focal length* and the camera *format* size. This capability is usually described in degrees. A lens with a really wide FOV—say, 165°—can see a broad area.

Format: This is the size of the camera imaging device. Today, most security camera formats are ½ (6.4mm) or ⅓ inch (4.9mm) format.

Imaging device: The imaging device is the portion of the camera that converts light to an electrical signal.

Lens: the camera's "eye," the lens focuses light reflected from people and objects onto the imaging device of the camera. The *aperture* is the iris of the lens, which expands and contracts to control the amount of light entering the camera through the lens.

Lens focal length: This describes the magnification of the lens. The longer the focal length of a lens is, the more narrow its angle of view is.

Lines of resolution: This refers to how many image lines are transmitted to broadcast the image. The higher this number is, the clearer and crisper the image will be. Higher-resolution cameras generally cost more than lower-resolution cameras. A typical rating for a color security camera is 300 to 400 lines of horizontal resolution. Black-and-white security cameras generally have 500 to 700 lines of resolution.

Lux: This is a measurement of light. The lower the lux value is, the less light is required by the camera to record.

Pixels: This is a term for active picture elements. These are the number of light-sensitive elements within the camera imaging device.

Not-So-Anonymous Tip

You'll find a number of online purveyors of VSS listed in the glossary of this book. For a good online glossary of these and other VSS terms, check out www.sharp–security.com/ glossary/cctv.htm.

Don't let this terminology scare you off. Both bricks-and-mortar and online dealers of VSS are usually happy to help you choose the right cameras and other surveillance equipment, if you can just describe the purpose and area in which you intend to use the system.

Installing a Wireless System

Wireless VSS are easier to install than are their hard-wired cousins. Wireless VSS operate through transmitted radio signals; a camera or a transmitter sends a video signal to a receiver. The receiver is connected to a TV, a VCR, or some other monitoring equipment, but that's the only cabling you have to do when setting up a wireless system. No wires need to connect the transmitter and the receiver.

A typical wireless system includes some variation on these basic components:

➤ One or more cameras or transmitters

➤ A receiver and an antenna

➤ A power supply (usually a 12-volt DC supply)

➤ Cabling to connect the receiver to a monitor or a VCR

Sound the Alarm!

Don't get me wrong! I'm not offering information here to take the place of the installation and user information that accompanied your VSS equipment when you bought it. *Always* follow the manufacturer's instructions when installing, connecting, and using any system, including VSS.

To this basic setup, many people add a motion detector and a VCR. If you just want to broadcast the signal to a monitor rather than record the images, you can hook up the receiver to a television or monitor instead of a VCR.

Many of the same tools required for wireless and hard-wired alarm systems will be needed for your VSS installation. To install a wireless VSS, you really need only a pencil (to mark your drill spots), a drill, a screwdriver, a ladder, and a small wrench (for tightening those cable ends, if your fingers are too big to get a good grip on those little devils).

Before you start hooking up anything, though, you have to decide where you want to put all this stuff. I can help with that! Read on.

Figuring Out Your System's Point of View

When deciding where to locate your camera system, you (of course) need to refer to the floor plan(s) that you drew up in Chapter 18, "Smile, You're on Hidden Camera!" Decide which areas you most want to cover with video surveillance, and then measure the areas so that you have a good idea what kind of *lines of sight* (*LOS*) and field of view (FOV) your system will require. The LOS determines how far from the receiver the transmitter can be. The FOV determines the length and width of the area that the camera can actually monitor.

Your surveillance camera equipment will be graded to tell you how wide (in degrees, remember) its FOV is and how many lines of resolution it transmits. And don't forget that you can always get help in choosing and locating your VSS components from any reputable dealer.

One important formula you should know, however, is how to calculate the best *resolution-limited FOV* (the distance from your camera lens at which an object can be clearly viewed). To calculate this distance, you divide the camera's lines of resolution by 16 (the minimum lines per foot required to identify someone on videotape). So, if a camera transmits 350 lines of resolution, you divide that number by 16, to get 22. That means that the camera's resolution-limited FOV is 22 feet. Anything beyond that distance won't be clearly transmitted (or recorded) by your system.

Talk the Talk

You'll often see the term **lines of sight (LOS)** when reading about the transmitting capability of a wireless system. That term just refers to how far from the receiver the transmitter can be located and still broadcast a clear image. A typical system may have about 300 feet LOS, but that distance will vary, depending upon interference and obstructions.

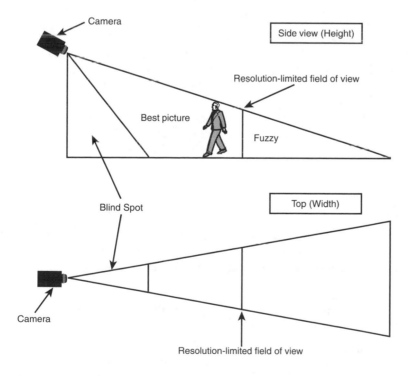

Although your camera may be able to pick up images for a long distance, its resolution-limited field of view will determine just how far from the lens a camera's subject can be clearly viewed.

Security Password

Most surveillance cameras, in general, and all outdoor surveillance models, are clearly marked to designate the temperature ranges within which they'll operate. Outdoor cameras typically operate within a range of −15° to 130° Fahrenheit.

Security Password

Most surveillance system receivers are connected to the monitor or the VCR with standard cable—you know, cable TV wire. This cable is shielded to cut down on interference and video distortion.

You'll also need to be certain to install the camera where it won't be interfered with—by either human hands or the elements. Here are a few rules of thumb for siting your camera:

➤ Put the camera where it will have a clear view of the area you want to monitor. Usually, near the ceiling is best.

➤ Locate the camera so that it isn't directed right at a light source—that will cause backlighting and diminish the quality of the image that the camera transmits.

➤ Put the camera where it won't be subject to lots of dust and where the temperature won't go above or beyond the camera's limits.

In addition to placing your surveillance cameras in the right locations, you'll also need to take some care in locating the receiver. Again, you'll want to make sure that you're within the system's signaling distance, and you'll need to avoid too many interfering objects or structural features. And keep the cabling away from your home's electrical equipment and power and telephone lines.

Depending upon the strength of your surveillance system's transmitter, it will be capable of sending signals through one or more walls. The beauty of wireless systems, though, is that you can move them around easily. Test the system components in place before you bolt anything down, to make sure you're getting the best view of the area and the best signal transmission and reception.

Installing the System

When you've decided where all your components need to go, you're ready for the easy part: mounting and connecting the system. Begin by mounting the camera. Follow your manufacturer's instructions, which will probably offer some variety of these steps:

1. Use your camera's base as a guide, and mark the screw-hole locations on the wall where you intend to install the camera.

2. Drill starter holes for the screws.

3. Screw the base onto the wall, and then attach the camera to the base. Connect any necessary cables between the base and the camera.

Connecting the Components

Connecting the components is a simple operation: They're connected much the same way as your cable TV and TV/VCR. Simply connect the camera to the transmitter with the cable supplied with your system. Aim the antenna in the direction that the signal will be transmitted (toward the receiver), and then plug in the transmitter. Then turn on the power and (on multichannel systems) choose the channel you want to use.

Next, you're ready to hook up your receiver, another really simple operation. Put the receiver where you want it to be located, point the antenna toward the transmitter, and choose the same channel that you chose when you set up the transmitter (if necessary).

Cabling the receiver to a TV or VCR is easy, too. Just run the video output from the receiver to the video input connections on your VCR (or directly to a monitor). On a standard TV, the cable will be connected to the "signal in" port. On a standard VCR, the cable will be connected to the "video in" port and the VCR will be connected to your TV in the normal way. Manufacturers use different jargon to label ports or connections, so be sure to read the instructions that come with your VSS components.

When your transmitter and receiver are hooked up and the monitor (TV or whatever) is on and displaying an image, adjust the camera or cameras to make sure that they're aimed and focused accurately. Your system may have controls that adjust the vertical and horizontal focus, brightness, and so on. Almost all cameras can be positioned manually and locked into place with a wing nut.

Security Password

If you're installing an outdoor camera, try to locate it so that it's protected from rain and direct sun. You'll also need to be sure that obstructions aren't going to create "blind spots" in important areas of surveillance.

Security Password

If you're running the surveillance video through a VCR, and you want to watch live surveillance through your TV, make sure that your TV is set to channel 3 or 4 or the video input (depending upon your system and setup).

Special Concerns for Outdoor Installations

The basic source of electricity for the VSS typically is household current, but your system also may be powered by batteries. To connect interior components, you just have to plug the things into an outlet, either directly or through a DC converter. Installing an outside camera can be a bit more difficult, though. For example, if you need to run a new 110- to 120-volt electrical line to an outdoor surveillance component, call an electrician.

Measure the area you want the camera to be able to "see," and check to see whether the camera will face the sun or artificial lights at night. Be sure that you purchase a camera designed for the weather or climate where it will be installed.

Not-So-Anonymous Tip

To avoid glare and image "wash-out," mount an outdoor surveillance camera below evening lighting sources, and aim it downward to reduce the effects of direct sunlight into the camera.

For about $50, you can install a black-and-white surveillance camera that has night vision technology so that it can record in the low-light of dark areas in your yard (it's rated at .5 lux, which means that it needs less light than you'd get from the average candle). For about $200, you can buy a motion-triggered weather-proof camera that can film at 1 lux illumination. Most outdoor cameras come with cable, a TV control unit cable and jacks, mounting brackets, and any necessary power adapters.

Remember, you may need to install your exterior camera 15 to 20 feet high for best viewing results and to keep it up where thieves can't disconnect it easily. And don't permanently attach the camera until you test it out, to make sure that it's broadcasting well and doesn't have any big blind spots in its FOV. It would be a shame to have to climb all that way back up and start all over.

Hooking Up a Nanny-Cam

If you've decided that you need interior covert video surveillance (otherwise known as a nanny-cam), then I recommend a good-quality wireless camera that is disguised as a smoke detector, a clock, a book, or some other innocuous knickknack. These cameras are professionally built, well-disguised, and easy to set up and move. They are more expensive than putting together a pinhole or other hard-wired system, but they're easier to install and are totally lacking in those ugly wires and cables that scream "something's going on here!" to anyone who sees them.

These covert systems are set up just like any other wireless VSS; put the camera in the location of your choice, aim it so that it's broadcasting to the receiver, plug it in, and you're ready to go.

Recording What Your System Sees

Now that you have your cameras set up, you can set up the VCR to record the action; unless you plan to spend all day watching the monitor, recording is a pretty essential step in most surveillance systems. Most home systems simply use a standard VCR hooked up in the manner I previously described. Check your system's specifications to determine whether you can adjust the recording time, and how long your system can record on a single tape.

The VSS receiver connects into the VCR, as I described earlier. To set up your system for recording, make sure you set the VCR to its AUX (auxiliary) setting—otherwise, it'll record some television program instead of the surveillance. Follow your manufacturer's instructions for recording, but in general, the process will be something like this:

1. Turn on the VCR and select the right inputs.

2. Turn on the monitor.

3. Set the VCR to record.

4. If you're recording sound and audio, adjust the volume control to the right setting.

5. Begin recording (check your VCR's instructions if you have special settings that I haven't mentioned here); you can turn on the TV or other monitor to see exactly what image is being recorded.

> **Not-So-Anonymous Tip**
>
> Keep in mind, if you're using covert surveillance, that you'll want to be sure the recorder is hidden, too. Try keeping it in a locked cabinet, or at least behind closed cabinet doors, so that no one can see that it's on.

If you don't want to leave the VCR on continuously while you're away, you can use the VCR's preset option to program a date and time for the recording to start and stop. This option can come in handy if you want to record during a specific period of time during your absence—say, during the hours you expect your housekeeping service to be working in your home.

If you don't know specifically when you want the VCR to begin recording, you can include motion detectors, timers, alarm control panels, or other triggering methods in your VSS system. Many of these hookups go well beyond the basic installation, though, so I suggest that you consult with a pro for that type of installation.

One wireless system available for about $50 utilizes a motion detector that operates by sending a signal to a receiver attached to your VCR. You simply attach the motion detector in the area where you want to trigger surveillance recording. When the sensor detects motion, it sends a signal to the receiver attached to your VCR to tell it to start recording.

An Eye Toward the Future

Many home improvement, security, and computer suppliers offer automated home systems that probably represent the future of home security technology. These systems let you use your personal computer to program your home's lights, appliances, and, yes, its home security system. You can buy systems today that let you patch your surveillance view into a desktop or laptop computer, with signals broadcast by satellite, just like wireless phones.

The prices of today's systems vary, but you can find automated home hardware and software kits on the market for about $100 to $200. The system works by networking motion sensors, key-chain remotes, appliance and lamp modules, and hand controllers through your personal computer. The systems typically come with software, a PC interface, a remote control unit, lamp and appliance modules, a transceiver, a wall switch, and a motion detector.

The Least You Need to Know

➤ Video surveillance systems aren't terribly difficult to install, but I recommend that you stick with the wireless variety unless you're extra handy with end-cuts and soldering irons.

➤ Siting the camera is a critical part of placing your VSS; put it where it has the best unobstructed view and where its transmitter is within signal range of the receiver.

➤ To install a wireless system, you mount the camera (or cameras), connect and aim the transmitter, connect and aim the receiver, and wire the receiver into a monitor (TV, VCR, or other).

➤ Outdoor cameras need to be aimed away from the sun and artificial lighting as much as is possible; you also need to do what you can to shield them from rain, dust, and other elemental nasties.

➤ If you want to record your surveillance, you need to make sure that the receiver is hooked into a VCR, and follow your VCR instructions for recording.

Part 6

Putting a Lid on Other Issues in Home Security

Alarms, sirens, surveillance systems—do you really know whether or not you have a legal leg to stand on when you're using these security measures? Well, I'll tell you what I know about these security issues and help point you to places where you can get the full scoop. And I have a few more crime-busting tips to share, too—like the latest in car-theft prevention devices and what you can expect on the security system horizon.

Finally, let's talk worst-case scenario. Even the best security plan doesn't guarantee that you'll never be the victim of a crime. In the last chapter of the book, I tell you what to do when things go wrong: how to contact the people you need to contact, preserve evidence, and follow through with your insurance company and the incident investigators to make sure that you get the best outcome to a bad deal.

Chapter 20

Here Comes
the Judge!

> ## In This Chapter
>
> ➤ Know your rights
>
> ➤ Who gets caught in your man trap?
>
> ➤ Understanding courts, torts, and other messy legal issues
>
> ➤ Beware of dog
>
> ➤ Taking the risk out of home security

Anyone who watches the news knows that nothing is simple in the eyes of the law. So, whereas you may think that those antipersonnel mines are a perfectly reasonable way to keep the neighborhood kids from cutting through your backyard, some folks might think your "self-protection" measures are a bit extreme.

Now, you and I are both smart enough to know that I can't (shouldn't, won't, don't want to, and you can't make me) offer legal advice to you in the pages of this book. But I can give you some general observations and guidelines about some of the pitfalls you may want to guard against when guarding against crime. With that legal protection in place, read on to get my spin on some home security hazards you may want to avoid.

A Homeowner's Rights of Protection

Depending upon your state laws, you undoubtedly enjoy some rights as a home-owner. The thing to keep in mind, though, is that for every homeowner right, you also probably have a homeowner responsibility. Knowing both sides of this coin can help shield you from potential lawsuits and damages.

For example, every state has laws regulating the level of force that a homeowner can legally use to defend himself or herself, and his or her home and family. While spe-cific laws vary from state to state, most states hold that you're justified in using rea-sonable force against another person to protect yourself or a third person from what you reasonably believe to be the imminent use of unlawful force.

But, in most states, you're justified in using deadly force *only* if you reasonably believe that that force is necessary to prevent serious bodily injury to yourself or a third per-son, or to prevent the commission of a forcible felony. That means that unless you have a real reason to think that someone is going to seriously hurt you or someone else, you aren't justified in trying to kill that person. That's not an altogether unrea-sonable rule of thumb, as I'm sure most of you will agree.

Security Password

In the previous chapters of this book, I've tried to help you weave a web of protection around your home and family—whether through identifying and changing risky behaviors; by reducing, spreading, or transferring risks; or by installing alarm or video surveillance sys-tems. You'll recall that at each step of the way, I've mentioned certain legal concerns of which you should be aware. In this chapter, I discuss, in general terms, your rights and re-sponsibilities with respect to protecting your home and family. As I've mentioned before, to get specific information on your rights and responsibilities, you need to check the laws of your jurisdiction. Use the information that I give you here as a "heads-up" for some is-sues that may require some deeper digging.

This is the whole "rights and responsibilities" issue that I mentioned earlier. You have a *right* to defend your home, but you have the *responsibility* to be reasonable about it. So, if you interrupt a burglary in progress, and the thief turns and bolts out the door, it isn't reasonable for you to chase him outside and shoot him in the back as he runs away. In spite of the old vigilante creed of "Shoot 'em down and drag 'em back inside," gunning someone down as he flees is a very bad idea. You're likely to be found out, and it's highly *unlikely* that your action will be judged a reasonable show of force.

Let's Be Reasonable About This

In spite of the dangers of going too far, some states do provide protection for homeowners who use reasonable force to protect themselves and their property. But what is reasonable, you ask?

Well, I'm afraid there isn't a clear-cut definition of *reasonable force* that is useful in every situation, in every state, in every home. Every time force is used in self-defense, the officials in charge examine the facts and circumstances surrounding the incident and make a judgment based on the results of that examination. In general, though, reasonable force is something that seems appropriate to the nature of the incident itself. So, yelling at a trespasser, "Hey, get off my property!" is certainly a reasonable action. It doesn't physically harm the trespasser, but it gives the person an opportunity to stop committing the offense. On the other hand, cranking off a round of buckshot into a trespasser without warning would rarely be considered reasonable by a court of law.

Talk the Talk

By its very nature, the term *reasonable* gives a highly subjective spin to the qualifier of **reasonable force.** By definition, *reasonable* means fair and moderate, not excessive or extreme. And in the final analysis, a judge or jury will determine what's reasonable and what isn't. So whether you're planting pangi sticks at the bottom of a tiger pit in front of your door or polishing up your "burglar bayonet," just remember to ask yourself, "Can I *reasonably* expect a court of law to find my actions *reasonable?* If not, you'd better start looking for more moderate, fair, and nonexcessive forms of self-protection.

Citizen's Arrest! Citizen's Arrest!

If you missed the episode of *The Andy Griffith Show* where Gomer arrested Barney for an illegal U-turn, let me tell you that I resent your youth. No, I mean, let me tell you that your local laws may empower you to use reasonable force to "arrest" someone if you have probable cause to believe that the person committed a felony.

So, let's say that you're walking down the street, and you see someone in front of you picking the pocket of a guy walking next to him. You slowly move forward and grab the pickpocket, push him to the ground, and yell for someone to call the police while you hold the struggling sticky-fingers to the sidewalk. You've just made a citizen's arrest; you may be a hero—or you may end up on the wrong end of a lawsuit.

Or, let's say that you hear someone breaking into your house at night, and you grab your trusty crossbow and use it to corner the thief in your living room. If you hold the thief there until the cops arrive, you've made a citizen's arrest. But you'd better call the cops right away, if you want to avoid any hint of unlawful behavior on your part. (And try extra hard not to pull that trigger!)

Not-So-Anonymous Tip

Some states place a dollar value as a definition of a felony. For example, in some states, if you steal less than $100, it's a misdemeanor rather than a felony.

Sound the Alarm!

In almost every state, citizen's arrests are legal only if they occur *when the crime is taking place.* So don't run over to your neighbor's house and hold him at gunpoint until the cops arrive because you saw him speeding on the way to work yesterday.

The legalities of making a citizen's arrest are about as unstraightforward and complicated as you would imagine them to be. As much trouble as the police have in making a "clean" arrest without a warrant, you can believe that it's no walk in the park for Joe Citizen to play cop-for-a-day, either. Let's dig through a few of the legal terms involved in the definition of a citizen's arrest:

➤ A *felony* is a crime that is punishable by more than one year in prison and/or a fine. Now, the incarceration time for the crime changes from location to location, so a felony in my area may not be a felony in yours. But *in general,* most home burglaries count as felonies in most states. If you don't know what constitutes a felony in your area, you have no way of knowing how shaky the ground surrounding your citizen's arrest may be.

➤ *Probable cause* exists where the observable or knowable facts and circumstances are sufficient to convince a reasonable person that a crime took place and that the suspect committed the crime. That gets into the whole "reasonable" issue we just talked about; basically, though, it's saying that you must have a logical reason for believing that someone committed a crime before you can detain that person in a citizen's arrest.

In general, you should consider three things before you attempt a citizen's arrest:

➤ Do you think that a court of law would find that you have grounds for making the arrest (that probable-cause factor)?

➤ Do you think that the courts would find your actions (and level of force) reasonable?

➤ Is your action necessary to stop the crime?

In any event, you need to be certain that you call the police *immediately* after you detain someone in a citizen's arrest. The quicker the police arrive on the scene, the better (for you and the detainee).

I think this little foray into the legalities of detaining or even injuring someone whom you believe has committed a crime should convince you that the best policy is to *deter* crimes rather than try to apprehend or punish the criminals. That's what this book is all about.

Man Traps, Booby Traps, and Other Ways to Get into Trouble

In April 2000, I visited England. As chance would have it, my visit coincided with one of the most sensational "personal protection" trials ever to take place in that fair country. Evidently, some farmer whose house had been burgled a couple times in the past decided to take matters into his own hands (literally). He booby-trapped his home and slept with a shotgun. Finally, when two hapless would-be criminals broke into his home one night, he shot them, and one of them died from his wounds.

The farmer received a stiff jail sentence for his actions, but the whole country was up in arms debating the case. Great Britain buzzed for weeks and weeks as people on both sides of the Atlantic voiced their opinions on the legality, illegality, rights, and wrongs of using deadly force in self-protection, the condition of rural policing, homeowners' rights, and so on. The fact that this guy—rightly or wrongly—felt so besieged as to be justified in rigging up his home like a mini-fortress was disturbing to nearly everyone who read of the case. When does your right to protect yourself step over the line into vigilante justice and the social chaos that it provokes?

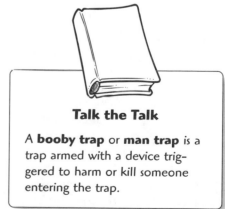

Talk the Talk

A **booby trap** or **man trap** is a trap armed with a device triggered to harm or kill someone entering the trap.

If you think the issue of the use of *booby traps* or *man traps* is less risky here in the United States, you're wrong. In many states, if someone is harmed in a booby trap that you set on your property, you may be liable for damages. Laws vary from state to state, but in most areas, it's illegal to set man traps on your property, even if you've done so to protect yourself or your property.

Security Password

Personal liability may not be limited to damages that you inflict on intruders with a gun or an explosive. In November 1999, the Fresno, California, Fifth District Court of Appeal ruled in *People* v. *Henderson,* 99 C.D.O.S. 9291, that pit bulls can be considered deadly weapons. If you keep a hungry pit bull tied near your doorway, don't be surprised if you're sued by someone it's bitten—even if that someone has entered your property without your permission. Read more about doggie don'ts later in this chapter.

Sound the Alarm!

Many states prohibit or regulate "fright" booby traps through the State Fire Marshall's Office or some other regulatory agency. Stay away from using these things: They aren't as effective at protecting you and your property as the security systems we've discussed, and they're usually illegal and dangerous. If someone is injured by one of these relatively ineffective devices, you could be held liable.

These traps can take any number of forms: People have been known to rig up shotguns to fire when a door opens, grenades to go off when someone walks through a doorway, or dynamite to explode when a car's ignition is activated. If you can think of it, someone has probably tried to use it to trap, injure, or even kill someone else entering their property.

Not only are booby traps illegal, they're also very likely to harm innocent people, such as firefighters, mail carriers, utility workers, children, or any innocent person who might knock on a door. One policeman I know was investigating a report of a suspicious vehicle in a rural area. As is usual in these cases, he went door to door, checking homes in the area to see if they had been burglarized. After knocking on the door of one home, he peered into a window from the porch. The door he'd been standing in front of had a shotgun wired to it! My friend later found out that the frustrated homeowner had been burglarized before and had decided to take things into his own hands. Unfortunately, his actions put himself in legal jeopardy and risked the lives of innocent people.

Some booby traps are designed to frighten people, not kill or injure them (case in point, an *un*loaded shotgun wired to a doorknob). For example, traps known as "auto burglar alarms" produce a loud whistle or bang and smoke when the ignition of a car is started. "Door bombs," sold at many fireworks stores, contain a small amount of friction-sensitive explosive and cause a bang like a gunshot when the door they're wired to is opened. These devices may very likely scare a would-be thief and bring attention to the location, but they're also dangerous and illegal in many states.

You Need to Know a Bit About Premises Liability

I'm about to tell you something that may shock you: The United States is a very litigious country. People get sued or sue someone on a daily basis, and it's not unusual to hear of bizarre and extraordinary cases in which someone is awarded millions of dollars over something as commonplace as spilled coffee. But a very real and common lawsuit occurs when someone is injured on somebody else's property.

Don't run screaming in fear that I'm about to launch into a diatribe on the legal nooks and crannies of *tort* law. But you should be aware of some legal concepts regarding your liability if someone is hurt on your property. After all, any discussion of home security would be incomplete if it didn't at least make mention of this real danger that threatens every homeowner.

Considering the climate of tort law reform and the differences in the way varying jurisdictions interpret and apply the law, I can give you only a general view with regard to premises liability. Still, this discussion should help you understand some basic legal principles that will help you, as a homeowner, avoid some potential liability issues.

You may not know it, but you owe a *duty of care* to most people who come onto your property or into your home or apartment. That means that you're responsible for doing the right thing to reasonably ensure that no one gets hurt on your property. The level of your duty of care, however, is determined (in most cases) by what kind of "visitor" you're dealing with:

Not-So-Anonymous Tip

Because accidents will happen, liability insurance such as casualty insurance should be a part of any complete home security plan. If you don't have it in your current homeowner's plan, you have a gaping hole in the safety net of your security plan.

Talk the Talk

A **tort** is the commission of a wrongful act, whether done on purpose or by accident, that results in the person acted upon being injured. Negligence resulting in injury is usually considered a tort, so failing to do something that you were supposed to do can also get you a front-row seat in the courtroom.

➤ An *invitee* is typically defined as someone you've invited onto your property as a social guest or to conduct business. Typical invitees are the contractor you hired to clean your gutters, the boy who mows your lawn, or the mail carrier. In most jurisdictions, your duty of care to an invitee is to keep your premises in reasonably safe condition.

➤ A *trespasser* is someone who comes onto your property with no invitation or any other right and who intrudes for personal purposes—for example, a thief, a hunter, or a vandal. To trespassers, your duty of care is usually that of refraining from reckless or extreme conduct that would injure the person (remember those booby traps?). You're usually considered liable if you harm a trespasser.

➤ In some jurisdictions, a *licensee* is someone you didn't invite onto your property, but who isn't there for personal gain, either. Other jurisdictions consider a licensee to be someone who has permission to come onto your land, even though you didn't invite them. This could be someone who comes to your door by mistake, such as a door-to-door charity drive collector, or a census worker. If you know children to play on your property, and you don't object or do anything to stop them, the courts may consider that you've conferred licensee status on them, too. You owe it to licensees to do nothing to intentionally harm them and to warn them of hidden yet potentially dangerous conditions that exist on your property and that could threaten the licensee—thus the "Beware of Dog" signs and high, protective fences around backyard pools.

So, if you invite people onto your property (for business or pleasure), you need to do all you can to guarantee their safety while they are there. If people come onto your property without your permission, even for the purpose of helping themselves to something of yours, you can't set out to harm them just because they're on your property. If people come onto your property unannounced but with no evil in mind, you need to be certain that you've done nothing to hurt them and that you've posted warnings to let them know of any latent dangers that lurk in your home or grounds.

Limiting Your Risk of Liability

If someone is injured on your property and a judge or jury determines that the person is something other than a trespasser, the court will also want to determine whether the accident or injury was foreseeable. *Foreseeability* refers to the reasonable anticipation that certain things will happen as the result of an action or situation. In other words, something is foreseeable if a reasonably intelligent person could have predicted that it would happen, based on the actions or circumstances that preceded it (known in nonlegal circles as "I *told* you so!").

If an injury was foreseeable, based on a condition that exists on your property, the court may say that you're liable for damages—and smacking yourself on the forehead and groaning, "Oh my gosh, I feel so silly" is unlikely to get you off the hook, in most of these situations. A better approach may be to look around your yard, house, or apartment and ask yourself what hazards, big or small, exist there. Then ask yourself what you can do to:

1. Eliminate the hazard (cover up the well).

2. Isolate the hazard (fence in the dog or the pool).

3. Warn people about the hazard so that they won't injure themselves (post warning signs prominently around your property).

It's a Dog-Eat-Dog World

Do you own a dog? Did you know that many states have laws that make the owner of a dog that bites automatically responsible for the dog-bite injuries, regardless of the dog's propensity for biting? Using the three-part approach to limiting your liability, what are your options?

Not-So-Anonymous Tip

If you own a dog, check your homeowner's policy to make sure that it covers you if your dog misbehaves and nails someone in your yard. Your liability in any case may vary, depending on local regs; you may be deemed liable for physical and property damage and medical expenses, and, in really bad cases, you may even be criminally liable for a really vicious and predictable attack. Many areas have what's called a "one-bite" rule that says your dog's entitled to one slip-up. Other areas don't. If you're worried about your ferocious Fido landing you in the clink, check your local laws.

You can't totally eliminate the possibility that your dog will bite someone if it gets an opportunity. You can isolate the hazard by fencing in your property and keeping the dog inside the fence. However, because people may come onto your property without your knowledge, you need to post signs warning them that the dog is loose on the grounds and may bite them.

Security Password

The Centers for Disease Control and Prevention (CDC) estimates that in the United States, dogs bite nearly 5 million people a year, and more than 800,000 dog attacks every year are serious enough to require medical care (more than half of those attacks are against children). Insurance companies have estimated that they pay more than $100 million annually to settle dog–bite claims.

Even if you've posted warning signs, if someone comes onto your property and the dog attacks them, the signs alone may not save you. Entire areas of law are being constructed around dog bites, and this is an area of continuing legal decisions and developments. If you own a dog, you'd better find out what the local laws dictate for the dog's access to the public. Also find out what legalities surround dog attacks in your area. You may need to take serious measures to protect yourself against liability resulting from your dog's behavior.

Some Parting Thoughts on Judgment—Good and Bad

Throughout this book, I've recommended that you always use common sense in directing your plans for home security and your actions in securing it. Here are a few common-sense ideas to save yourself from as much homeowner heartache as you possibly can:

➤ If you have a dog, don't let him run loose. When you take him for walks, keep him on a leash; when you put him out, be sure he's in a fenced-in yard (invisible or otherwise). If your dog is ever outside and unleashed on your property, you probably should put up a "Beware of Dog" sign.

➤ Don't leave ladders, rakes, power tools, yard chemicals, pruning sheers, shovels, toys, garden hoses, power cords, or bicycles lying around on your lawn, sidewalks, or driveway. This isn't being a neatness fanatic—it's protecting yourself from lawsuits.

➤ If you have a pool, be sure to follow your jurisdiction's pool and fencing codes.

➤ Make sure that your steps, stairs, and walkways are well-lighted.

➤ Fix broken steps, and fill in those nasty, ankle-twisting yard holes.

➤ If you live in a cold-weather climate, arrange to have snow and ice removed from walkways, and keep a bag of salt or other ice-melting material handy for use on your porch and walkways.

➤ Keep any toxic or dangerous materials that you have on your property safely stored away and in properly labeled containers.

Not-So-Anonymous Tip

Here's a general home-security liability checklist of questions you should ask yourself when pondering the legality of your system:

➤ Does my jurisdiction have a time limit on how long an outside alarm siren or bell may sound and how loud it can be?

➤ Does my jurisdiction prohibit programming an automatic telephone dialer to call certain numbers (such as the police or 911)?

➤ Does my jurisdiction impose fines for false alarms?

➤ Does my jurisdiction limit where covert surveillance cameras can be placed or how they can be used in my home?

The Least You Need to Know

➤ Knowing your responsibilities as a homeowner is an important part of managing your home security plan.

➤ Many areas of premises and homeowner liability law revolve around the concepts of reasonable care and probable cause. If your actions wouldn't look reasonable in a court of law, you shouldn't use them to defend yourself or your property.

➤ You're almost always endangering yourself if you install a man trap or a booby trap on your property. They're illegal in many states, and they carry the very real risk of hurting an innocent person.

➤ Your responsibility to keep people safe on your property is determined in part by whether you invited them there.

➤ You can limit your liability by eliminating hazards on your property, isolating the hazards, or at least warning people that the hazards exist.

➤ Learn about the dog-bite laws in your area, and protect yourself from liability by controlling your dog per the rules and making sure that your homeowner's policy covers you against loss due to your dog's behavior.

Chapter 21

I ♥ My Car: Guarding Against Vehicle Theft

In This Chapter

➤ Some alarming facts about car theft

➤ Alarm it!

➤ Other "you can't touch this" antitheft devices

A lot of people are stealing a lot of cars out there, folks. The National Insurance Crime Bureau (the source for most of the statistics I throw out in this chapter) estimates that approximately 1.3 million cars, trucks, and motorcycles are stolen every year in the United States, at a cost of more than $7 billion. Because only about 14 percent of vehicle thefts result in an arrest, we can assume that car thieves are not one of our country's endangered species.

In previous chapters, I've talked about some of the common techniques used by car thieves and some of the common-sense ways you can avoid becoming someone's free ride. Here, I'm going to talk about some of the anti–auto-theft alarms, systems, devices, and magic spells (just kidding) available to you today. From the simplest steering-wheel lock to some very sophisticated computer-based technologies, let's talk car-theft prevention!

What Are You Protecting Your Car From?

I lived in Chicago for a while (great town, great people, and, oh, those Devil Dogs!), and someone up there stole my car. The police duly took a report and said they'd "get on it," but they didn't encourage me to hold my breath waiting on my auto-Lassie to come home. For months I watched the streets, confident that I'd see my faithful car and could then jump in a cab, yell, "Follow my car," to the driver, and track the felons to their lair. When I mentioned my determined vigil to a city-wise friend of mine, he burst out laughing and said, "That car hasn't been in one piece since about 20 minutes after it left your parking spot. It's gone forever—get over it!"

Security Password

Every car theft doesn't end in permanent good-byes; nearly 85 percent of stolen vehicles are recovered. And most stolen cars are between two and seven years old.

Talk the Talk

Since 1968, **VIN (vehicle identification number)** plates on most U.S. and foreign cars have been attached to the left side of the dash; the VIN is a unique number assigned to each automobile to provide positive identification (and easier tracking) of automobiles.

Well, the tactlessness of this remark aside, he was right. Depending upon what kind of vehicle you lose to theft, it may or may not make it out of the experience in one piece. And even if it does, it may be spirited off to points unknown—in its home country or overseas—eliminating almost any chance that you'll ever see it again.

What makes the difference, you say? Well, by knowing what thieves want to do with your vehicle, you know how to make it less attractive to them. For example, my 20-year-old car was in showroom shape and had a huge, fast engine, which made it a much-in-demand classic on the stolen-car market. Had I known that, I wouldn't have been so casual about parking it out on the street and ignoring it for weeks at a time, and I might have etched my *VIN* numbers on the windshields, engine block, and other pertinent parts.

In the interest of doing all you can to protect *your* ride, take a quick look at what happens when a vehicle is stolen.

Chop, Borrow, and Steal

Most cops will tell you that there are three flavors of auto theft. *Temporary theft* is when someone steals a car to use it for a short time or a single purpose—for a joyride, as a getaway vehicle, or for point-to-point transportation. If you lose your auto to a temporary theft, you stand a good chance of getting it back again (although it may be badly trashed).

Temporary theft is usually a crime of opportunity, and the thieves typically target cars that are easy to get and (if they can find them) that are *fast*. Sports-car enthusiasts, listen up. To protect yourself from this kind of theft, you can use physical deterrents, a car alarm system, and a good dose of common sense in where to park and store your car.

In a less rosy scenario, your stolen car could find its way rather quickly to a *chop shop,* where it would be stripped down to its frame and sold off, piece by piece. Sometimes car thieves will do a *quick strip* right by the side of the road, and strip a car of its stereo, car phone, tires—whatever they can quickly remove—and then simply leave the carcass there for the cops to find.

Any car can fall prey to this crime; if you own an older car that's in good shape (like mine, sniff, sniff), thieves may be particularly interested in parting it out on the classic car market. This kind of vehicle theft is best prevented by protected parking, audible alarm systems, and lots of well-advertised identity marking (which I talk about later).

The third common type of auto theft is the quickly growing *export* market. Especially in port cities, luxury cars may be stolen "to order," loaded on a flatbed, driven onto a boat, and then shipped off to foreign destinations, never to see their homeland again. You can get a lot more money for certain model luxury cars in some foreign cities than you can in the United States, so this type of theft can be quite lucrative.

The more luxurious the car, the more attractive it will be to an export thief. To prevent this kind of theft, you need an on-vehicle tracking system, alarms, and some highly refined immobilizing systems or devices.

So what are those systems and techniques I mentioned for protecting your car from being shipped oversees? Or hacked up in a chop shop? Read on, and I'll tell you more.

Talk the Talk

Ever heard of a **salvage switch?** That term refers to a clever type of auto theft, wherein the thief buys a car that has been totaled, making sure to also get the title to the vehicle. Next, the thief steals a car of the same make and model, and switches the VINs. The stolen car assumes the wreck's identity, and the thief has a nice "legally" numbered car for the price of a wreck.

Not-So-Anonymous Tip

If you want to find out just how popular your car is with thieves, both in your state and around the country, visit www.insure.com. This site not only posts the Highway Loss Data Institute (HDLI) figures on which car models are being stolen most often around the country, it also lets you enter your own state (even city) or car model to find out whether you're driving a hot commodity for theft.

Security Password

Some surveys have shown that 20–30 percent of drivers have on more than one occasion walked away and left their car keys in the ignition.

Sound the Alarm!

Unless you run the local auto-repair shop or are otherwise exceptionally savvy when it comes to automotive electronics, you need to pay someone to install your alarm system. The wiring systems in cars today are too intricate and involved for an amateur to mess around in. Not only can a wiring mistake immobilize your security system, it also could mess up the rest of your car's electronics.

Alarm It!

Car alarms have come a long way in the past few years—and aren't we all glad? Who didn't get tired of hearing all of those car alarms wailing away at 3 A.M., with not a person in sight paying any attention to the warning?

Many late-model cars come with their own built-in security features, which may include anything from power locks and remote dome-light control to a tracking chip and monitoring service. But what are the typical features you can choose from if you're buying an alarm system for your car?

➤ **Keyless entry.** This system lets you unlock your car doors and/or trunk using a handheld remote. Most keyless entry systems are part of a basic alarm system.

➤ **Dual-stage sensors.** Sensors are the triggers that set off the alarm, and they usually are connected to your doors, hood, and trunk. Some systems also include glass-break sensors that monitor your windows. A dual-stage sensor triggers a quick series of beeps if the car is jostled, but it will fire into full-stage siren songs if the action is repeated or if the car gets a big jolt. (This type of sensor helps avoid those false alarms that drive us all so crazy.)

➤ **Interior/exterior sensors.** These sensors pick up motion on the seats or when someone steps into the vehicle (if you have a jeep or other open-air vehicle, this can be a good way to augment the traditional closed-vehicle sensors).

➤ **Remote starting and disabling.** These remotes will start your car from more than 500 feet away, and you also can buy them with an engine-disabling option (see the next section of this chapter). If you activate that, you shut off the gas to the engine, interrupt the electrical circuit to the starter, or initiate some other disabling action to prevent the car's engine from starting.

Not-So-Anonymous Tip

If you really don't want to have to bother with your car security, I recommend that you go for a *passive-setting* system. These alarm systems automatically arm themselves within a few minutes of your exit from the vehicle. You don't even have to aim the remote and push a button! Auto insurers love these things because they don't depend on the energy or attention of the car's owner. Some states even offer discounts on auto insurance if you have a passive-setting system in your auto. Ask your insurance rep to fill you in.

Most of these options can be combined in a car alarm system that should cost less than $250 to buy (installation extra, of course). You can get a basic siren, a few sensors, and a remote for around $100.

Some Physical Deterrents

What about those boots, collars, and clubs that everyone used to use to protect their car from theft? Well, you can still get them, and they often can prevent a casual thief from jumping in your car and splitting in a hurry. The jury is out on the effectiveness of some of these devices, though. Crooks seem to view each new antitheft device as a personal challenge, and it rarely takes the criminal community long to come up with a way to thwart the best physical deterrent. But these things can still offer some protection, and they continue to be popular with auto owners. So here are your options:

➤ **The boot.** Not just for cops, anymore, you can buy these babies and put them right on your tire. Until the boot comes off, the car can't be moved without a tow truck. Tire boots cost anywhere between $80 and $200.

Security Password

Immobilizers can interrupt the car's startability in one or more places. For example, a single-point immobilizer may just cut off the fuel pump. A double-point immobilizer could interrupt the fuel pump and the starter, and a three-point model might add another ignition interrupter elsewhere in the wiring system. The more interruptions, the better the chance that the immobilizer won't be easily overridden by a high-tech low-life.

➤ **Column collars.** These large metal collars are used to protect the column and ignition switch from access, but they have to be taken off and then put back on each time you drive and park the car. They aren't cheap (costing $100 to $200), and they don't work on some car models. They're not a great solution, in most cases.

➤ **Steering-wheel bars.** These metal bars lock the steering wheel in place, but they don't prove to be really effective these days. And because they have to be applied each time the car is parked, people tend to get lazy and stop using them. But they're cheap—$25 to $50 will get you one of these devices.

➤ **Case-hardened steel ignition lock.** This prevents thieves from popping out the lock cylinder (a favorite technique for steeling a car). These are effective in slowing down, if not completely stopping, a car theft. Expect to pay more than $100 to have one of these installed.

➤ **The immobilizers.** A new breed of theft deterrent is in the air, and so far, this approach seems to work. By immobilizing a car's engine, fuel supply, transmission, or other critical moving part, the device prevents someone from being able to start or move the car. Depending upon the sophistication of the system, it can cost anywhere from $90 to $550 to buy an immobilizing system and have it installed.

If You Can't Stop the Theft, You Might Catch the Thief

Lots of luxury cars today come with highly sophisticated security tracking devices as standard issue. The specific devices vary, but in general, they rely on a microchip or transponder installation within the vehicle's electrical system. These devices will not only inform you (via a remote pager) that your car's engine has been started or that the car's door has been opened, but they'll also send out a signal that can be tracked by satellite to show exactly where the car is being taken.

If your straight-off-the-lot auto costs around $70,000 or so, you'll probably have one of these systems at your disposal. If you want to pay to have one installed yourself, it's going to cost you anywhere from $400 to $1500, depending upon the level of sophistication your heart desires. And you'll have to pay a monthly fee for the tracking and in-car navigation service.

Talk the Talk

Your insurance company or your local police department may sponsor VIN **etching** programs in your area. If so, you can get your car windows etched free (or nearly free) through the program. Call your insurance agent or local law enforcement office to find out if there's a program planned (or in place) in your area.

Now how about a few not-so-Star-Wars-like ideas for tracking down your car after the fact? Well, you could go with an advanced marking plan—*etching* your VIN number on the windows, radio and speakers, wheels, and other parts of your car. You can also post a sticker in your window indicating that the car's components have been engraved and that the numbers are registered for theft tracking. (Many of your car's parts are already uniquely engraved, but these very visible identifiers can offer an additional "get lost" warning to potential thieves.)

Window etching is done with an etching solution and stencils, in a process much like that used by some home hobby buffs to etch flowers and monograms on wine glasses. You can get the etching material (including the etching cream, stencils, and application brush) from craft stores or on the Internet for about $20. If you pay a pro to etch your windows, it may cost around $100.

Will it work? It might. And if you own an older car that could be highly valued for its bits and pieces, you definitely might make it less attractive to a would-be thief by letting him or her know that its parts won't come "clean" of their owner's mark.

Not-So-Anonymous Tip

Some insurance companies will deduct up to 5 percent off the cost of your auto insurance policy if you get all your car windows etched.

Don't Forget These "Don't Steal My Car" Basics

Before you spend a dime on vehicle alarms or antitheft devices, make sure you're following these common-sense car-protection basics:

➤ Always lock and remove your keys (even when it's cold outside and you are sure you are going to be inside the convenience store only a couple of minutes).

➤ Lock valuables in the trunk. Never leave personal identification or credit cards in your car.

➤ Whenever possible, park in a garage or in a well-lighted, highly traveled area.

➤ Make a copy of your title and vehicle registration, and always have your license plate number written down somewhere at home. You'll need all of these numbers if your car is stolen.

➤ When parking at the curb, turn your tires completely toward the curb and set your emergency brake. This makes it more difficult for a thief to steal your car.

➤ Don't hide spare keys on your vehicle. If you're prone to locking keys in your car, put a copy of a door key in your wallet or purse.

➤ Hide one of your business cards somewhere inside the door of your car (this could help police determine that your car *is* your car, even if the thief has switched the VIN).

➤ Remove all electrical or electronic devices that use the cigarette lighter receptacle when you park the car. Insert the cigarette lighter or close the cigarette lighter ash-tray door, and put the electronic stuff in the trunk.

Vehicles may be stolen for a variety of purposes; after all, theives steal things for their reasons, not yours. The type of car you own and where you live may increase the risk of your falling victim to auto theft. The greater the risk of theft, the more layers of auto-theft protection you should implement.

The Least You Need to Know

➤ Vehicles might be stolen for a temporary purpose, for stripping down and selling as parts, or for shipping overseas for sale to foreign buyers.

➤ You can protect your car with audible alarms, visible deterrents, and physical deterrents. You may need more than one type of protection, depending upon the make and model of your car (and the habits of car thieves in your area).

➤ Most physical deterrents, such as wheel locks and column collars, are easily overcome by car thieves. Immobilizers have a better chance of stopping a theft—and work better the more places they immobilize your car's systems.

➤ Etching VIN numbers on your car windows may deter a thief from stealing the car for sale with a switched VIN.

➤ Some common-sense antitheft actions are free but require that you think about protecting your car each time you park it.

Chapter 22

When Bad Things Happen to Good Security Plans

In This Chapter

➤ First things first

➤ Preserving evidence

➤ Making sure about insurance

➤ Notifying friends and neighbors

➤ Can lightning strike twice?

➤ Prosecution without persecution

No matter how carefully you plan or how good your security plan might be, you can't guarantee that you'll escape every calamity life has to offer. Even the most protected people and the most elaborate security systems in the world have suffered losses. But take heart! I'm going to show you how to cut your losses by making the best of a bad situation.

In this chapter, I'll explain to you how to deal with a fire, a break-in, or other incident when it occurs, and how to follow up for the best possible response from law enforcement and emergency workers—and your insurance agency, too.

First Things First

Although each situation is different, there's a number-one rule that you should follow if you have any kind of incident, whether it's a fire, a break-in, or any other loss: *Keep the situation from getting any worse, and summon help.* How do you keep things from getting worse? By *not* doing a couple of things:

➤ *Don't* take unnecessary risks.

➤ *Don't* do anything that will get in the way of help getting to you.

➤ *Don't* destroy evidence or do anything else that might inhibit an investigation.

What to Do if a Fire Breaks Out

If you followed my advice earlier in the book, you have a fire escape plan in place. If your smoke alarm wakes you up, put the plan into action. Get everyone out of the house, account for everyone, tell everyone to stay together, and then go next door or to another nearby phone and summon help. Bang on doors, yell "Fire!" and do whatever you can to get help as quickly as possible.

Don't go back into the house to telephone for help or to rescue *stuff*. A fire can spread through a room in seconds and engulf an entire home in a matter of a few short minutes. What seemed like a small threat when the alarm went off might be very dangerous by the time you get everyone out and assembled. If you're trapped, injured, or killed by going back into a burning house, it's safe to say that you've broken the number-one emergency rule by making the situation worse.

That being said, you also should use your common sense. If you start a small kitchen fire, grab your fire extinguisher and try to put it out. But at the same time, you should tell everyone else in the house to get out, go to the prearranged meeting spot, and call 911, just in case. But don't try to fight a fire if it threatens to block your only escape route or is clearly beyond the handheld fire extinguisher stage. If you can't get the fire out almost immediately and it's spreading, get out.

After you've evacuated a burning house, make sure that you get a safe distance away from it and out of the way of firefighters. If necessary, take care of anyone who's injured until medical help arrives. Don't go back into a fire scene until the fire department gives the okay. People have been burned and injured when walking and sifting through rubble after a fire has been extinguished.

Not-So-Anonymous Tip

If you have a cordless or cell phone, you should keep it next to your bed and incorporate it into your escape plan—pick it up and take it with you as you evacuate. You rarely want to hang around in a burning house to phone 911, so it's best to call from outside the house, after everyone is assembled in your prearranged meeting spot.

If you need a refresher on how to put together an emergency escape plan or a general fire-prevention brush-up, reread Chapter 10, "Low-Cost Common-sense Fire Safety Techniques."

After a Burglary or Theft

You've heard it before, but I'll say it again: Don't ever go into your home if you suspect that someone has broken into it. They could still be in there, and even if they aren't, your messing around in there could destroy evidence that might help investigators track down the dirty crooks who robbed the joint.

If you enter your home and then realize that there's been a burglary, follow these two steps:

1. Leave the house, *retracing the path you took when you entered it.* Don't walk around surveying the "damage"—get out immediately. The less disturbance you make to the scene of the crime, the better you preserve the evidence.

2. Call the police, and say that you have just discovered that your house or apartment has been broken into and that you think the burglar may still be in the house (that may help speed the police on their way to the scene).

If you've gone to a neighbor's house to call for help, don't allow that person (or anyone else but the police) to be a hero and go in after the bad guys. If you've called 911, they'll ask you to stay on the phone until help arrives. If possible, watch your house (or ask someone with you to watch it) from a safe distance; if you see someone leave your property, note every detail of their appearance and give it to the 911 dispatcher, or tell the police as soon as they arrive.

Sound the Alarm!

A burned home is filled with potential hazards, such as jagged glass, exposed nails, loose bricks, weakened floors, and hot embers. Most experts will tell you to wear protective gear, such as boots, hard hats, and gloves when you go back into a burn site.

Sound the Alarm!

The last thing you want to do is come face-to-face with someone who's robbing your house. You put the burglar in a fight-or-flight position, and there's no telling how he'll respond. Many a homeowner has been injured or killed when interrupting a burglary in progress. If you think that your house has been broken into, retreat, retreat, retreat.

Not-So-Anonymous Tip

You're in an emergency situation, you see a bad guy, and you want to remember *everything* about what he looks like—but how? Well, cops are trained to memorize the features of any suspect by "scanning" the person from top to bottom and remembering things in that order: hair (or lack thereof), skin color, eyes, mouth, facial hair, body build, estimated height and weight, clothing, and shoes. And don't forget distinguishing features like a tattoo, a limp, missing teeth, or acne. Of course, get license plate numbers of any vehicles, and tell the police what direction (in car or on foot) the suspects were traveling in when you last saw them.

Not-So-Anonymous Tip

After you've met with the police after a break-in or theft, make sure that you get the name and contact information of the officer in charge before he or she leaves. If you gain important information or need to follow up on the progress of your case, you'll need to know who to call. Your insurance company will want a police report, too, so the officer in charge will be responsible for that paperwork.

Of course, all of this becomes a little bit trickier if the crime scene is your car, truck, or van. What you do after a vehicle break-in is determined to a large degree by the circumstances. For example, if it's broad daylight and there are plenty of people around when you discover that your car has been broken into, follow the advice I gave earlier. Don't touch anything, go immediately to a phone, and call the police (this probably isn't a 911 call, though—just call the local police number). Then go back to your car and wait there (without touching anything) until the police arrive.

However, if it's 3 A.M. and you go out to find that your car (the last in the parking lot) has been broken into, you may be in danger yourself if you hang around on the street. In that case, you may not have any choice but to get in and (if your car's drivable) drive to the nearest 24-hour convenience store or other well-lighted, populated spot, and call the cops from there.

Use your judgment; you don't want to put yourself in danger to help catch a car thief. On the other hand, when you get in and drive the car, or even check through your glove box to see if anything's missing from there, you'll destroy evidence and possibly damage the chance for investigators to find the culprits. And that's really the topic of the next section of this chapter.

Be an Evidence Preservationist

There's an old crime-scene investigator's saying (and I actually know some old crime-scene investigators): "Whenever you enter a crime scene, you bring something with you, and when you leave, you take something away—even if its only air." Now, they're not talking about a dishonest cop making off with a victim's VCR. What they mean is that by walking through the scene of a crime, you may contaminate the scene with your footprints, track in dirt and leaves, or drop hair and clothing fibers that will confuse the scene and make sifting through the evidence more difficult.

And with those same big feet of yours, you can destroy footprints or pick up hair and fibers left by the criminal, instead of leaving all the evidence in place where it could help investigators solve the crime. The air—well, you can have that, but it's still not right to mess up the crime scene.

The crime scene is more than just a location where a crime took place. It's actually a record of that crime. For example, it's the route the criminal took as he entered and left the scene. And it's the air that criminal breathed, it's his hair and clothing fibers, the salt and oil from his skin, and the tool marks that he left behind. The crime scene is the witness to the crime.

Tire marks in the mud at the curb in front of your house may be those of the burglar's car; that piece of torn denim hanging on the chain-link fence behind your house may belong to the thief. Or maybe he left footprints in the mud or snow in the alley behind your apartment.

All of these are examples of what can be valuable *trace* evidence that the police can use to help solve the crime. Generally, trace evidence is very small or hard to detect and is also extremely fragile. A patent footprint on a dusty floor could be easily overlooked and destroyed by the untrained observer. And we've all heard about the value of fingerprints. The bottom line to preserving evidence is to leave everything absolutely untouched—don't enter or walk through the crime scene until the police give you the okay.

The police can "develop" latent finger prints through a variety of methods including dusting for prints, use of chemicals, and even laser technology.

Security Password

If you have touched something or been through an area of the crime scene, let the police know. They'll need to know who has been in the scene since the crime took place, and they may need to take *elimination prints* from you. Elimination prints are fingerprints of all nonsuspects who may have been in an area. The police can compare these to prints they took from the scene and can eliminate matches from evidence. The police may also want elimination hair samples and shoe prints.

When they let you back into your home after a break-in, the police may ask you to look around for things that seem out of place or that don't belong. Was that dirty glass on the counter when you left? Did anyone you know leave that cigarette butt by the back door? Is food missing from the refrigerator, or have things in there been moved around? Anything that a criminal left behind can help catch him. Be alert— you know better than anyone else what belongs where in and around your home.

Most of all, be patient. Believe me, I know that anyone whose house has been robbed just wants to get in there and see what has been taken. But keep that old crime-scene investigator in mind and remember what he said about destroying evidence. Whatever is gone is gone; what's left behind may be critical to catching your thief.

Be Sure About Insurance

I've told you before that maintaining adequate insurance coverage is an important part of your overall home security plan. But when it comes time to get your agency the cold, hard facts that they need to process your claim, well, it can seem like a cold, hard process. Anyone who has experienced a loss is upset; you just have to do what you can to keep your cool and get down to business with the insurance company as quickly as possible.

Report your loss to your insurance company as soon as you reasonably can. Go get that list of valuables and photographs that I had you prepare, and go through it to determine what's gone and what isn't. (See, I told you that list could come in handy.) Present the insurance company with a detailed list that includes the missing items and their value. If you have any receipts or other identifying paperwork, make sure to have it ready as well. The police will want a copy of the list, and that will include registration numbers and marks, as well as the other identifying information for missing items.

If you missed it before, you can read all about creating a good insurance record of your possessions in Chapter 12, "Your Name Here _____: Branding Your Stuff."

Not-So-Anonymous Tip

Not sure what's gone, what's there, and what's what? Don't despair. Get out the records you made for your insurance company and tick through your list of valuables. If you've made videotapes in and around your home, take a moment to view them so that you can refresh your memory about any items that may have been stolen or moved without your knowledge.

Talk to Your Neighbors

All that time you spent meeting and greeting your neighbors will really pay off if you suffer some sort of break-in. Although the police will probably interview your neighbors, too, lots of people are uncomfortable talking with the police. You may uncover a lot more information on your own than the cops can turn up in a typical *neighborhood check*.

Dishing with your neighbors about your break-in pays two ways: First, you may learn valuable information about something that someone saw or heard during the crime. And second, you're letting everyone in the area know that a criminal's afoot. They can be on the lookout and extra aware of anything or anyone suspicious. And you may find out that they suffered a similar crime last month; the police will want to know if they have a repeat offender in the neighborhood.

Talk the Talk

A **neighborhood check** is a police term for the routine questioning they undertake with neighbors and merchants in the area of a crime, to see if they noticed the suspects or anything unusual.

Security Password

Do you have to be your own Sherlock Holmes to get to the bottom of some crime that has been perpetrated against you? No, but the police are busy. If people aren't at home when the police conduct a neighborhood check, they may not be able to get back to the area for some time. And you aren't the only victim on their list, either. You have the biggest stake in solving your crime, so anything you can do to gather helpful information and funnel it to the cops is in your best interest.

Not-So-Anonymous Tip

Surprisingly, many people don't report minor thefts or attempted break-ins to the police. They figure that the loss was minor and that the police can't do anything about it, anyway. But because these little things go unreported, the police may not have a complete picture of what has been going on in your neighborhood. No matter how inconsequential a crime may seem, make sure to tell the police about it.

Here are some helpful questions to ask:

1. Has anyone in your neighborhood hired any handymen or subcontractors lately? If so, who were they?

2. Have your neighbors had any thefts or losses recently, or have they heard of anyone else having any?

3. Who was around at the time of the burglary? You may not know exactly when the burglary took place, but you know that everything was fine when you left at 7:30 in the morning and not fine when you got back at 6:00. Who was at home in the neighborhood during the day? What about the mail carrier, meter reader, local joggers, dog-walkers, yard workers, and gardeners? These people may have seen something unusual or suspicious but then explained it away because they didn't know that anything out of the ordinary had happened. Figure out who was around, and talk to them or ask the police to talk to them.

Whenever you uncover any information, turn it over to the officer in charge of investigating your crime *immediately*. Hot information is always more valuable than old news.

Your mail carrier may have thought it unusual that your front door was standing open when he delivered your mail; ask anyone in the area to remember anything they saw or heard at the time of the crime.

Can Lightning Strike Twice?

If by lightning you mean a theft, break-in, or burglary, the answer is "Yes." You wouldn't believe how many times burglars go back to the well, so to speak, and break into the same house they burgled before. The reason? They know that the insurance company probably replaced all your stolen property with bright, shiny, new stuff. So why not get that, too?

Once you have been the target of a burglary, expect that you will be targeted again. After all, the crooks know your property, they may know your schedule, and they certainly know what kinds of things you're likely to have lying around the house.

And remember what I said a few chapters back about the relative intelligence of the average thief. Whatever you see in the movies, these guys ain't suave, sophisticated geniuses-gone-wrong. You're probably much smarter than they are, so learn from your past experience. How did the thieves get into your house before? When did they break in—what time of day was it, and where were you? At work? On vacation? Upstairs in bed?

Put systems in place or upgrade your existing systems to combat the crime you already suffered. This is one time when it makes perfect sense to close the barn door after the horse gets out. After all, you replaced the horse, didn't you?

For a fast refresher on crime-busting basics, see Chapter 9, "Fast, Easy, Cheap Crime-Fighting Basics."

Prosecution Without Persecution

The cops caught your thief! That's reason to celebrate, right? Well, maybe not a lot. That person isn't a thief unless a court of law says so. The prosecutor is going to have to prove that this presumed-innocent person the police have brought before the court is, indeed, the dirty so-and-so who kicked in your front door and stole the family silver (and your most beloved home entertainment center with that huge remote and beautiful surround-sound system).

The burden of proof is heavy; the prosecutor has to prove the defendant guilty beyond a reasonable doubt. And because most of the time burglaries have no witnesses, the prosecution may be relying on other types of evidence, such as trace evidence from the crime scene (fingerprints, clothing fibers, and so on), stolen property that was found in possession of the suspect, or a witness who bought stolen merchandise from that person.

Both you and the suspect get your day in court; remember, everyone's innocent until proven guilty.

Not-So-Anonymous Tip

You shouldn't hesitate to take notes of relevant information and developments of your case, from the moment the crime takes place until you appear in court. If they catch the crook, a lot of time will undoubtedly pass between the time of the crime and the day you appear in court. If you've taken notes, you'll be able to use them when you meet with the prosecutor, and you can use them to prepare for your testimony, if you're called.

One of the most important witnesses the prosecutor calls may be you, the victim of the crime. If you want to help the prosecutor, you have to be clear, consistent, and thoughtful in the evidence you present if you're called as a witness. The prosecution will have to build the case from all the facts and circumstances, so you'll need to be able to testify about what time you left the house, when you returned, what you observed, how you know that recovered items are yours, and so on.

And you have to be a credible witness, too, which means that you need to tell the truth. If you're lying, the judge or jury is likely to spot it. The prosecutor will go over your testimony with you beforehand; you'll know what questions he or she is going to ask you. Be prepared; reflect and review your own notes or materials before you testify.

Because you're likely to be called as a prosecution witness, the prosecutor will ask you questions on *direct examination*. When the prosecutor is finished, the defense will have the opportunity to go over your testimony on *cross-examination*.

And, again, try to forget all the courtroom scenes you've ever seen on television or in films. Answer questions from both the prosecutor and the defense attorney without being sarcastic or smarmy, hold the witty repartée, and don't get all aggressive with anyone. Don't get carried away and exaggerate any of the details of your testimony. The prosecution already knows that it has a case; overstating the facts will only give the defense an opportunity to attack your credibility. You'll be most effective if you're positive and firm in your answers; that comes from being prepared and telling the truth (don't I sound like your old Scout leader?).

Your willingness to cooperate with police and testify if needed is an essential part of your overall home security plan. Remember the deterrence triangle I discussed way back in the first chapter of the book? Well, criminals need to understand that they face severe sanctions when they're caught violating the law. That happens only if we all step up and take on criminals through crime prevention and through participating in the criminal justice system.

Talk the Talk

Direct examination is the first questioning of a witness by the party on whose behalf the witness is called to testify. So, if the prosecutor calls you to testify on behalf of the prosecution, that round of questioning is the direct examination. When the defense attorney (the opposition) asks you questions, that's the **cross-examination** phase.

The Least You Need to Know

➤ No matter what incident occurs—fire, break-in, theft, or other security snafu—your first rule of action is to keep the situation from getting any worse and summon help.

➤ If you have a fire, get everyone outside to your preassigned meeting place, then call for help.

➤ If you suspect someone has broken into your home, don't go in—go elsewhere and call the police. If you've already entered your house, leave by retracing the steps you took when you entered and call for help. Don't walk around looking at the damage—you may destroy evidence.

➤ When you contact your insurance company to report losses due to a theft or fire, have your record of possessions ready. If possible, review photos and videotapes of your home to refresh your memory about what you had and where it was located.

➤ Talk to your neighbors after a break-in, both to alert them that the neighborhood has experienced a robbery and to gather from them any information on suspicious activity they may have seen or heard around the time of the event.

➤ If your house-thief is caught and you're called upon to testify in court, remember to be honest and don't exaggerate the details in your testimony.

Glossary

aggravated assault   An assault committed with the intent to commit an associated crime, such as rape, robbery, or murder.

all-risk (insurance) coverage   Insurance that covers everything except specific exclusions written into an insurance policy.

B&E (breaking and entering)   The illegal entry into a residence or business with the idea of committing a theft or felony assault.

block captain   A Neighborhood Watch leader, usually responsible for calling meetings, contacting outside agencies for extra information or special assistance, welcoming new members, and so on.

booby trap   A trap armed with a device triggered to harm or kill anyone who enters the trap. Also called a man trap.

carbon monoxide   An odorless, invisible gas that is a by-product of the incomplete burning of certain fuels, such as gasoline, kerosene, and natural gas. Inhaling high levels of this gas results in *carbon monoxide poisoning,* whose symptoms include weakness, dizziness, blurred vision, grogginess, disorientation, and finally coma and death.

cat burglar   Someone who enters homes at night, usually for the purpose of stealing credit cards, money, jewelry, and other valuables that people tend to toss on tables and counters before going to bed for the night.

chop shop   An operation that specializes in stripping stolen cars of accessories, parts, and other desirables that can be sold and traded on the car parts market.

closed-loop configuration   A wiring configuration used in home security systems in which the contacts are closed when the system is "at rest" (that is, when nothing's happening). If a door is protected with a closed-loop-configured sensor, when the door is opened, the magnet separates from the magnetic switch, the circuit is interrupted, and the alarm sounds.

column collars   Large metal collars used as antitheft devices that protect a vehicle's column and ignition switch from access.

console or control panel   The "brains" and the command center of a security system. It houses the controls with which you program, arm, disarm, and check your system; it receives information from the sensors and displays warning messages, triggers alarms, or sends the signals to a central station or monitoring facility.

continually monitored alarm   A security system that is monitored 24 hours a day by a monitoring service. For example, in a continually monitored system, if a sensor triggers the system, an audible alarm may sound, the homeowner may receive a paging message, and the security service's monitoring center may send one of its officers or dispatch police, fire, or another appropriate agent to your home.

double-cylinder deadbolt locks   Deadbolt locks that require a key for opening from either side of the lock. These are very secure types of locks, but some areas prohibit their use on exterior doors because of the potential difficulties in exiting in case of a fire or other emergency.

dual-stage sensors   A car sensor that triggers a quick series of beeps if the car is jostled but that will fire into a full-stage siren blast if the action is repeated or if the car gets a big jolt. This type of sensor helps avoid those false alarms caused by someone jostling the car in passing.

dupe numbers   Numbers stamped or molded into keys (by the manufacturer) that identify the cut pattern of the key. These numbers can be used to duplicate the key, even without an original key as a pattern.

duty of care   The legal notion that you are responsible for doing what you can to reasonably ensure that people don't get hurt on your property.

E911/Enhanced 911   Extended 911 service, in which a number is assigned to each residence and is automatically recorded (along with a location) when a 911 call is placed from that location. If the call is interrupted, the dispatcher has an address and location to which emergency help can be routed, even if the caller was unable to supply that information.

felony   The definition varies from jurisdiction to jurisdiction, but in general, a felony is a crime punishable by more than one year in prison and a fine, or a crime that involves the theft or destruction of goods equal to a specific dollar amount established by the jurisdiction.

foreseeability   The reasonable anticipation that certain things will happen as the result of an action or situation. In other words, if your front porch has rotten boards and someone falls through them and is injured, the court will probably consider that the accident was foreseeable, so you should have fixed the boards or blocked off the area before anyone got hurt.

gravity of harm   The amount of damage suffered as a result of a loss due to a crime, accident, fire, or other incident.

hard-wired security system   A system that is connected by wires and cables linked throughout a home or building.

home invasion   A break-in in which someone deliberately uses force against a homeowner to get into his or her house.

home security system   Anything that you plan and do before the fact to decrease the opportunity for a crime or accident to occur.

ISO rating   A rating issued for firefighting companies across the United States by the Insurance Services Office (ISO), a New York–based independent industry advisory organization. The ISO bases its ratings on the agencies' capability to receive reports of, respond to, and fight fires.

keypads   Security system input devices that let you operate a security system by entering your unique security code.

lamp modules   A security system feature that turns lamps on and off at set times or that flashes them when an alarm is triggered.

larceny   The unlawful taking of personal property (stealing, to you and me).

liability   Your responsibility for damages resulting from accident or injury.

local alarm   An alarm that sounds both inside and outside the premises when triggered by someone going through a door or window, or by motion around or within the house. Local alarm systems warn occupants and those in the area that the system has been tripped.

magnetic switch   A part of a magnetic sensor used (typically on a door or window) to trigger an alarm in the security system. The magnetic switch separates from the sensor body, opening or closing the electrical circuit to trigger the alarm.

motion detectors   Sensors that detect movement within a specific range inside or outside your home. The most common type, passive infrared (PIR) motion detectors, work by sensing body heat as it moves across an area's background temperature.

named (insurance) coverage   Insurance that covers only what is detailed in the policy; if it's not mentioned, it's not covered.

NCIC   The National Crime Information Center, an agency that maintains a central computer resource used by police and law enforcement groups around the world. For example, the police maintain a bank of registration numbers for stolen goods and registered goods for sale; the police can enter the registration numbers of your stolen goods into the NCIC computer and then track them as they turn up on the market.

Omnia Presence doctrine   A doctrine that holds that most people don't break the law because they believe that the police are everywhere and always ready to strike.

open-loop configuration   Electrical circuits that, in security systems, are triggered when sensor connections are closed. In other words, the connections are open when all is well. Open a door, and if you snap a magnetic switch up so that it connects to a magnet on the door frame, you trip the alarm.

palisade fencing   A type of fencing that permits viewing of the enclosed space from outside the fence. This type of fencing allows neighbors, law enforcement officers, and passersby to see activity within your yard, a real benefit if that activity is generated by someone attempting to break into your home.

panic buttons   Wall-mounted or portable (necklace-type) sounding devices that emit an alarm or trigger a call for help when a button is pushed for a specified period of time (such as 2 seconds).

passive-setting auto alarm system   An alarm system that automatically arms itself within a short specified time after you exit your vehicle.

perimeter sensors   Sensors (typically magnetic contacts or glass-break sensors) located on doors, windows, and other entry points around the home.

personal liability   Your responsibility for paying obligations as a result of an accident, injury, or other incident.

probable cause   A legal condition that exists in which the observable or knowable facts and circumstances are sufficient to convince a reasonable person that a crime took place and that the suspect committed the crime.

prop bars   Security bars, typically used to physically prevent a door or window from being opened from the outside.

property crime   Burglary, vandalism, and motor vehicle theft.

public safety agencies   Government departments responsible for the safety and welfare of citizens (like you and me). These agencies include police, fire, and highway patrol departments, as well as emergency medical dispatch teams and disaster relief organizations such as the Federal Emergency Management Agency (FEMA).

reasonable force   The force that a judge or jury would deem fair, inexcessive, and necessary as a measure to prevent further harm or to protect you or your family from danger.

remote control devices   Portable controls with which you can arm, disarm, monitor, or otherwise control your security system from outside the home. Some of these devices turn lights on and off, open and close garage doors, and perform other convenience functions.

remote starting and disabling   Remote devices that will start your car from more than 500 feet away and that can also interrupt the vehicle's gas or electricity flow to disable the car in case of theft.

response time   The amount of time that it takes an agency to respond to an alarm or call for assistance.

risk assessment   Here, a detailed analysis of what risks threaten you, your home, and your property.

salvage switch   A type of auto theft in which a thief buys a car that has been to-taled and then steals another car of the same make and model. The thief then switch-es the VINs of the two cars, giving a nice legal VIN to the stolen car, which the thief now owns free and clear for the price of a wreck.

security strobe   A kind of outdoor security lighting that is connected to an alarm system. When the security alarm goes off, an outdoor light flashes to tell police or neighbors exactly where the alarm is located.

sensors   A vital part of security systems. Reacting either to motion, heat, sound, or the breaking of a magnetic contact, the sensors trigger the system alarms or warnings. Typical sensors include magnetic contacts, motion detectors, and glass-break detec-tors.

simple premises alarms   Alarms designed to sound a warning to the home's occu-pants that a single type of danger is present.

sirens or sounders   Security devices that emit an audible alarm and that can be mounted indoors or outdoors, or contained in remote devices.

smoke detectors   Single-unit or hard-wired security devices that sound an alarm when they detect smoke. *Monitored smoke detectors* are part of a central security system and are on 24 hours a day (even if the burglary protection is turned off) so that the system can react to fire emergencies at any time.

special units   Police officers in larger cities placed in teams or groups and assigned to specific kinds of tasks, such as investigation, patrol, and so on. The term also de-scribes the officers' area of specialization.

strikeplate   That part of a door-locking mechanism that is opposite the door knob and locking bolt. The locking bolt "strikes" and enters the strikeplate when the door is closed and locked.

susceptibility profile   The results of your risk assessment that indicate the security problems you're most likely to deal with. Your susceptibility profile is based on your living habits, your history of security problems, the general security conditions of your home's construction and the area in which you live, and the skill and staffing of local public service agencies.

target hardening   Anything you do that makes it more difficult for a criminal to get to you or your valuables (locked doors, fencing, bolted-down equipment, and so on).

telephone dialer   A self-monitored system in which a system trigger causes the di-aler to automatically dial four telephone numbers that you've programmed into the unit. When the call is answered, the system plays a prerecorded message for help.

temperature-sensor alarms   Alarms triggered by falling or rising temperatures, usually included in a home security system to warn of freezing temperatures in areas where water pipes are located.

temporary theft   When someone takes your car for a joyride (or to be used as a getaway car) and then abandons it. You stand a good chance of getting your car back if it's taken in a temporary theft, but it may be in a less-than-pristine condition when you find it.

tort   The commission of a wrongful act, whether done on purpose or by accident, that results in the person acted upon being injured. Negligence resulting in injury is usually considered a tort.

Tot Finders   A program used by many area fire and police units in which parents register the names, ages, and sleeping locations of their children with the public service agency. In case of a fire or other emergency, rescue workers then know specifically what young occupants may need to be rescued from the home.

volt-ohm meter   An electrical meter used to check whether current is running through a wiring system.

VIN (vehicle identification number)   A numbering system, in use since the late 1960s, in which each car, truck, or other motorized vehicle is issued a unique identification number for tracking the vehicle through sales, theft, and other changes in ownership. The number is displayed on a metal plate, usually located on the left side of the dashboard under the windshield.

water-sensor alarms   Alarms triggered by sensors (usually a float switch) detecting rising water. Water-sensor alarms are becoming increasingly common in home security warning systems for residences in flood-prone areas.

wedge alarms   Portable, inexpensive, battery-operated alarms that are placed under a door like traditional wedge doorstops but that sound a loud alarm when someone attempts to open the door.

window etching   A vehicle antitheft measure in which the VIN number is etched on all of the vehicle's windows to help identify the vehicle and to discourage thieves from believing that they can easily disguise a stolen vehicle.

wireless security systems   Security alarm and monitoring systems that are not connected to a home's central wiring system. Wireless systems are battery-powered and rely on radio waves that bounce between a sending and a receiving unit.

Resources

The world is awash in great resources for information about home security. In this appendix, I've listed those that I find particularly helpful and interesting, as well as some sources that serve as important "launching pads" for further information. When you're planning your home security system, don't forget to take advantage of as many outside sources of information as you can find. The more research you do, the tighter your home security plan will be. Happy hunting!

Crime Statistics and Prevention Information

National Association of Town Watch
www.nationaltownwatch.org

The NATW is a nonprofit organization that develops and promotes neighborhood crime- and drug-prevention programs. State, local, and regional law enforcement agencies belong to this group, along with private citizens, businesses, civic groups, and others who are interested in protecting their communities from the destabilizing effects of crime. The NATW Web site offers ideas for participating in the National Night Out program, a yearly "night out against crime" event sponsored by the NATW. You can also access an order form for Community Watch Block Captain's Handbooks.

National Crime Prevention Council
www.ncpc.org

The National Crime Prevention Council has been around since the early 1980s, providing education and training for crime prevention to communities around the United States.

The NCPC Web site has a lot of really helpful information, including a 1999 survey on Americans' attitudes and ideas about crime. It's worth a visit to what is now the official home of McGruff!

National Insurance Crime Bureau
www.nicb.org/

The National Insurance Crime Bureau is a not-for-profit organization that receives support from approximately 1,000 property/casualty insurance companies. The NICB partners with insurers and law enforcement agencies to facilitate the identification, detection, and prosecution of insurance criminals.

www.disastercenter.com/crime/

Want to know how the crime rates have changed in your state over the past 40 years? This site offers links to crime statistics for every state in the country, as well as overall national crime stats.

www.nashville.net/~police/risk/

This site offers self-rating questionnaires for determining what risks you face for home intrusion, street assault, robbery, and more.

www.neighborhoodwatch.com

This site includes good information about joining and maintaining a Neighborhood Watch program.

www.sustainableusa.com

This organization promotes a number of initiatives for maintaining and improving the safety and livability of our nation's cities, towns, and neighborhoods. At this site, you'll find an interesting discussion of how making neighborhoods more "walkable" can actually make them safer and healthier places to live—an interesting source of information on ways to make your neighborhood more secure.

Fire Safety and Prevention

www.alpha-tek.com/burn/profiles.asp

At this site, you'll find first-person accounts of individuals who have survived fires in and around their homes. You'll get a close look at how fires break out, what it's like to be caught in a house fire, and the long and painful experience of recovery. As you read through these first-person profiles, you'll gain a new respect for the tried-and-true fire-prevention maxims offered in this book and the online and print resources that it mentions.

www.firesafetytips.com

A commercial Web site of the Fire Escape Systems company, the site offers good fire safety information and links to its product list of fire-escape ladders.

www.testyoursmokealarms.com

This site has a wide range of good information regarding fire safety, rescue plans, a room-by-room plan for fire prevention, fire safety for special-needs residents, and good general information about residential sprinkler systems, along with a wealth of other helpful information.

www.usfa.fema.gov/safety/sheets.htm

The United States Fire Administration office (which is a division of FEMA) hosts an informative site with good information on fire prevention and survival, fire-safety product recalls, rural fire safety management tips, and more.

Home Security Products and Installation

www.business-home-security.com

This is another home-security products site, with equipment ranging from alarm systems to spy cameras, theft deterrents, security VCRs, and more.

www.home-security-systems.youdoitsecurity.com

This site offers a wide range of home security and surveillance equipment, along with a good list of do-it-yourself home security products.

www.homedirector.net

This isn't touted as installable through a do-it-yourself project, but Homedirector's product is a pretty interesting home-automation tool. You can use this system to get everything from the typical sensor-triggered alarms and warnings to room-by-room monitoring (from remote locations), networked Internet access from multiple points through a single connection, onscreen warnings of alarm triggers, and more.

www.prowlercam.com

This site offers ProwlerCam shareware, Windows 98 security camera software. Even if you're not interested in setting up surveillance cameras around your home, this site gives you a good look at how security camera software works so that you can see for yourself how useful it would be in your home, office, or business.

www.remodelingcorner.com

If you're interested in learning more about "smart" technology and its role in home security, check out this site. It has a do-it-yourselfer's guide to wiring your smart-technology home, in addition to articles on installing and using home security systems. If you're thinking of installing your own security system, this site is a good first stop for how-to information.

www.sharp-security.com/glossary/cctv.htm

Another online source for video and audio surveillance systems, this site also hosts a really helpful glossary of terms related to surveillance equipment and installations.

www.spycameras.com

This site offers a wide range of video surveillance system (VSS) equipment, with prices and installation options.

www.x10.com/homepage.htm

This company goes beyond offering home security products and equipment—it also sells a full range of home entertainment and home automation equipment. If you're interested in wiring up the ultimate obedient home, you may be interested in looking at X10's ActiveHome software/hardware kits that can control everything from your garage door to your security system, home entertainment center, and bedroom lights.

General Information

www.dictionary.law.com/

This is a good online source of definitions for legal terms that you may need to know when studying premises liability regulations in your area or other laws that impact your rights as a homeowner.

Index

J-K-L